PRIVATE PLANS AND PUBLIC DANGERS

The Story of FDR's Third Nomination

by Bernard F. Donahoe

PRIVATE PLANS AND PUBLIC DANGERS

UNIVERSITY OF NOTRE DAME PRESS

The New Deal—the "Roosevelt Years"—will long be a fascinating subject for historians, researchers, scholars, and all readers with an interest in politics, particularly those with a special interest in the ideals and purposes of the Democratic Party. The period will be explored again and again throughout the years, for in addition to the passionate bias of many for or against the whole concept of the New Deal, there will long remain the possibility of doubt, conjecture, supposition about the accomplishments, failures, and motivations of the men who played the major roles.

Private Plans and Public Dangers: The Story of FDR's Third Nomination seems to me to cover the years from 1937 until the conclusion of the Democratic National Convention of 1940 most adequately. As he carefully details their behavior, Bernard Donahoe painstakingly probes the minds and hearts of those men who were so vividly in the forefront, as well as those who, remaining in the shadows, also contributed very greatly in the events that culminated in the breaking of the Nation's traditional unwritten law of two terms only for each President.

This twofold approach distinguishes Brother Donahoe's earnest search for the reality behind the scenes in this historical drama. He has written an account that I believe will be read, referred to, and quoted by historians for years to come.

James A. Farley

September, 1965

PREFACE

The third-term nomination and election of President Franklin D. Roosevelt in 1940 was a unique phenomenon in the history of American politics. This uniqueness was subsequently insured by a Constitutional amendment. The general assumption not only of Roosevelt's associates and the journalists of that day but also of historians since then has been that the third term was dictated by the need for governmental continuity and experience in the face of a grave international threat. Lyndon Johnson, for example, who played an active part in securing a third nomination for Roosevelt, has written this author, "It was inconceivable to me that under the circumstances in which our country then found itself that we would make any effort to change our leadership at a time when continuity of leadership was of such extreme importance."

These sentiments have been echoed and reechoed by others many times.

Unquestionably, the advent of World War II did play a major role in overcoming the reluctance of American voters to abandon the anti-third term tradition and even in convincing some members of the Democratic party that a third nomination did not spell political suicide. The importance of the war, however, can be and, I believe, has been overemphasized. To be sure, unique problems called for unique measures to meet them, but the war was not the only unique problem—probably not even the most pressing problem—facing the Democratic party and the Amercian people in 1940 and the years just preceding. The panic and the resulting depression of 1929 had through eleven years baffled Americans of every economic stratum and every shade of political belief, and the solutions suggested by politicians and professional economists reflected this nearly universal bewilderment.

Whether one considers the New Deal a revolution in American politics or merely the logical continuation of the march of progress (or decadence) begun during the Progressive Period, it is clear that most Americans in the nineteen-thirties regarded it as a rather sharp departure from the political philosophy and practices of the preceding decade. Its wisdom was debated hotly, not only in the nation as a whole but also within the ranks of the Democratic party, and by 1940 there had evolved two rather distinct schools of thought on the value of the men and philosophy behind the New Deal. The nomination of the President that year held the key to control of the party for one group or the other.

Perhaps the international crisis was the deciding factor in President Roosevelt's victory over Wendell Willkie; the point would be difficult to prove one way or the other. The struggle for the Democratic nomination, however, began well before Americans became concerned over affairs so far beyond their borders, and by the time they did become concerned the lines within the Democratic party were drawn for a 1940 showdown. The intra-party struggle between 1937 and 1940 left President Roosevelt with little or no choice but to surrender party and national leadership to men he regarded as too conservative on domestic issues or stand for renomination again himself. It was this consideration as much as, or more than, the outbreak of the war which motivated most of the political decisions which eventually led to the third nomination. Undoubtedly other factors entered also, but in the end it was the liberal-conservative split which presented the nation with its first and only successful presidential candidate for three consecutive terms.

This development is shown by tracing the split in the party from 1937 through 1940 and noting its effects on the many logical successors of the President. Roosevelt never lacked for would-be successors, either liberal or conservative. By 1940, however, there was virtually no possibility for any of the men he considered sufficiently liberal to gain the nomination. On the other hand, there would have been relatively little difficulty in nominating a "moderate" who saw eye-to-eye with him on foreign policy. A study of the growth of the third-term movement from 1937 on attempts to distinguish how much of it was spontaneous and how much carefully planned by the New Deal "palace guard."

It is a pleasant duty to acknowledge the thanks I owe the many people who made the writing of this book possible. I am especially grateful to Professor Vincent P. DeSantis of the University of Notre Dame Department of History, who prevented many errors by his generously patient and critical reading of the text. Thanks are also due Brother Donatus Schmitz, C.S.C., and Professor Marshall Smelser, who were responsible for the opportunity to begin the work. I owe a debt of gratitude to a number of librarians and archivists for their assistance and permission in using a number of collections of papers. Elizabeth Drewry and the excellent staff at the Roosevelt Library, Hyde Park, were particularly helpful, as was the staff at the Manuscripts Division, Library of Congress. I should also like to thank Reverend Thomas McAvoy, C.S.C., Archivist of the University of Notre Dame, and Thomas Walker for permission to use the Frank Walker Papers; Doris M. Reed, Curator of Manuscripts at the Lilly Library, Indiana University, and Mrs. Watson, widow of Paul McNutt, for permission to use the Paul McNutt Papers; Josephine Harper, Manuscripts Librarian of the State Historical Society, Madison, Wisconsin, for permission and assistance in using the Merlin Hull, Charles Broughton, Harry Bolens and Raymond Robbins Papers; Mr. E. Taylor Parks of the

State Department for permission to use some otherwise closed portions of the Cordell Hull Papers; and Professor Joseph Huthmacher of Georgetown University for showing me through pertinent portions of the Robert Wagner Papers. I am also very grateful to James A. Farley, Congressman Claude Pepper, and Benjamin V. Cohen for taking the time to give me the benefit of their intimate knowledge of the facts around which this book is based as well as their candid opinions of various phases of the problems. I am also very much indebted to Brother Linus Foy, F.M.S., President of Marist College, Poughkeepsie, New York, and Brother Thomas Buckley, C.S.C., principal of Mackin High School, Washington, D. C., whose kind hospitality made it possible for me to spend many weeks at the Roosevelt Library and the Library of Congress. The pleasant surroundings and convivial atmosphere provided by them made the work a pleasure. Despite a great number of generous helping hands, it goes without saying that any errors in the work are my own.

B. F. D.

September, 1965

CONTENTS

	FOREWORD	v
	PREFACE	vii
I	THE PROTAGONISTS	1
II	THE RUPTURED PARTY, 1937	31
III	THE REBELLION GROWS, 1938	55
IV	THE TURNING POINT, 1939	91
V	BY PROCESS OF ELIMINATION	127
VI	JEFFERSON'S LAST STAND	165
VII	CONCLUSIONS	191
	NOTES	197
	BIBLIOGRAPHY	235

Franklin D. Roosevelt began his second term as President of the United States in January, 1937. To a casual observer he may have appeared as the head of a political juggernaut which was his to command for the next four, and possibly eight, years and which would, at the nod of his head, roll mercilessly over all opposition. He had just finished inflicting what was in some respects the worst defeat in the political history of the country on Republican Alf Landon. Roosevelt's popularity with the American people was so universal that some pundits were already heralding the beginning of a new "Era of Good Feeling."

Beneath the apparently placid surface of the mighty Roosevelt political machine, however, the combustible elements were already beginning to overheat dangerously, and it needed only one false step by their organizer to blow the whole thing sky high. The problem was that of any successful political coalition: many of the forces which had backed Roosevelt in his drive for a second term were mutually antagonistic. With the beginning of his second term—presumably, though not assuredly, the last—the fight for future control of the party was only a matter of time, the winner to be announced at the 1940 Democratic National Convention.

The internal struggle for power within the major political parties of the country was certainly not new. Traditionally, the eastern wing of the Republican party opposed that of the West, and the southern Democrats tended to disagree in some matters with their brethren in the North. What was to make this particular contest so significant and so bitter were the new elements and new alignments initiated during the "First New Deal." By the middle of Roosevelt's first term his enemies were suggesting that he and Eleanor were singing in duet:

> You kiss the Negroes
> I'll kiss the Jews.
> We'll stay in the White House,
> As long as we choose.[1]

By the end of his first term, however, it was clear that the Rooseveltian kissing activities had ranged far beyond Negroes and Jews. A whole group of minorities, large enough to almost dwarf the hard core of the Democratic party, had been kissed and had swung aboard the New Deal bandwagon. Indeed, as one historian has noted, Roosevelt saw the traditional party organization as merely the vehicle for a great liberal reform coalition primarily for the betterment of the one-third of the country that was "ill-housed, ill-clad, ill-nourished."[2] He scarcely mentioned the Democratic party in the 1936 campaign; it was for the New Deal that he was fighting, and the Democratic party and the New Deal were definitely not synonymous. Where, for example, a conservative Democratic candidate for Congress was running against a pro-New Deal independent in 1936, or where a conservative state party faced vigorous liberal opposition, the force of presidential influence was generally swung against his own party or not swung at all, despite the silent or whispered opposition to this policy by National Chairman Jim Farley. Cases in point were Nebraska, where Roosevelt ignored the Democratic candidate and endorsed independent

George Norris; Minnesota, where he insisted on an alliance of Democrats and Farmer-Laborites; Wisconsin, where Roosevelt backed the liberal La Follette Progressives; and Massachusetts, where he refused to support James M. Curley, the Democratic candidate for senator.[3] This approach was certainly not a pragmatic one to roll up as large a vote as possible in November. While Roosevelt was still governor of New York, he told Rex Tugwell, "We'll have eight years in Washington. By that time there may not be a Democratic party, but there will be a progressive one."[4]

William Allen White, writing in 1937, listed the elements in the mighty Roosevelt coalition of 1936 as the conservative, solid South, northern city machines, radical labor, farmers, Negroes, the unemployed, and liberals of all classes.[5] Aside from the omission of the white collar workers, 61 per cent of whom indicated they favored Roosevelt in 1936,[6] the list is largely complete and accurate. The first two groups formed the bone and sinew of the traditional Democratic party, whereas the other five, decidedly independent and selective about what political group they supported, were attracted by Roosevelt and the New Deal. What made bitter conflict within the party inevitable was not only the resentment of professional Democrats at the usurpation of power and office by rank outsiders, who had certainly not fought the party's battles through good years and bad, but the very real ideological split between the two groups of factions, which was far from normal in previous intraparty power struggles. At stake was the future economic, social, and political course, not only of the party, but of the nation as well. When one took all the elements of the Democratic coalition into consideration, one discovered, in the words of General Hugh Johnson:

> . . . a new party, not a recognizable Democratic Party, but a one-man Roosevelt Party, conceived with superficial cleverness, but stuck together with spit and tied into a unit with haywire—a composite of inconsistencies. You get, at the very party heart and center, the Solid South, tied in with Northern Pro-Negro policy. You get farmers coupled up with industrial workers on principles which are intrinsically contradictory.[7]

Traditionally, the Democratic party's principles had been Jeffersonian and its national leadership largely southern; northern city machines like Tammany in New York and the Kelly-Nash organization in Chicago tended to concentrate their interest on more local matters.[8] The party had long stood for low tariffs, states' rights, frugal government, low taxes, and, in the South, white supremacy. Except for a relatively brief Wilsonian honeymoon, it was not noticeably any more friendly to organized labor than the Republican party.[9] President Hoover's chief fault in 1932, according to congressional Democratic leaders, was his reckless spending. In their determination to balance the budget they even attempted to join conservative Republicans in jamming through a sales tax. Wrote Congressman Robert Doughton, no radical himself: "It looks like our national Democratic leaders have betrayed us. Mr. Garner and Mr. Rainey, Speaker and Floor Majority Leader, stand on the Republican platform of the sales tax."[10]

The ideas were largely southern, but northern politicians objected to that very little as long as their machines were kept well oiled with federal patronage. Generally the two wings of the party were able to compromise their differences fairly well before and after the 1924 fiasco. Made up of professionals, both wings depended on unquestioning, tight discipline. Shocking indeed to the leaders of these groups was the "theft" of their party by labor leaders, radicals, political amateurs, former Republicans, social workers, and congenital "do-gooders." Yet it was precisely from groups such as these that Roosevelt drew not only a great deal of his support but the administrators and idea men who put together much of the New Deal.

Typical of such irregular liberal support was the Washington Commonwealth Federation, a combination of liberal Democrats, production-for-use people, and the Unemployed Citizens' League, which had infiltrated and virtually captured the Democratic party of that state. By 1938 it planned (1) to support President Roosevelt if he chose to run in 1940, or (2) to support the man he considered his logical liberal successor, or (3) to bolt the Democratic party if President Roosevelt and the New Dealers thought a third party movement necessary because of the nomination of a conservative candidate. When asked by party chairman Farley why the organization did not call itself the Washington Democratic Federation, leader Howard Costigan replied tartly: "We're not Democrats. We're New Dealers. This is neither a Democratic nor Republican state. It is progressive."[11]

Labor, too, had been an important factor in the 1936 triumph. In 1932 fully one-fourth of the Democratic campaign funds had been furnished by bankers. In 1936 it was only three per cent.[12] The slack was largely taken up by the C.I.O. unions, which contributed about $770,000 to the war chest. Labor's Non-partisan League, formed to solidify the labor vote behind Roosevelt, claimed credit for Democratic pluralities in Illinois, Indiana, and Ohio.[13] Labor leaders, particularly John L. Lewis, regarded their contributions as a shrewd investment, and they expected a good rate of return on it. "Is anyone fool enough," asked Lewis, "to believe for one instant that we gave this money to Roosevelt because we were spellbound by his voice?"[14] However Roosevelt may have felt about the contribution, labor-baiting conservatives within the party felt no particular obligations, and a clash was inevitable.

A combination of the Agricultural Adjustment Act and bad weather succeeded in raising farm prices fifty per cent by 1936, and one poll indicated that at least fifty-nine per cent of the farmers were grateful enough to vote Democratic.[15] Indeed, the normally Republican western farm states voted for Roosevelt en bloc, and Landon could not even carry his own state of Kansas. Ironically, farm prosperity spelled political trouble for the New Deal. Usually conservative and Republican except when in dire economic straits, farmers might be expected in better times to be repelled by New Deal labor and relief policies. The reliefers, on the other hand, were so appreciative of New Deal efforts on their behalf that eighty per cent of those polled expressed their approval of the Democratic party in 1936.[16]

As long as the New Deal could hold such disparate groups as these together, conservatives within the party would find their influence diminished. Nor could the big-city machines be counted on to throw their weight toward a return to the old order. Though politically powerful bosses like Thomas Pendergast, Ed Kelly, Frank Hague, and Ed Flynn might resent to some extent their lack of influence on some federal policy and federal policy makers, such annoyances were minor compared with the over-all benefit of having a name like Roosevelt to head the national ticket and ample amounts of federal patronage at the local level at their disposal. Professional politicians from all areas, however, were angered by Roosevelt's tendency to ignore party lines in his appointments. Undoubtedly it was a result of his desire to bring able liberals into the government regardless of political labels, but it tended to undercut state and local organizations. On one occasion Roosevelt explained his philosophy in this way:

> People tell me that I hold to party ties less tenaciously than most of my predecessors in the Presidency, and that I have too many people in my Administration who are not active party Democrats. I must admit the soft impeachment. . . . the future lies with those wise political leaders who realize that the great public is interested more in Government than in politics.[17]

What all this portended, of course, was a shift not only away from Bourbon conservatism, which had largely been accomplished in the first term, but even away from the older party leaders, who had, for the most part, gone along with the New Deal. A whole new political alignment appeared to be in the making, with the liberals taking over the Democratic party completely and forcing the old guard to accept their principles and leadership or leave the party. According to Tugwell this conception was never absent from Roosevelt's consideration, and practically all his policies and actions, except those adopted to meet direct emergencies, were aimed at this goal.[18] Both Tugwell and Raymond Moley agree that that was what was behind the sharp New Deal turn to the left in 1935.[19] To attract the support of the great body of American progressives, the national economic planning policy, which had produced the N.I.R.A. and the first A.A.A., had to be scrapped for the more traditional trust-busting, Wilsonian approach. The major obstacle to the plan was, of course, the group of conservatives who were firmly entrenched in the party and had no intention of leaving. The question of who was to obtain control of the promised land and who was to wander in the desert could be determined only by the party and the nation at large in 1940. In the meantime, however, energetic spadework and sharp in-fighting were called for.

To be sure, the ideological split can be exagggerated. The vast majority of professional politicians appear to have been far more interested in supporting policies and candidates whose popularity would insure their party's success—and their own jobs—than the wisdom or lack thereof of the policies and candidates. Like the majority of American voters, their position was somewhere between the two ideological extremes. They were important, however, because by weight of numbers they held the balance of power between the wings of the Democratic party. To pinpoint some of the more important individuals and policies involved, a closer study of each faction is necessary.

Party Factions: The New Dealers

Assisting President Roosevelt in his effort to liberalize the Democratic party was a group of advisers and assistants most often grouped together under the title of "New Dealers." Even before he was elected President, he was gathering about himself the nucleus of a "Brain Trust," largely made up at that time of Columbia University economists, for the purpose of developing the New Deal program. As one former member of the group noted, such men were indispensable to Roosevelt. They supplied him with the facts he needed to formulate his policies as well as providing a good many ideas of their own.[20] Frank Walker, who was probably as close to him as any man, believed that he never really read a book in his life. His facts and ideas were picked from the brains of other men.[21] And right from the beginning there was a conflict between the idea men and the professional politicians. Even the headquarters were in different hotels during the 1932 campaign, the politicians meeting at the Biltmore in New York under the direction of Jim Farley, and the idea men at the Hotel Roosevelt a block away.[22] By 1937 most of the members of the original Brain Trust had departed, but another group had moved up to take their places. The change in personnel and ideology was probably not as radical as some historians have made it out to be.[23] But there was some change in both. The concept of national planning and mutual benefits for all elements of the national economic structure, which inspired much of the first-term legislation, came under heavy fire from liberals and conservatives alike, and was largely cancelled by the Supreme Court. It was then abandoned in favor of a more Wilsonian second New Deal, marked by the traditional liberal and progressive distrust of bigness in business, large-scale operations, and centralized planning and management.[24] With the shift in philosophy the Brain Trust gave way to the New Dealers. There was, of course, also a good deal of continuity in the liberal administration advisers. Even those who began appearing in the spotlight for the first time after 1936 had, for the most part, been in government service for some years before; the difference was that they were now moving into the inner circle of advisers and thereby into the limelight which inevitably surrounds the occupant of the White House.

Top ranking leaders of the New Deal group were cabinet members Harold Ickes, Secretary of Interior; Henry Wallace, Secretary of Agriculture; and Frances Perkins, Secretary of Labor. Not quite on a par with them in the prestige of his office but in many ways more influential was presidential confidant and W.P.A. Administrator Harry Hopkins. As a group they were noteworthy for competence, integrity, and lack of any important political connections. Not one of them was a professional politician. "Honest Harold" Ickes had been a Bull Moose Republican with a political record consisting largely of a relatively unsuccessful thirty-year vendetta against Chicago's machine politicians. Henry Wallace was also a Republican until the election of 1928, and he was registered as a Republican in Iowa as late as 1938. Harry Hopkins and Frances Perkins had both been social workers who had held positions in the Roosevelt administration when F.D.R. was governor of New York. None of them had the sort of background necessary to understand and sympathize with the needs and desires of professional politicians. Insofar as the New Dealers were a cohesive force, united to do battle with the conservatives in the Cabinet and in Congress, both Henry Wallace and Frances Perkins were somewhat on the fringe of this group. Their philosophy was acceptable enough, but they were not often in the councils of the inner circle of the New Deal.[25]

Behind these leaders was a remarkable group of dedicated, competent, and intelligent followers, all of whom had achieved influential positions on the basis of sheer ability. Undoubtedly the element within the group which attracted the most notice from friends and foes alike was the Tom Corcoran-Ben Cohen team. By 1937 the "jolly hot dogs," as Hugh Johnson had dubbed the pair, were receiving much of the praise and blame for the legislative program of the New Deal. Whether antibusiness Brandeisians[26] or merely power-hungry Machiavellians,[27] their influence with the President caused intense resentment among the party regulars, and Corcoran's enthusiastic but often tactless lobbying methods tended to exacerbate the situation.[28] The more publicized and politically active of the two, he was described as "the Duke of Buckingham" by one writer,[29] and "the most fearsome force throughout the entire reaches of the government" by another.[30] As one hostile observer put it, he might easily have resigned to take a private law practice with a salary in six figures, but "there is no fun equal to that of experimenting on a nation."[31] For the quiet, shy Ben Cohen there was far less animosity, perhaps because it was recognized that he had no desire for any personal power and remained in public service more or less against his own inclinations. The most hostile of New Deal critics could only write that Cohen was so brilliant that "Dr. Roosevelt enjoys having him around as a chilled man enjoys sitting near a stove."[32]

Whatever may be said for or against the legal skills of Corcoran and Cohen, when it came to reshaping the Democratic party, they had the same handicaps that afflicted the other New Dealers. They had neither political experience nor any great understanding of politicians, as the next three years were to prove. Nevertheless, their power was very real and feared, not only because they had the ear of the President but also because of Corcoran's many loyal connections in all parts of the executive branch, many of whom he had recruited from eastern law schools. Their own official positions—Corcoran was an attorney for the Reconstruction Finance Corporation and Cohen was general counsel for the National Power Policy Committee of the Public Works Administration—were hardly the measure of their influence.

Others of the inner circle were no less impressive in their abilities and no more impressive in their political backgrounds. The chairman of the Board of Governors of the Federal Reserve System, who would become increasingly influential during the second New Deal, was a Utah banker, Marriner Eccles, a Keynesian long before he read Keynes. William O. Douglas, chairman of the Securities Exchange Commission, was an ex-college professor whose advice would become increasingly valued by Roosevelt,[33] and Robert Jackson was an upstate New York lawyer whose work in the Justice Department was beginning to attract attention. Behind them was a squad of brilliant young economists, analysts, and lawyers from the various departments and commissions of the executive branch of government. Herman Oliphant, an economist from the Treasury Department, Isador Lubin from the Labor Department, Mordecai Ezekiel from Agriculture, Lauchlin Currie under Eccles, Leon Henderson and David K. Niles under Hopkins, made up the nucleus of the group.[34] Allied with them but holding no offices in the federal government were Felix Frankfurter of the Harvard Law School and Samuel Rosenman, a justice of the New York Supreme Court and frequent presidential speech writer.

Essentially they formed a sort of palace guard or junta and were, in effect, an extension of the President's political personality. They would last as long as the presidency was held by Roosevelt or one of their group and no longer, and they were well aware of it. However much they might differ on details of what the New Deal program should include, they were united in their desire to make over the Democratic party as an instrument of reform—and to stay in power. They were the champions of the newer elements in the Roosevelt coalition—organized labor, farmers, Negroes, the unemployed, and liberals everywhere, and they tended to show little sympathy for and less understanding of big business.[35] As one New Deal sympathizer noted, their lack of tact in some respects was such that "they proceeded to spawn Roosevelt-haters with a fecundity that makes that of the rabbit seem the next thing to sterility."[36]

If President Roosevelt stepped down in 1940, it was presumed by many that he would choose his successor to carry on his program from this group if he possibly could. By 1937, however, even as the second term began, Stanley High noted an air of despair and impending doom among the group, as though they sensed a resurgence of conservatism.[37] The prospects of none of them looked particularly bright inasmuch as none had either political popularity or a base for political power. The problem for the more ambitious of them was to build up a following among party leaders of their home state as well as an impressive national image as the logical successor of Roosevelt, all within a period of three years. Several were willing to make the effort.

Two of them, Harry Hopkins and Henry Wallace, appeared to have the best chances of rising to the top. After President Roosevelt, probably no one was more closely identified with the New Deal than free-spending, tough-talking Harry Hopkins. This was both his strength and his weakness in 1937. He had the ear and affection of Roosevelt, the support of a huge and loyal staff, and the appreciation of millions of unemployed who had been aided by the Works Projects Administration. Characteristically, however, his political right hand man, David K. Niles, who was dedicated to the idea that Hopkins should be the next President, was not a Democrat himself, having headed the La Follette-Wheeler campaign in Massachusetts in 1924 and the Progressives-for-Roosevelt in 1936.[38] Moreover the expensive, boondoggling W.P.A. was a scandal to the conservatives in the party, and Hopkins was a favorite whipping boy. During the debates on a relief measure in 1937 Congressman Jed Johnson of Oklahoma remarked:

> The gentleman from Tennessee (Sam McReynolds), as well as several other speakers, have based the burden of their opposition to giving the President the amount he is asking for in this bill on the grounds that they do not like the W.P.A. Administrator, Mr. Harry Hopkins. In fact, it seems a popular pastime to criticize and condemn Mr. Hopkins.[39]

The House did not limit itself to mere criticism. It added a clause to the relief bill cutting Hopkins' salary from $12,000 to $10,000, partly out of spite and partly because they feared his potential political power.[40]

Hopkins himself was not lacking in ambition. His biographer, Robert Sherwood, says he was aiming at the presidency at least by 1936, if not 1935.[41] It was noted by others that when he had first come to Washington in 1933 he had been indifferent and impatient with politicians and politics, whereas in 1937 he could be seen cultivating and showing deference to a number of the "key men" in Congress.[42] By December of 1937, however, he had run into difficulties far greater than any number of conservative opponents. Although it was announced that he was in Mayo Clinic with a serious case of stomach ulcers, it was cancer that caused the removal of a large part of his stomach. From that time on his health was precarious at best.[43]

Both Hopkins and Wallace were originally from Iowa. The difference was that whereas Hopkins had left Iowa for New York shortly after his graduation from Grinnell College, Wallace lived there, published a farm journal there, and was well known in the state. Thus, there was some possibility that he might be able to develop some support among the local politicians. Like Hopkins he headed a large federal organization and had a staff which was personally devoted to him. If there was any political planning for the future in the Agriculture Department in 1937, however, it was not evident. Wallace was not a politician by nature, did not work very hard at it, and certainly had no great talent for it. Yet, for all that, he was an outstanding liberal, and no one counted him out as a likely candidate for 1940. His future political life, it seemed, would depend largely on the ties he was able to make with the local Iowa politicians.[44]

A far more likely means of retaining the presidency for the New Deal than the candidacy of any member of the Administration, however, was a third nomination for Roosevelt. It was true that the precedent denying a third term to any President, dating back to the founding of the nation, was a strong one, but it was just as true that a number of previous Presidents would have gladly shattered it had not circumstances—not reverence—prevented it. It was also true that Roosevelt seemed to love to break precedents and that, according to a *Fortune* poll taken in April of 1937, 52.6

per cent of the American people favored a third term for him.[45] So alarmed was Democratic Senator Edward Burke at the danger that as early as January 6, when Congress had barely gotten organized, he introduced a constitutional amendment to limit the office of President to one six-year term with no re-election.[46] It was never brought to a vote, but it did reflect the conservative state of mind before any real split in the party ranks had developed.

There is no evidence at all to suggest that Roosevelt was even considering the possibility of a third term as early as 1937, though it soon became evident that he had no intention of reducing his own political potentialities as "Cousin Ted" had done by pledging himself not to run. The closest he came publicly to ruling out a third term was his speech at the Democratic Victory Dinner on March 4, when he stated:

> My great ambition on January 20, 1941, is to turn over this desk and chair in the White House to my successor, whoever he may be, with the assurance that I am at the same time turning over to him as President, a nation intact, a nation at peace, a nation prosperous. . . .[47]

Privately he was slightly more positive. When Senator Sherman Minton of Indiana wrote him that "your 'adoring' Cousin Alice" (Alice Roosevelt Longworth) had given him forty to ten odds that the President would be the candidate in 1940, and ". . . I don't mind losing my senatorial toga or my political life following you but I can't afford to lose forty dollars," Roosevelt replied gaily, "In the strictest of confidence, if you have any doubt, I will gladly take that forty to ten off your hands!"[48]

During the fierce battle over the President's Court-packing plan in the spring and early summer of 1937, however, Roosevelt realized the threat of third term was a potent weapon not to be lightly blunted. Concerning the growing power of the party conservatives he remarked to Farley, "This comes from telling them I would not be a candidate again."[49] Quickly he reversed his field. Calling in his congressional leaders, he told them firmly that the fight for a reformed Supreme Court would go on, but if it should fail he would take the issue to the country in 1938 and

1940. It was a shaken group of advisers that left the White House after that conference.[50]

The question of a third term was largely a matter for private speculation by the politicians until the latter part of June, when it suddenly became of wider interest thanks to the crisp announcement by Governor George Earle of Pennsylvania, "I am for Franklin Roosevelt for President in 1940 unqualifiedly and finally."[51] The motives of Governor Earle, who was considered by many as the front runner for the 1940 nomination himself, were, of course, questioned. Sneered Senator Burton K. Wheeler, "Governor Earle reminds me of John Alden. Why don't you speak for yourself, Gov?"[52]

The President's first press conference following the Earle statement has become rather famous as a masterpiece of humorous but firm uncommunicativeness. When Robert Post of the New York *Times* asked, ". . . can you tell us or would you say whether you would accept the nomination?" the President groaned, "Oh, my God! This is hot weather. Bob, go into the corner over there and put on the dunce cap and stand with your back to the crowd." Seconds later he told a persistent Fred Perkins of the Pittsburgh *Press*, "My God, you will have to join Bob in the corner."[53] The President thus inaugurated a policy of silence which was to be as important as any other single factor in determining the outcome of the 1940 Democratic National Convention.

The national response to the open suggestion of a third term was rather unfavorable, and it was evident that the Court-packing bill had eaten into the President's popularity with the American people. A *Fortune* poll showed that only 36.9 per cent of those asked favored the President's proposal to reform the Court, whereas 38.1 per cent wanted a retention of the status quo and 18.9 per cent favored some other means of reform. At the same time, those in favor of a third term declined from 52.6 per cent in April to 45 per cent in July. It was observed by the editors that the Supreme Court struggle had cut into the President's popularity as no other issue ever had.[54] The examples of Hitler, Mussolini, and Franco were especially grim warnings against one-man rule just at that time. Even the liberal *Nation* editorialized: "There is only one thing for Mr. Roosevelt to do. He must 'unqualifiedly and finally' announce that he will not be a candidate in 1940 to succeed him-self."[55] It might be added, however, that despite the apparent loss of popularity by the President, Charles Oursler of *Liberty* magazine told presidential secretary Grace Tully that a poll *Liberty* was mak-ing showed that the vast majority of editors, industrialists, business and labor leaders believed he would be the first third-term President in history.[56]

Within the party the Earle suggestion did not engender any very great enthusiasm either. Jim Farley was quoted as saying it was too early to talk about 1940, although privately he himself was discussing it a bit.[57] For several weeks the papers were quoting statements for or against by a number of state governors until the United Press finally took a poll to see how the Democratic gov-ernors as a group stood on the issue. Six openly favored a third term; three were opposed to it as a matter of principle; and twenty-nine shrewdly kept their own counsel.[58] It was not an overwhelm-ing vote of confidence in the President's ability to control his own party in the future.

As it might be expected, the sharpest criticism of a possible third term came from conservative, anti-New Deal Democrats. One indirect effect of their opposition was the defeat of the Presi-dent's program in Congress as part of an effort to discredit its author.[59] Nevertheless, by the end of the first session of Congress in August of 1937 it was reported by one journalist that those hostile to Roosevelt were becoming extremely jittery over all the discussion of the third term, since it was thought it might deaden the public reaction to the shock of broken precedent.[60] They did more than their share, however, to keep the issue a topic of con-versation. Senator Wheeler announced at the close of the con-gressional session in August that he would oppose anyone seeking a third term, since "the matter goes beyond partisan or personal considerations."[61] A short time later Senator Edward Burke of Nebraska charged that Roosevelt was already an active candidate for a third term, and his colleague, Senator William King of Utah, reported that friends of the President were already lining up work-ers in several states.[62]

So seriously did the conservatives take the threat of a con-tinuation of the New Deal under President Roosevelt (or any other

New Dealer) after 1941 that in September one of them, Senator Burke, announced the formation of a group of both pro- and anti-New Deal congressmen for the purpose of preventing the President from either serving a third term or naming his successor. He charged that the re-election of Roosevelt would mean "dictatorship, the like of which this country has never seen," and he added that the group was also opposed to Henry Wallace and Senator Robert La Follette, Jr., since they would be under obligations to Roosevelt and might appoint him to the Supreme Court.[63] The names of the members of this cabal were not revealed, but there was no great mystery about who were the anti-Roosevelt men in Congress. If Senator Burke expected to arouse great public support with his announcement, he was disappointed. There was no public response whatever, and the group, as such, was heard from no more as an organized antithird-term force. There was simply no public backing for it.[64] With the possible exception of the northwestern part of the country, where reporters accompanying the President on an early fall vacation trip found Democrats generally favorable,[65] most of the nation was increasingly hostile to a third term,[66] but not hostile enough to take an interest in Senator Burke and his colleagues.

Besides the President and members of his Cabinet, several other liberals appeared to have good to fair chances of moving into the White House in 1941. According to Stanley High, the President himself would have preferred Robert La Follette as a successor in 1937.[67] Since La Follette was not a Democrat, however, the only likelihood of his running for the presidency would be as a third-party candidate. It was conceivable to a number of people that the conservatives might regain control of the Democratic party; the way would then be clear for an amalgamation of New Dealers, Wisconsin Progressives, third-party radicals from other states, and organized labor to unite behind La Follette, and with the support of Roosevelt to win the election.[68] In 1937, however, Roosevelt was a long way from giving up on the Democratic party.

The leading heir apparent among the liberals was the man who seemed to be driving the third-term bandwagon for Roosevelt, Governor George Earle of Pennsylvania.[69] The Gallup Poll for April of 1937 showed Earle in second place among Democratic contenders, right behind Jim Farley, who was not regarded as a

New Dealer or even a serious candidate at that time.[70] In many respects Earle looked like an ideal candidate. He was from a very wealthy Philadelphia Main Line family and had been a Republican until 1932. Converted to the New Deal, he contributed $35,000 to the Democratic campaign chest that year and was rewarded by being appointed Minister to Austria. Brought back to Pennsylvania to run for governor in 1934 by Senator Joseph Guffey, he was the first Democrat to win in that state in forty-four years.[71] He had, in that office, compiled an outstanding liberal record which included a balanced budget, a "little Wagner Act," an unemployment compensation act, a public utility act, and the first state Bureau of Civil Liberties in the nation.[72] Politically, he could count on the support of organized labor and the shrewd backing of Senator Joseph Guffey and his machine.[73] Although he denied having any ambitions to live in the White House after 1940,[74] it was noted that at the President's second inauguration Earle's suite at the Carleton Hotel, the hall leading to it, and the lobby below were jammed with Earle-for-President enthusiasts and, further, that he was giving an unusual number of speeches outside of Pennsylvania during 1937.[75]

The other frequently mentioned contender among the liberal Democratic governors was Frank Murphy of Michigan. Like Earle, Murphy's election to the governorship broke a Republican stranglehold on his state, and his cool-headed handling of the tense sit-down strike crisis of 1937 had given him national stature. An unmarried ascetic who neither smoked nor drank (even tea or coffee), he was noted for scrupulous honesty and fairness during his career as judge, Mayor of Detroit, High Commissioner of the Philippines, and governor.[76] He was, however, a Roman Catholic, and, further, it was apparent by the end of the year that the sit-down strikes were doing him a great deal more harm than good. Had there been only the strike at General Motors, which ended in February, Murphy would have emerged a top-notch presidential possibility with no blemish on his record.[77] Alfred P. Sloan, Jr., of General Motors testified that everyone concerned was "indebted to the Governor's untiring and conscientious efforts," and John L. Lewis added, "The Nation is the beneficiary of his statesmanship."[78] Roosevelt, who had appointed him High Commissioner of the Philippines in 1933 and called him back to run for governor in 1936, wired him: "Yours has been a high public service nobly performed for which I desire to express the thanks of the Nation."[79]

But as the year wore on and the sit-down strikes spread, the feeling developed that had Murphy carried out the court orders promptly in the General Motors strike and evicted the strikers, the epidemic would have been avoided.[80] In the Detroit Athletic Club automobile manufacturers could be heard complaining that "Murphy has given industry the worst rooking it has ever had."[81] Many thought he had loaded the dice for labor, but labor itself was not so sure. The General Motors strike had come to an end when it did because of a sharp, private ultimatum delivered by Murphy to John L. Lewis.[82] By the end of 1937, as the labor situation became more chaotic, Murphy was publicly talking and acting a good deal tougher toward labor. Nevertheless, it seemed most unlikely that the southern conservatives in the party would ever support for the presidency the man who had been Governor of Michigan during the time the rights of private property had been so seriously abused by the sit downs.

Party Factions: The Democratic Right

Conservatism within the Democratic party generally meant opposition to most of the New Deal policies. The term "conservative" is a relative one; most of the members of the party usually grouped together under it claimed to be liberals, Jeffersonian liberals. Many of the more prominent members of this group, led by Al Smith, had "taken a walk" out of the party in the 1936 campaign, but by 1937 there still remained a relatively small clique of Democrats in Congress which was unalterably opposed to the radical trend the party was taking and did not hesitate to say so. Of particular concern to them was the Administration's consistent policy of deficit spending, its sympathy for organized labor, the general extension of federal power at the expense of the states, and the extension of executive power at the expense of Congress. The southern conservatives were also deeply concerned about the obvious Administration interest in the Negroes.

Although there was considerable sympathy for these views by

most of the party leaders in Congress, only a small minority in the House and Senate stated its opposition to the New Deal openly prior to 1937. As the second term began, the group appeared to be politically impotent, and there was a strong belief in some circles that it would soon follow Al Smith out of the party.[83] But appearances were deceptive. Several factors account for the eventual resurgence of the group during the period under consideration, the most important of which were the top-heavy Democratic majorities in both houses of Congress, which made party discipline difficult if not well-nigh impossible, the remarkable political astuteness of some of the conservatives, and some colossal blundering on the part of the New Dealers.

At this time the most influential and doctrinaire conservative Democrats were in the Senate, and two of them, Harry Byrd and Carter Glass of Virginia, provided much of the moral leadership. Because of an antiquated state constitution and a political machine which Tammany might well have envied, their seats in the Senate were perfectly safe from any indignation their constituents might have felt for the positions they took.[84] Hence, they were free to be as critical of Roosevelt as they wished. Senator Byrd had been relatively hostile to the New Deal right from the start, but Carter Glass, although he had refused the position as Secretary of the Treasury under Roosevelt partly because he feared the New Deal meant fiscal irresponsibility, had supported some of the earlier measures.[85] By 1934, however, he publicly stated:

> I think the sooner Washington is rid of impatient academicians whose threatening manifestoes and decrees keep business and banks alike in suspension, even in consternation, the sooner and more certain will we have a complete restoration of confidence and resumption of business in every line of endeavor.[86]

On another occasion he expressed his political frame of reference very clearly and thereby that of many of his colleagues as well:

> Perhaps I am a relic of constitutional government—I am rather inclined to think I am. I entertain the misguided notion that the Constitution of the United States as it existed in the time of Grover Cleveland is the same Constitution that exists today. . . .[87]

By 1940 Glass was writing bluntly of one Senate liberal, "I frequently tell Bob Wagner that he has become Public Enemy No. 1. I have a warm personal regard for him; but he is a group socialist."[88]

Others who agreed with the Virginians were Millard Tydings of Maryland, who had supported only one major New Deal measure (National Industrial Recovery Act) since 1933, Peter Gerry of Rhode Island, David L. Walsh of Massachusetts, Josiah Bailey of North Carolina, "Cotton Ed" Smith of South Carolina, Edward Burke of Nebraska, and Royal Copeland of New York. Tydings stood four square for fiscal responsibility, twice submitting proposals for joint resolutions which would have provided that Congress could not appropriate more money than its estimated income without making a very definite provision for the payment of the debt.[89] Gerry and Walsh were both strong supporters of Al Smith, and Bailey and Smith were southern Bourbons. For many years Senator Smith had won every primary campaign on his own personal platform of states' rights, white supremacy (protection for southern womanhood), and tariff for revenue only. His major concern was what the "one gallus" farmer wanted.[90] Ed Burke was an unpleasant surprise to the New Dealers. He had been elected to the Senate in 1934 under the auspices of the Arthur Mullen machine in Nebraska and with the implicit aid of Roosevelt, whose use of Burke's definition of the New Deal in a speech during the primary campaign was considered very helpful.[91] After his victory in the primary Burke wrote gratefully to Roosevelt that he was ready to meet anti-New Deal opposition at every turn.[92] The first turn was the Utilities Holding Company Bill, and Burke not only met the opposition but joined it as well. In August of 1936 he made it official by resigning from the Democratic National Committee with a letter to Farley in which he stated: "I cannot work for the election of any candidate masquerading as a Democrat who is a Democrat in name only and who neither understands nor cares at all for the fundamental principles of the Democratic party."[93] Senator Royal Copeland was a doctor and a former Republican mayor of Ann Arbor, Michigan. Taking advantage of his popularity gained from writing popular health treatises for the Hearst papers, he ran for the Senate in New York in 1922, was elected, and was unbeatable thereafter.[94] His thinking in large measure seems to have been shaped by his association with Hearst.

Though these were some of the more important conservatives, it would be a mistake to think that there were not a good many other Democrats, both in the Senate and in the House, who quietly shared the views of these leaders. As White House correspondent Raymond Clapper pointed out, neither voting records nor a Congressman's public statements were necessarily a good indication of his liberal or conservative leanings or, indeed, of his influence on legislation. A relative conservative like Walter George of Georgia had a far better New Deal voting record than a relative liberal like Robert Bulkley of Ohio. Voting records do not show proposals and votes for crippling amendments, consistent opposition in committee and even on the floor; they merely show that when the "Yeas and Nays" were taken, the lawmaker bowed to the inevitable and kept his record of administration support clean.[95] One of the most powerful New Deal opponents in Congress was John J. O'Connor, chairman of the House Rules Committee. It was neither his votes nor his debating power that slowed up liberal legislation, but his ability to bottle up legislation he did not favor in the Rules Committee.

Although this conservative clique naturally wanted very much to capture the 1940 presidential nomination and control of the party for one of its own, and though newspaper columnists occasionally remarked on what a fine President Senator Harry Byrd of Virginia would make,[96] it was generally agreed that the best they could hope for would be to prevent Roosevelt from naming a successor from among the more radical liberals or taking a third term himself. Indeed, if they were able to do that much, many—including the New Dealers—believed it would be a victory for conservatism, since the nominee would necessarily then have to come from the ranks of the party regulars.

Party Factions: The Democratic Center

Undoubtedly the majority of Democrats, both in the legislative and executive branches of government, were neither New

Dealers nor hide-bound conservatives in early 1937. For many of them, especially those from the South, office-holding was a life-time career, and they had found that the road to power and prestige was party discipline and party regularity, not crusades for or against policies and ideals. When up to this time the President had stamped a measure with the party label, they had generally gone along with him regardless of their private views on the matter. Perhaps their philosophy was best expressed by Vice President Garner, one of the most influential of the group, when he told some representatives who were complaining about the President's character and judgment, "Now look here. It doesn't matter what kind of a fool you think he is. He's your fool just as long as he's President and the leader of your party."[97]

Because of the one-party system and the very slow turnover of its politicians once they were elected, many of the most powerful members of the orthodox center of the party came from the South. They included Senate Majority Leader Joseph Robinson of Arkansas, Speaker of the House William Bankhead of Alabama, and such perennial Democratic leaders as Pat Harrison of Mississippi, Tom Connally of Texas, Walter George of Georgia, James Byrnes of South Carolina, and a great many others of similar weight. Though by and large their sympathies lay with the conservative wing of the party more often than with the liberals, they voted consistently with the Administration. Pat Harrison, who was described by many at the time and since as an anti-New Deal or anti-Roosevelt man, remarked after a sharp disagreement with the President on a tax bill, "I concede to none of my Democratic brethren a greater degree of loyalty to the President than I. . . . In the future, as in the past, I shall resolve every doubt in favor of Administration policies, and vote for them."[98]

The northern regulars were no more inclined to be wild-eyed reformers than their southern brethren, but they were more inclined to be sensitive to Administration pressure, which might be either direct, in the form of the "loaves and fishes" of federal patronage, or indirect, in the form of a request for a vote delivered through the local boss who was responsible for the incumbent being in Congress in the first place. Senator F. Ryan Duffy of the rather moribund and conservative Wisconsin Democratic "machine," for instance, never seemed to consider voting against the Administration, though he was not known to have any strong liberal convictions personally. In like manner, Senator William Dieterich, the representative of the Kelly-Nash Illinois machine in the Senate, had a perfect New Deal voting record between 1933 and 1938.[99]

Some of the most influential of party regulars were, of course, in the Cabinet itself. The most important and powerful of these, politically speaking, was the Postmaster General and National Democratic Committee Chairman, James Aloysius Farley. Short of the President, probably no Democrat was more respected and genuinely loved by members of his own party. Although President Roosevelt brought in the votes, Chairman Farley handed out the jobs. And he handed out jobs more efficiently and more fairly than anyone could remember it ever being done. What was more important, he handed them out to and through regular party members. Late in the Hundred Days he laid down three rules for the hiring of federal employees: (1) that the candidate should be qualified for the job, (2) that he should be a Democrat, (3) that a written request from the state leaders should be in the National Committee files for every person appointed to a federal position.[100] This, of course, meant that control of patronage was in the hands of the party regulars. Nevertheless, even the New Dealers, who naturally tended to be rather idealistic about the appointment of government workers, generally had nothing but praise for the way he handled the "spoils" until later in the second term, when they began bypassing him in order to get men who "thought right" into offices of importance.[101]

Other members of the Administration who might be classed as orthodox Democrats, or at least *persona grata* with those who were, included Cordell Hull, Secretary of State; Dan Roper, Secretary of Commerce; Attorney General Homer Cummings; Secretary of War Harry Woodring, and, one of the most powerful of all, Reconstruction Finance Administrator Jesse Jones.

It was generally conceded that if President Roosevelt did not run for a third term in 1940—and there were few in 1937 who thought he would—his successor would probably come from this orthodox group, regardless of Roosevelt's desire that a New Dealer succeed him. By and large, a compromise candidate of the orthodox persuasion would be far more satisfactory to the conservatives in the party than to the liberals. At the very least the party would be turned back to the professional politicians, and there would almost surely be more emphasis on fiscal responsibility and "business confidence," neither of which even got lip service from the New Dealers. One young Congressman summed up the liberal attitude succinctly when he remarked, "It will cost a lot of money, but what the hell is money where lives are involved?"[102]

Quite obviously, one did not have to be an archconservative to be considered right-of-center by Democratic liberals in 1937 and thus eliminated as a presidential possibility as far as the New Dealers were concerned. As important a cog in the Roosevelt political machine as Chairman Farley, who had supported every New Deal policy with perfect loyalty, though without much interest or understanding, fell into the category of candidates unacceptable to the liberal wing of the party. Indeed, few even took him seriously as a candidate for higher office, despite the fact that his name was at the top of the Gallup Poll throughout most of 1937 as the man most likely to succeed Roosevelt.[103] Delbert Clark of the New York *Times* probably voiced the opinion of most observers when he noted that although Farley undoubtedly liked the idea of being President, "the chance of his nomination is so slight as to be negligible."[104] The editors of *American Mercury* predicted that the voters "would laugh in every hamlet from Calais, Maine, to Coronado, California, if the Honorable James Aloysius Farley should announce himself for the presidency."[105] Indeed, in most discussion of possible 1940 candidates Farley's name did not even come up except to observe that he would have great influence in determining who it would be.

Farley himself may have had other ideas. The evidence is conflicting. Molly Dewson, of the Women's Division of the party, recalled that right after the 1936 campaign was over and Roosevelt safely back in office, Farley asked her one day what she thought of Frank Murphy as the candidate for 1940 (or another prominent Catholic politician—she was not positive it was Murphy). When she replied that having been in the Bible Belt in the 1928 campaign, she was convinced that no Catholic could win for a great many years, she noticed that Farley looked so disappointed and grim that she could not get it out of her mind. A week later it finally dawned on her that he had been "feeling out the ground in his own behalf."[106] Farley, on the other hand, denies that he ever sought the presidency for himself; his highest ambition was the vice presidency.[107]

Roosevelt, though he had no religious bias himself, knew very well the severe handicap Farley's religion would be to achieving either office. More fundamental, however, was his belief, shared not only by the inner circle of liberals but by most other political observers as well, that Farley was no New Dealer.[108] He had nothing to do with making policy and, indeed, seemed to have no interest in it. On one occasion the President remarked to Grace Tully:

> Grace, you know the manner in which I go around the Cabinet table, starting with Cordell (Hull) and giving each one an opportunity to tell what is on his mind. Well, it's a curious thing that in all these years I have never heard Jim Farley make a constructive suggestion or even criticism regarding anything of importance to the country as a whole. He makes a routine report on the Post Office Department but he has no idea of the broad objectives of this Administration.[109]

Moreover, Farley's complete loyalty to the Administration was somewhat taken for granted. Raymond Moley remarked that if Roosevelt had chosen to speak on the Koran, Farley would have enthusiastically gotten the product into as many hands as possible.[110] Frank Walker observed that Farley never disagreed for any length of time with Roosevelt; they might differ briefly on some point, but Farley always wound up with the same statement, "You're the Boss! Whatever you say goes with me. But I just wanted to express the viewpoint of some who have talked."[111] As far as the more radical liberals outside the Administration were concerned, Farley disgraced himself in 1937 when he supported Democrat Jeremiah Mahoney for Mayor of New York against the darling of eastern progressives, Fiorello La Guardia. "As for Jim Farley," steamed a *New Republic* editorial, "he proved once again that he is a machine politician whose ideals have never risen above the ward clubroom, utterly unfit for any public office."[112] A Democrat was a Democrat to Farley, and everyone else was the opposition and that was precisely what liberals objected to in him.

Secretary of State Cordell Hull also had friends, chiefly in Tennessee, who were eager to begin work for his candidacy. He was far too canny a politician, however, to offer himself as a target so early in the season, especially since all his attention was concentrated on the increasingly bleak foreign situation. Accordingly, he informed his would-be backers that he had no interest in the presidency, and even if he did, it was too early to begin taking organizational steps.[113] So successful was Hull in keeping his name out of the domestic political picture before 1940 that he was largely exempt from the usual sniping other candidates were facing.

Another party regular of President Roosevelt's own official family who appeared to have a chance for the presidency in 1940 was R.F.C. Administrator Jesse Jones, a self-made millionaire many times over and probably the most popular of all Democrats with the business community. He was careful to keep his fences mended in Texas by frequent trips and consultations with state leaders and by sending his speeches out in pamphlet form by the thousands,[114] but he was, nevertheless, not highly regarded by the leaders in his home state and carried little political weight.[115] He was considerably less popular with the New Dealers and President Roosevelt, chiefly because he did not care for Roosevelt's brand of liberalism and occasionally indicated as much in public. He was reported to be "shocked" by the appointment of the liberal Hugo Black to the Supreme Court in August of 1937,[116] and in December he was highly critical of the government's taxing program in one of his many speeches to businessmen. On that occasion he drew a sharp four-page scolding from Roosevelt, which ended with the suggestion, "I think we must all be very careful not to make general assertions but to separate the sheep from the goats and talk in terms of actual facts."[117] Frank Walker believed Jones would have been eliminated from the Administration a good deal sooner than he was except that Roosevelt knew he was a symbol of big business and the President did not want to cut the last connection between the New Deal and the business community.[118] Though the demand for the candidacy of Jones was "as loud as the tramp of a timorous kitten," as George Creel observed,[119] a successful conservative or congressional challenge to presidential control of the party by 1940 could have placed him among the leading dark horses.

A somewhat more colorful threat for first place on the 1940 ticket was former governor Paul V. McNutt of Indiana, who had made quite a name for himself as chief executive. Spectacularly handsome and apparently a born politician, he had moved like lightning from being youngest dean in the history of the Indiana University Law School to National Commander of the American Legion to first Democratic governor of Indiana since 1916. In that office his record was sensational, if somewhat mixed. Working with heavy Democratic majorities in both houses of the legislature, his administration in 1933 passed laws more rapidly than Congress during the Hundred Days. On the credit side of the ledger McNutt reorganized the entire state government for a saving of $2,000,000 a year and tremendously increased political power for himself, balanced the budget of the debt-ridden state and left a $10,000,000 surplus by the time he retired from office, and poured enough money into the state public school system to save it from the total ruin it seemed to be heading for when he took office, while at the same time paying more money out for teachers' salaries than any previous governor. Further, he had been able to construct a powerful political machine and leave a man totally loyal to him in the governor's chair when the state constitution forced his retirement.[120]

The debit side of the ledger, however, was in some ways more impressive. One McNutt innovation which contributed mightily to his power was the "Two Percent Club," a "voluntary" organization consisting of those state employees who contributed two per cent of their salaries for the use of the Democratic organization. Although the Republicans found it advisable not to make it an issue in Indiana after 1934, when McNutt challenged them to make public the sources of their funds, its unsavory appearance of political extortion was to prove a millstone about his neck in his efforts to climb higher. Another McNutt-inspired act which had a slightly gamey air about it was the beer import system, whereby the state was divided into districts and the businesses able to import beer into them limited by franchise. The question in some people's minds was: Was the act passed to insure the good behavior of liquor dealers by making the franchise too valuable to risk in illegal operations, as advertised by the McNutt administration, or was it passed to obtain huge campaign contributions and other favors from companies interested in a franchise?[121]

These were shadows in the McNutt past which might have been forgotten had the Governor not also made some rather bitter and extremely influential personal enemies. Organized labor and unorganized liberals throughout the country were infuriated by his use of the National Guard and martial law for months in Sullivan and Vigo counties, which eventually resulted in the breaking of several bitter strikes. These actions plus the emergency powers given him by the legislature earned him the unenviable nickname of "the Hoosier Hitler."[122] Even earlier, however, McNutt had made an enemy of Jim Farley, which was hardly the way to rise in the ranks of the Democratic party. At the 1932 convention Farley had asked McNutt for help in pushing the Roosevelt nomination across in the crucial second ballot. McNutt replied that "an overwhelming majority of Indiana Democratic leaders feel they should not be hampered by instructions." He was further quoted after the ballot as saying, "Not only were we in a position to do Roosevelt some good with our own Indiana vote, but our action would have brought half a hundred more."[123] It was the wrong time to gloat over his political influence. Thereafter Farley had little or no use for McNutt.

McNutt climbed aboard the Roosevelt bandwagon with a vengeance in 1936 and received by way of reward the appointment as High Commissioner of the Philippines upon his retirement from office as governor. The appointment was made in early February of 1937, but the word was already out that McNutt would be a serious candidate in 1940. At Farley's testimonial dinner in January, Roosevelt mentioned that he was uncertain whether the appointment had been a wise one. Vice President Garner observed that he did not know him personally, but he did know that he was a candidate for 1940, and the Philippines might be just the place for him. "Do you think," cracked Farley, "the Philippines will be far enough"?[124]

These were the figures who seemed to tower highest on the horizon as President Roosevelt took the oath of office for the second time on a cold, rainy January morning. It was clear at that time that if he were able to keep his great coalition in harmony until 1940, his word would be decisive in the choice of his successor, perhaps not even excluding one of the politically weak New Dealers. What upset all such calculations, however, was the disruption of the coalition. Within two months after the second term began, the party was in turmoil and discipline virtually gone. Moreover, it became increasingly apparent as the year wore on that the hostilities could be smoothed over only by the abandonment of much of the New Deal program as well as the President's virtual abdication of party leadership to conservative and orthodox Democratic congressional leaders. Several new presidential hopefuls were swept to the fore as a result of their leadership in the battle against presidential power and leadership, and it was soon evident that a three-year struggle was beginning for control of the Democratic party and the presidency in 1940.

CHAPTER II

THE RUPTURED PARTY, 1937

What had begun with the appearance of an "era of good feeling" was in reality from the beginning an era of bad feeling. The smashing victory of 1936 had filled the New Dealers with confidence and determination that the Democratic party should not be allowed to fall back under the control of the "reactionaries" if it could possibly be avoided. In May of 1937 Roosevelt told Secretary of Treasury Henry Morgenthau that the time had come to attack the opposition within the party, and he was prepared to do just that.

> Did you notice how downcast Jack Garner was at Cabinet? Well when I saw Jack before Cabinet, rather than give him a chance to attack me, I attacked him. People like Garner, Senator Bailey, Walsh of Massachusetts and numerous other conservative Democrats, knowingly or not, are getting prepared

for a conservative Democratic party. They won't go
along with any reform measures, and they are only
interested in balancing the budget.[1]

In New Deal circles, gossip and criticism of the party conservatives became more open and more witty as Roosevelt, to an
increasing extent, fell under the influence of men like Felix Frankfurter, Tom Corcoran, and William O. Douglas, all of whom,
according to a disapproving Frank Walker, had intellectual su-
periority complexes and fresh, new, false philosophies.[2] Although
presidential speech-writer Stanley High was repudiated by the
White House when he wrote an article for the *Saturday Evening
Post* ("Whose Party Is It?"), repeating some of the comments
New Dealers were making about the party conservatives, Arthur
Krock pointed out that High's reporting was not inaccurate. Anyone could hear the same kind of talk in a good many places around
Washington where the New Dealers gathered.[3] And when they
had specific, unpleasant things to say about some of the more conservative members of the government, there were always pro-New
Deal newspaper columnists like Drew Pearson, Robert Allen, Jay
Franklin, and others who were glad to pick up "leaks" from
"sources close to the President" or "usually reliable sources" with
which to scourge the opposition.[4] After being on the receiving
end of a few of Harold Ickes' indirect barbs of this sort, Jesse Jones
"felt like swatting him in the jaw."[5] He had a lot of company in
that respect.

If at the beginning of the second term the New Dealers and
their chief were prepared to open an all-out offensive against conservatives for control of the party in 1940, the opposition was not
loath to take up the gauntlet. The attitude of professional politicians toward Administration advisers was put succinctly by the
relatively liberal Sam Rayburn when he told Raymond Moley in
1933, "I hope we don't have any — — Rasputin in this administration." The party leaders who helped nominate and elect Roosevelt, observed Moley, had no intention of putting up with palace
politics and palace politicos.[6] According to Rex Tugwell the
Southerners—with a few exceptions like Hugo Black, Lister Hill,
and Sam Rayburn—hated Roosevelt with a vengeance, whatever

they might profess in public. Chief among the haters, he believed, were "the malicious little man from Uvalde," Vice President Garner, and Jesse Jones.[7]

Increasingly, too, political chieftains like Jim Farley and his successor, Edward J. Flynn, came to dislike the political meddling of the amateurs. The governmental, fiscal, or foreign policies of the New Dealers might be matters of complete indifference, but when their political activities began to undercut the authority of a Farley or a Flynn and even threaten a split in the party, they were adding to their list of enemies. By 1938 Farley would be snarling to Roosevelt, "Between you and me, I'm getting a bit fed up with Corcoran and his crowd. . . . I'll be able to handle them in my own way and at my own time. They're merely peanuts in a sugar barrel."[8] When at about the same time Roosevelt asked Ed Flynn for a political favor in the New York primary battle, the Bronx boss replied bluntly that "if Corcoran or any of his ilk had anything to do with the campaign, I would immediately withdraw."[9]

So stirred up were a great number of the stalwart Senate Democrats by early 1937 that newly elected Senator William Smathers of New Jersey was shocked to find about half of them talking about the need to turn the party in a conservative direction. After talking to a number of them, he came to the conclusion that the chief reason for the trend was pique and jealousy that they had not been consulted by the Administration, which had, instead, relied on the advice of "two kids, Corcoran and Cohen, who never ran for public office, who are impractical and theorists."[10]

Perhaps the resentment felt by the party regulars for the liberals and New Dealers would best be expressed by General Hugh Johnson in his 1940 Jefferson Day Address when he said:

> It is these veteran Democrats who have borne the heat and burden of all these close contests, not the Schwellenbachs, the Peppers and the Mintons, nor yet the Hopkinses, the Ickeses, Corcorans or Wallaces. It has been the Pat Harrisons, the Joe Robinsons, the Jimmy Byrneses, the Georges of Georgia, the Cordell Hulls and, saddest of all, the loyal, faith-

ful Farleys. They have carried the fight and torch
and all too often gotten kicks in the pants for their
pains.[11]

If the regulars were unable to "get rid of the interlopers and
usurpers" and "throw out the strange doctrines . . . and return to
the faith and house of our father," it was not for lack of effort.[12]

The Supreme Court: Casus Belli

It was President Roosevelt himself, with his ill-conceived
Court reform plan, who precipitated open revolt within the party
and presided over the apparent dissolution of his own grand coalition, although there were also several other major issues tearing
Democratic party unity to shreds in the first half of 1937. Perhaps
no single issue in itself could have caused more than a temporary
rift in the ranks, but several together in a rather short span of time
were able to create permanent suspicions and hostility or at least
bring them out in the open. The Court plan provided the trigger
for the uprising because many of the more timid anti-New Dealers
could base their opposition to it on patriotism rather than conservatism and because once the breach was opened the personal
animosity and bitterness it engendered made it impossible to close.
Moreover, it appeared to many observers that the key to control of
the Democratic party in 1940 lay with the Seventy-Fifth Congress,
and many in the Seventy-Fifth were prepared to use it to lock
out any possible third-term attempt as well as any New Deal sympathizer. Defeat of the President's program appeared to some to
be the surest way to eliminate eventually the President and his
immediate retinue from the political picture.

Although Roosevelt had told Congress in his State of the
Union Address of January 6 that what was needed for national
progress was not an alteration of the Constitution but an increasingly enlightened view of it,[13] no one was prepared for the scheme
he so disingenuously proposed a month later. Ironically, the New
Dealers had nothing whatever to do with the drafting of the bill;
it was done almost entirely by Attorney General Homer Cummings, a party regular. Nevertheless, once submitted it became a

rallying point, one way or the other, for the pro- and anti-New Deal forces. Although the bill provided for the reform of the entire federal court system, the controversial point was that giving the President authority to appoint one additional justice for each member of the Supreme Court over seventy years of age who refused to retire, up to six additional justices. Presumably, instead of seeing his program cancelled by a series of five-to-four decisions, as had happened during the first term, Roosevelt would be assured of at least a ten-to-five margin in cases involving future New Deal legislation. The bill became the center of a nation-wide debate between its introduction on February 5 and its final rejection by the Senate on July 22, and the outcome proved to be a sharp blow to New Deal prestige and power.[14]

Some historians have maintained that the Court fight was not a genuine liberal-conservative battle, pointing to the presence of liberals on both sides of the argument.[15] The fact is, however, that both in Congress and in the nation as a whole there was a general rallying of liberal forces behind the bill, making the split in the Democratic party more liberal vs. conservative than executive vs. legislature or loose vs. strict construction.

There was no question that the conservatives inside and outside the party were determined to deal the Administration a paralyzing blow. Within a matter of days the entire Democratic right wing in the Senate had announced opposition to the plan, and it was supported throughout the struggle by like-minded Republicans across the aisle, who, few as they were, caused the Administration great embarrassment by simply keeping quiet so that the bill could not be made a party issue.[16] So close, in fact, was this cooperation between conservative Democrats and Republicans that the *New Republic* reported that it appeared likely the Republicans would close up shop and join the "Wheeler-Burke" faction of the Democratic party.[17]

Acutely aware that an exclusively conservative coalition against the President was doomed to defeat from the start, the opponents of the bill knew that a Democratic liberal would have to be found to lead the fight for them. There was no difficulty in locating the man. At a dinner at the home of Millard Tydings, Senator Burton K. Wheeler of Montana was chosen floor leader for the opposition. Wheeler's liberalism was unquestioned. He had been Robert La Follette's running mate for the Progressive Party in 1924, an early supporter of Roosevelt, and a staunch supporter of most New Deal measures. The steering committee for the bill's opposition, however, was almost an honor role of Democratic conservatives. Besides Wheeler it included Josiah Bailey of North Carolina, Harry Byrd of Virginia, Edward Burke of Nebraska, Walter George of Georgia, Millard Tydings of Maryland, David I. Walsh of Massachusetts, Peter G. Gerry of Rhode Island, Bennett Clark of Missouri, Frederick Van Nuys of Indiana and Tom Connally of Texas.[18] Clark, Van Nuys, and Connally were party regulars who had generally been counted on the side of the New Deal program; from this time on their relation with the Administration became frigid.

There was, it is true, a number of genuine liberals throughout the country such as Amos Pinchot, Oswald Garrison Villard, William Allen White, John T. Flynn, Morris Ernst, and, privately, Felix Frankfurter, who were also quite hostile to the plan. In the Senate, Joseph O'Mahoney, a former protégé of Postmaster General Jim Farley and a liberal, stated that he considered the bill "obnoxious, undemocratic, and an insult to the Senate," and he would never be able to stand for it.[19] Non-Democratic progressives William Borah, Gerald Nye, Lynn Frazier, Henrik Shipstead, and Hiram Johnson also joined the opposition. Sam Rosenman told Roosevelt he thought many of the defections could be attributed to the reluctance of lawyers in general to tamper with the Supreme Court,[20] but Josephus Daniels was probably equally correct when he blamed the loss of men like Borah and Johnson on traditional tendencies of progressives to balk unless their program was used or "unless they could call the 'figgers.' "[21]

The members of the Senate were split into three groups on the issue. Roughly thirty members were in favor of the bill, thirty were opposed, and the others were considered on the fence.[22] The New Dealers, almost to a man, were in favor of the bill, and the conservatives, to a man, were opposed. The fight was for the souls of the orthodox Democrats, and it was here that the split took place.

All during the spring and summer of 1937 Democrats were at

one another's throats over the question. In some cases, perhaps, there was genuine concern for the integrity of the Constitution on the part of the opposition, but to the Roosevelt supporters it was pure party treason, an excuse to discredit the Roosevelt leadership and New Deal liberalism in general. Even some Republicans were ready to compromise on at least two more justices if Senator Arthur Vandenburg was allowed to name one of them.[23] This indicates that politics rather than Constitutional scruples was behind much of the noisy anguish over the President's plan. Jim Farley voiced some of the cynicism felt by a number of Administration-supporting party regulars when he remarked, "When Senator O'Mahoney comes around for help on the sugar bill, his conscience won't bother him then, will it? Neither will Senator McCarran's when he wants something for his state. It's all in the point of view."[24] Old Josephus Daniels expressed the New Deal point of view when he wrote that the Court plan "sharply divides the sheep from the goats—that is those who truly wish to see the objectives set forth in the New Deal program to prevail and those who would like to see it fail."[25]

Roosevelt agreed that the goats ought to be separated from the sheep and as soon as possible. When Farley met him returning from a fishing trip in May to tell him the vote was so close that hostile John Nance Garner might have to cast the deciding vote, Roosevelt snapped, "Let him do it." To Farley's argument that the party might be split beyond repair he replied bluntly, "And good riddance too."[26] Clearly he underestimated the power of the opposition. To Paul McNutt he wrote confidently that "even if we have to part with some more of our ultra-conservative friends, we have the overwhelming majority of Democratic voters with us and a substantial majority of all the voters."[27]

The opposition leaders, on the other hand, were determined that if anyone were forced out of the ranks of the Democratic party, it would not be they. The spearhead of their counterattack was the sizzling report from the Senate Judiciary Committee rejecting the bill, which was bitter and so personal that according to Arthur Krock of the New York *Times* many in Washington thought it could be understood only in the light of the 1940 hopes of its authors. It appeared unlikely that any of the men who signed it would ever be on friendly terms with Roosevelt again, and it therefore represented a clean break with the President with a view to recapturing the Democratic party in 1940, just as the Republican Senators had recaptured their party in 1920.[28] Senator Marvel Logan of Kentucky was of the same opinion. The fight over the Court bill, he charged, was an out-and-out battle for control of the Democratic party, and an effort on the part of the conservative Democrats to break the President's hold on the party so that he would not be strong enough to name a successor in 1940.[29]

At least one of the signers of the report acknowledged that some of the public was also interpreting it that way, and he was troubled by the inference. Senator Carl Hatch of New Mexico remarked that he was getting letters from all over the country saying, "Now is the time to humiliate the President" and "Now is the time to beat Franklin D. Roosevelt." He wanted to make it perfectly clear, he said, that he had no intention of doing either when he signed the report.[30] O'Mahoney chimed in with the remark that there was not a derogatory adjective in the report, and the whole tenor of it had been misinterpreted by the press. Senator Logan retorted that if he himself really believed that President Roosevelt had done what the report said he had with the motives with which the report charged him, he would favor impeachment.[31] The futility of continuing this particular battle was brought home to the New Dealers on July 20, when Vice President Garner informed Roosevelt that he simply did not have the votes and was beaten.

Although there was some talk by Senator Joseph Guffey of Pennsylvania of punishing the "ingrates" who had opposed the plan, the issue might have been smoothed over in time, since the anxiety of the party regulars on both sides of the debate worked to avoid a split. Wrote Senator John Bankhead of Alabama, an opponent of the bill, to Roosevelt:

> I believe that we are now out of the woods. Be assured of my loyal support of every measure involved in the last election. I shall gladly cooperate in carrying out your social reform program. You have the same place in my heart that you have held for the last five years.[32]

Of equal or greater importance was whether Senator Bankhead still held the same place in Roosevelt's heart that he had held the previous five years.

Seventy-Fifth Congress and the President: The Battle Widens

The question of whether the President would attempt to challenge further the conservative group within the party after the Court fight with the view of smashing the malcontents, as his New Deal advisers were proposing,[33] was answered in the closing days of that debate as a result of the death of Senator Joseph Robinson, which left the office of majority leader open. The leading contenders for the post were New Dealer Alben Barkley of Kentucky and party regular Pat Harrison of Mississippi. Traditionally, there should have been no interference on the part of the Administration in the Senatorial caucus which chose Robinson's successor. Roosevelt chose to ignore the tradition and back Barkley, thus enraging not only the party conservatives, who considered Harrison much the safer man, but also a great many of the party regulars, who resented presidential interference in Senatorial affairs and generally liked Pat Harrison as a person. The famous "Dear Alben" letter, released to the press July 15, requested Barkley, in his capacity of acting majority leader, to carry on the fight to pass legislation embodying the objectives of the New Deal.[34] Despite the President's assurances to Harrison that he was not taking sides in the fight,[35] his real feelings were no secret, and the Democratic Senators again found themselves squaring off in what was generally a liberal vs. conservative alignment.[36] Heavy pressures were brought to bear by both sides. The Roosevelt forces through Mayor Ed Kelly of Chicago were able to change Senator William Dieterich's vote, while the Harrison forces put enough pressure on Senator Harry Truman through Tom Pendergast to force him to ask Barkley to release him from his promise of support.[37]

Barkley's margin of victory was a single vote. Though the balloting was secret, Senators were not shy about telling for whom and what they voted; it was widely known that Barkley's forces consisted chiefly of ardent New Dealers and freshmen Senators, whereas Harrison had the support of the conservatives and party regulars.[38] The anti-Court plan group was for Harrison virtually en bloc. Although the New Dealers could claim the victory, they did so at the expense of further alienating important party leaders.

Salt was further rubbed in some conservative Southern wounds when Roosevelt named liberal Senator Hugo Black of Alabama to the Supreme Court seat vacated by Justice Willis Van Devanter. Not only had Black supported the Court reform bill but he had also introduced the wages and hours bill, a measure deeply distasteful to Southern conservatives. Further, since Senate tradition ordained that presidential appointments of Senators to such positions should be approved without committee scrutiny by their colleagues, it appeared that no one could even protest what looked like the President's subtle revenge for the defeat of his Court bill. Tradition or no tradition, however, Senators Edward Burke and Hiram Johnson demanded the appointment be sent to committee.[39] The committee voted 13 to 4 to uphold the appointment, with two of the four nays coming from conservative Democrats Burke and William King of Utah.[40] Roosevelt was not the only one who ignored precedent in the struggle.

A third cause of party disharmony was rubbing tempers raw at the same time as the Supreme Court debate. On December 30, 1936, workers in Fisher Body Plant Number One in Flint "sat down." Within the next few weeks they were joined in their assault on the General Motors Company by members of John L. Lewis' C.I.O.-U.A.W. workers in other plants, and the massive sit-down strike battle was on. President Roosevelt was in a difficult position. He believed that the sit-down strike was illegal beyond the shadow of a doubt,[41] and he was being called upon by members of both parties to do something to express his disapproval or even break it by force. When reminded that the President had no authority in Michigan, one outraged Democratic Senator, Frederick Van Nuys, stated curtly, "Grover Cleveland did it [the Pullman Strike]."[42] But Roosevelt was opposed to bloodshed and believed the unions would learn of their own accord that the sit down was "a damned unpopular tactic."[43] Further, labor had supported him in 1936, was supporting him in his Court plan battle in 1937, and definitely expected some return on the investment. John L. Lewis made this brutally articulate when he publicly called upon the President to give the striking auto workers all the help that would be legal against the "economic royalists," since the union had supported him in 1936.[44] For the time being, Roosevelt's only comment on the situation was, "There come moments when statements, conversations and headlines are not in order," interpreted by the press as a direct slap at Lewis' effrontery.[45] Otherwise, he remained silent, leaving the strike negotiations to Secretary of Labor Frances Perkins and the Democratic governor, Frank Murphy.

The strike was successful at least to the extent that the popularity of the sit-down method among union men skyrocketed. All but the most ardent liberals in Congress were alarmed, and many were furious at labor's flagrant attack on private property and also at the President, who refused to intervene in any way. Some congressional frustration was expressed when Senator Jimmy Byrnes of South Carolina offered an amendment to a new Guffey coal bill making sit-down strikes illegal in the mines.[46] Although the Administration forces were able to muster enough votes after a fierce debate to defeat it, majority leader Robinson protested that throughout the discussion "there has run . . . implied criticism of both the President and the chief executive of Michigan."[47] Indicative of the way the party was splitting at this time was the fact that, besides the usual solid conservative bloc, some fifteen regular party Democrats voted against the Administration on the amendment, and all but two, Byrnes and Harry Truman, were also numbered among the enemies of the Court plan.[48]

Over the weekend the issue was smoothed out by substituting a joint resolution condemning both sit-down strikes and unfair labor practices of employers. This passed the Senate by a wide 75 to 3 margin.[49] As one member of the House remarked, any measure passed by the Senate by that majority "could not contain much fire anyway."[50]

Further labor troubles developed later in the summer when the C.I.O.'s attempt to unionize "Little Steel" resulted in widespread violence and terrorism. In an effort to mollify members of his own party and, more important, public opinion in general, which by this time was showing alarm at labor violence and irresponsibility,[51] Roosevelt allowed himself to be directly quoted as stating to both labor and management, "A plague on both your houses."[52] The political effects were not all that could have been desired. The conservatives and their allies among the party regulars showed no inclination whatever to soften their attitude toward the Administration (the remark was made less than a week before the defeat of the Court reform proposal), and John L. Lewis was furious. Said he bitterly:

> It ill behooves one who has supped at labor's table and who has been sheltered in labor's house to curse with equal fervor and fine impartiality both labor and its adversaries when they become locked in deadly embrace.[53]

The speech threatened to be more than merely splendid rhetoric. The tenor of the remarks indicated that labor was giving to no one and no party a blank check in future elections, and there was a genuine danger that the Democratic party might be split in three ways instead of two. Indeed, in August Lewis stated ominously, "The sabotage of the Democratic party by a small group of its more conservative members . . . shows that Democratic leadership is unable to carry out the pledges made in the name of their party in the 1936 campaign."[54] In attempting to cool down both conservative and labor elements in the coalition, Roosevelt was running the risk of falling between two stools.

Perhaps the falling out among Democrats which exhibited the deepest ideological roots was over the question of the unbalanced budget and, in particular, the part federal relief expenditures were playing in unbalancing it. To be sure, it was no part of Roosevelt's personal philosophy to engage in deficit spending on purpose. His budget message of January 8, 1937, predicted a "layman's balanced budget" in fiscal 1938 with a total balance and resumption of the reduction of the debt in 1939.[55] Toward the end of January, a number of party leaders, including Vice President Garner, majority leader Robinson, Speaker of the House William Bankhead, Senator James Byrnes, Congressman Sam Rayburn, and several others, lectured the President on the necessity of keeping the relief bill at around $1,000,000,000 or $1,200,000,000 at most to insure the balancing of the budget. When he argued that $1,500,-

000,000 would be necessary, one of those present polled the gathering and demonstrated that his entire congressional leadership firmly opposed him in the matter. At the time Roosevelt either promised to make the cut or gave the impression he was so promising.[56]

On April 20, however, to the dismay and anger of many, he once again demonstrated that he had no intention of being guided by party regulars when he sent to the House a request for $1,500,-000,000 for relief.[57] Under the chairmanship of conservative Clifton A. Woodrum of Virginia, the House Subcommittee on Deficiencies rebelled, and by a five-to-four margin cut the appropriation to $1,000,000,000. The full committee restored the missing amount, but in the debate on the question it was obvious that there was no consensus in the party, and, if anything, Roosevelt was in danger of falling between the same two stools he had tried to mount simultaneously on the labor question. The Workers' Alliance lobby demanded a $3,000,000,000 appropriation; Congressman Maverick wanted $2,500,000,000, while the Conference of Mayors fixed its figure at $2,200,000,000, as did liberals Gerald Boileau of Wisconsin and Jerry Voorhis of California.[58] The conservatives, on the other hand, led by Woodrum and Sam McReynolds of Tennessee, fought vigorously to stem the tide at $1,200,000,000. "No, we will not go back home and say we voted with the Republicans," shouted McReynolds defiantly. "We will say that the Republicans voted with us to save the Democratic party and the taxpayers of this nation."[59]

The so-called House rebellion was of short duration, however, and the bill sent to the Senate contained an appropriation of $1,500,000,000 as the President had requested. But in the Senate there was a new rebellion, led by men who had ordinarily been willing to support the President on almost anything. Majority Leader Joe Robinson tried to tack on an amendment requiring states, counties, and cities to put up 25 per cent of the cost of all W.P.A. projects but was beaten down by a 49 to 34 margin. That was followed by a much more extreme amendment by Senator Byrnes, demanding that the local governments furnish 40 per cent of the cost of such projects; it too was defeated. Significantly, however, Democratic leaders like Key Pittman, President Pro Tempore of the Senate, and Pat Harrison, chairman of the Senate

Finance Committee, were to be found in the ranks of the revolters.[60] The President was ultimately able to sign the bill substantially as he wanted it, but it was clear that deep fissures were developing in the party on the very touchy question of finance.

These were the major causes of the very obvious rent in the Democratic ranks, and for the rest of the New Deal legislative program for 1937 they spelled bickering, fighting, and ruin, largely as the result of the power struggle within the party. President Roosevelt suggested four major measures to the first session of the Seventy-Fifth Congress besides the reform of the Supreme Court. He wanted a new, comprehensive farm bill to replace the unconstitutional Agriculture Adjustment Act, a wages and hours bill, a bill for executive reorganization, and the creation of seven regional agencies patterned on the T.V.A.[61] In the end, not one was passed. What it added up to was a series of stunning blows to the Administration delivered in the house of its friends—or at least associates—and Harold Ickes in August noted that Roosevelt looked "punch drunk" from the punishment he was taking.[62]

After Congress adjourned, however, the President was refreshed and encouraged by a trip through the northwestern part of the country during which his popularity with the voters was amply demonstrated. He then called Congress back into special session in November to pass his four major pieces of "must" legislation. Before it convened, however, his prestige suffered another staggering blow when the nation's economy ceased its climb from the depths of the depression and began to lurch downward into a serious recession (or "Roosevelt depression"). Under the influence of his conservative Secretary of Treasury, Henry Morgenthau, he had cut back sharply on the W.P.A. rolls and stopped altogether further P.W.A. pump-priming in June of that year. As the recession gained momentum that fall, he became more determined than ever to restore business confidence by balancing the budget.[63] Whatever the President's relations with his congressional leaders, it was clear that within the Administration itself the conservative advisers were in the saddle, and the pump-priming New Dealers out in the cold.

If Roosevelt expected his show of fiscal responsibility to arouse any corresponding marks of good will on the part of either big businessmen or Democratic conservatives, he was doomed to disappointment. When Morgenthau informed a conservative audience of the Academy of Political Science in November that a balanced budget was the President's objective, someone laughed and the rest were silent and cold.[64] The economy continued to lose ground. In Congress the same group which had led the drive against New Deal legislation during the first session remained implacably hostile to Roosevelt during the special session. A week before Congress met, Senators William King and Ed Burke indicated they would oppose the President's program in the interest of state's rights and to prevent the growth of one-man rule.[65] The result was chaos.

When at one point the wages and hours bill was tied up in the House Rules Committee by Democratic conservatives and Majority Leader Rayburn was wheedling and cajoling members of his own party to sign the petition to force it out, Republican Minority Leader Bertrand Snell commented in wonder:

> I have just witnessed a very amazing spectacle on the floor of the House of Representatives. For the first time in my twenty-five years as a member I have seen a majority leader, with a majority of four to one, rise to appeal to his members to sign a petition to discharge his own Rules Committee from consideration of his legislation. That is definite proof of the statement I have often made: that the Democrats cannot efficiently run the House of Representatives.[66]

The result was a session of nearly utter futility. When Congress adjourned in December, not one of the bills requested by Roosevelt had been passed. Thus, one year after he was returned to power by one of the greatest pluralities in the nation's political history, he found his program frustrated, his coalition in shambles, and, most important of all, his hold on his party slipping badly. Prospective presidential candidates from the ranks of the conservatives and party regulars could look to 1940 with rising hopes, whereas liberals and New Dealers could only struggle through the year, trusting that the mass of voters was still with them. The worsening business outlook and increasing unemployment coupled with the year's labor problems made even that hope a rather dim one.

One significant development which immediately became clear from the fierce intraparty quarrel was that the President, unsuccessful in his effort to push his program through Congress, faced even greater difficulties in his efforts to create what he considered a genuinely progressive party. The conservative wing, it appeared, had at last found a champion behind whom it could rally and even entertain hopes of seizing the presidential nomination in 1940. The more moderate members of the party were already looking for a compromise candidate who would be generally satisfactory to both factions, and most of the candidates were expending considerable efforts to fit the description.

The Party Split and the Presidential Hopefuls

The apparently serious threat to liberal control of the administration, which appeared on the horizon like an ominous black cloud in the summer of 1937, was the short, round, red-faced Vice President from Uvalde, Texas, John Nance Garner, already sixty-nine years old but as vigorous and physically active as most men half his age. Prior to his sharp but not particularly clean break with Roosevelt that year, Garner had been party regularity personified. He had been elected to Congress in 1902, and his seat was never seriously contested thereafter. Like most Texas millionaires, he considered all Wall Street millionaires demons, and as House Majority Leader during the 1920's he developed something of a reputation of a liberal for his constant baiting of Secretary of Treasury Andrew Mellon.[67] Backed for the presidency in 1932 by William Randolph Hearst, he received the vice-presidential nomination when he allowed his supporters to swing to Roosevelt when they were most needed.[68] Extremely popular in both houses of Congress, he was famous for inviting legislators to his office to "strike a blow for freedom" with rye whiskey and "branch water." He had been quietly loyal to the New Deal during the first term, having pledged at the beginning of the term to leave all public speaking to Roosevelt; privately he gave the President the benefit of his wisdom with a salty frankness that Roosevelt seemed to enjoy.

Unlike a good many other party regulars, Garner's break with the Administration did not come about as a result of the Court-packing plan. His first reaction to it had been quite hostile—he was seen in the lobby of the Capitol holding his nose with one hand and vigorously giving the "thumbs down" sign with the other while the bill was being read[69]—but he soon came to the conclusion that even with six additional judges, the Supreme Court would eventually reassert its independence.[70] There were at least two and possibly three issues which aroused mutual suspicion and dislike between President and Vice President in 1937. Although he did not mention it, Garner was fearful and somewhat anxious even then lest Roosevelt consider breaking the two-term tradition. During the campaign of 1936 Frank Walker had coaxed him to come to New York to give one speech in behalf of the ticket. Going up to his hotel room on the morning of his arrival to meet him for breakfast, Walker found Garner talking to newspaper publisher Silliman Evans. After exchanging greetings, Evans left, and even as he was closing the door behind him, Garner turned to Walker and said bluntly, "Walker, I'm going along in this election with the Captain. It's a good thing and the Captain wants the election. But I'm against a third term. How do you stand on a third term, Walker?"

Walker could not remember any talk of a third term, or was he particularly in favor of one at the time, so he told Garner that he too was against a third term.

"Well," replied the Vice President, "I'm glad to hear that."[71]

Whether the possibility of a third term was still bothering him in 1937 or not, there were two differences with the President on which Garner minced no words. They were the unbalanced budget and the sit-down strikes. "The troubles with this country," he told Raymond Moley, "are too much John L. Lewis and too much spending."[72]

Garner's belief in fiscal responsibility was of long standing. He had been one of the leaders in the 1932 attempt by conservative Republicans and Democrats to balance the Hoover budget by a sales tax, and when that failed, he had been the leader in slamming through a series of excise taxes which had remained on the books ever since.[73] In 1934 he was pleading with Roosevelt to live within the nation's income, even claiming that the great popularity of the New Deal rested on the Economy Act of 1933,[74] and in 1936 he was telling his confidant, newspaperman Bascom Timmons, that it was time to give the country a rest and develop a more coherent program with reduced expenses and a balanced budget. The most effective speech of Roosevelt's compaigning, he thought, had been the one at Forbes Field, Pittsburgh, in 1932, when he had promised to balance the budget.[75] In early 1937 he was still trying to influence "the Captain" with warnings that people all over the country were asking ". . . when are we going to balance the budget?"[76]

Though his patience was tried by New Deal red ink, it was the sit-down strikes that brought Garner into open conflict with the President. When Senator Byrnes introduced his amendment to the Guffey coal bill outlawing sit downs in the mines and thereby caused a major flare-up in the Senate,[77] Roosevelt asked Garner and Senate Majority Leader Joe Robinson to the White House for a conference. It was, Garner reported, the hottest argument they ever had.[78] Garner was furious at the attack on private property which the sit downs represented; he was furious at the Communists in the C.I.O.; but most of all he was furious about John L. Lewis, who, he said, was using the strike to further his own personal and political power.[79] According to one report it was not long before both men lost their tempers and were using such language toward one another that a shocked Joe Robinson finally shouted them both down.[80] From that night on, Roosevelt and Garner, though publicly friendly, were going in opposite directions. A short time later, when Republican Arthur Vandenburg delivered a blistering speech on the subject of the sit-down strike, Garner left the rostrum to go down and congratulate him warmly in full view of the Senate galleries.[81] So angry was the Vice President that in the midst of the Court fight, in which he took little interest anyway, he packed his bags and went home to Uvalde. Now it was Roosevelt's turn to be furious, and Jim Farley dates the split between President and Vice President to the day of Garner's departure.[82] That, however, assumes that the break was purely one-sided, with Garner merely a passive outcast, which was not the case.

The newspapers, of course, immediately interpreted Garner's

departure as a split with Roosevelt over the Court fight, an impression the President was most anxious to dispel. On July 19 Garner gave a brief interview in Amarillo in which he stated that the vacation had been arranged long in advance and that he had told the President he would return to Washington any time he was needed. There was, he said, no basis for any rumor of a rift.[83] That was not completely accurate, however, as the letter Garner wrote to Roosevelt the same day indicates. Expressing genuine friendship and affection for the President, Garner said he was very sorry when Marvin McIntyre had told him he was "very upset" over his departure, and had he known it earlier he would not have left. The remainder of the letter, however, was an explanation of his two major differences with the Administration: the sit-down strikes, "which nearly got my goat," and excessive expenditures, about which "I am egotistical enough to believe that I know as much as most people." It was clear that Garner's back was up, and there was no mention of any offer to return when he was needed.[84]

On July 1 he sent Farley an even longer letter as a result of another "split in the Administration" article by Thomas Stokes of the Scripps-Howard newspaper chain. Again protesting that "I have almost gotten to love Roosevelt from a personal standpoint," he nevertheless spent most of the letter condemning the sit-down strikes and the unbalanced budget.[85]

With the Court fight going very badly, Roosevelt eventually swallowed his pride and, on July 7, wrote the Vice President to ask him to return. Part of the olive branch message included the comments that "if Congress does not run wild," the budget for the coming year would be balanced, and that most people had become "pretty sick" of the labor extremists on both sides. To this balm for the old Texan's wounded feelings, he added, "I want to tell you again how I miss you because of you, yourself. . . ."[86] To make sure Garner saw the need for a speedy return, he enclosed a large number of newspaper clippings which commented on his absence.

When Garner did return, however, it was on the special train carrying members of Congress back from Joe Robinson's funeral. While on the train, he had done some nose counting and was the bearer of the sad tidings that the Court-packing plan could not possibly pass. Roosevelt asked him to make the best deal he could with Senator Wheeler, who was well aware that he had won the fight and would take nothing short of unconditional surrender.[87] The President was furious, accusing Garner, though not to his face, of making no effort to compromise.[88]

The split between the two men never really healed, and from that time on Garner could usually be found sympathizing with, if not masterminding, Democratic opposition to the President, though always behind the closed doors of his chambers.[89] The result was a sudden discovery by conservatives across the land that Garner would make an ideal candidate in 1940. Senator Ed Burke announced that he was for Garner as early as September 5, and if Garner were not available in 1940, he would want a candidate with the same qualities. "What we need now," he said, "is someone with hard common sense rather than a sympathetic nature, particularly in financial matters. We need someone who can hold down expenditures and restore confidence so that industry and business can go ahead and expand, thus providing jobs." With regard to labor, Senator Burke felt Garner was qualified to be President because "he wouldn't stand for any nonsense, and he would make it known that the government doesn't owe a living to anybody unless he is willing to get out and work."[90]

Mayor Tom Miller of Austin, a firm supporter of the New Deal, became so alarmed at the enthusiasm for Garner that seemed to be mushrooming overnight that he complained in a Labor Day speech, "When one of the greatest Presidents in history still has three and one-half years to serve, it ill becomes his would-be friends in Texas and his enemies elsewhere to nominate anyone."[91]

The conservative plan, according to Kansas City boss Tom Pendergast, was for Garner to take the leadership of the Tory faction, prevent the spread of a revolt against the Administration which would totally rupture the party, direct the opposition against such New Deal measures as the conservatives could not stomach, and receive the presidential nomination in 1940. The conservatives, Pendergast reported, were confident they could prevent Roosevelt from naming his successor, though they were worried by the possibility of a third term. Hence, the all-out effort to make Garner the real leader of the Democratic party.[92] As for Garner himself, he was at this time protesting that he did not want to be President under any circumstances.[93] Perhaps he meant it at the time, but he was not adverse to serving as a conservative stalking horse, and there were three years in which to change his mind.

The belief that a compromise candidate acceptable to all factions would be needed by 1940 also brought into a quiet sort of prominence the name of Senator Burton K. Wheeler of Montana, although, as one observer noted, he would be a threat "only if President Roosevelt's influence in the party ceases to be a factor."[94] The analysis was a fair one. Wheeler followers might have presumed that he would be satisfactory to the New Dealers because his long record of liberalism made him essentially one of them (he was once nicknamed "Bolshevik Burt"),[95] and at least somewhat satisfactory to the conservatives because of his leadership in the fight against Roosevelt's Court plan (conservative Vice President Garner was quoted as remarking to Wheeler in the midst of the fight, "Burt, you're a real patriot").[96] In 1937 they would have been wrong on both counts. He was *persona non grata* with both groups. Extremely ambitious and a cagey, tenacious fighter, however, he was one of the ablest politicians to set his cap for the 1940 nomination, but several irretrievably bad guesses made his path toward the White House a rocky one.

The worst of these was his break with Roosevelt, which had been brewing for some time. Although one of the early supporters of the President's candidacy in 1932, he received few marks of gratitude. At first he had had high hopes for the vice presidency or, upon the death of Senator Thomas Walsh, a place in the Cabinet as Attorney General.[97] Instead, Homer Cummings, a close personal friend of his bitter Montana political rival, J. Bruce Kremer, received the Cabinet post, and Wheeler was forced to watch the Justice Department's considerable patronage in Montana channeled through Kremer. By 1934 the strain was beginning to show; it was noted that the Democratic National Committee sent no money to Montana for Wheeler's re-election campaign that year.[98]

When the President presented his Court plan, Wheeler saw a chance to settle a score with both Roosevelt and his Attorney General and perhaps further his own ambitions as well. Tom Corcoran reported to Harry Hopkins that he had tried to keep Wheeler in line but "he hated Cummings and walked out on us."[99] With that the feud was on. Mrs. Wheeler, who was reputed to be more ambitious for her husband than he was for himself, resigned from the Women's Democratic Club in Washington to carry on a full-scale war on Roosevelt and his entire family.[100] Liberal supporters of the President's plan, on the other hand, appeared to be more bitter against Wheeler because of his "treason" than they were against any of the conservatives. Said Senator Marvel Logan of Kentucky mournfully during the debate:

> Let me say to the Senator from Montana that I have great respect for his ability. He has been an outstanding member of this body for a long time; and there is no one more sorry than myself to see the company he is with at this time, when apparently he has turned his back on everything he has ever stood for since he has been in the Senate, and is lending aid and comfort to those who, he knows, would destroy the Government if they were not restrained.[101]

In Montana students at the state university formed a "Wheeler for Ex-Senator Club," and William T. Evjue, editor of the Madison *Capital Times*, leading Progressive paper of Wisconsin, wrote him, "I think that you have lost forever the support of millions of liberals."[102]

Nor did the bitter feelings end with the Court fight. In October, well after the adjournment of Congress, Wheeler spoke to a Milwaukee audience of the "mess in Washington created by young lawyers from Harvard and Columbia Law Schools who have never practiced law and never heard of Wisconsin or Montana except in a geography book."[103] "Wheeler," said Roosevelt bitterly, "is not a progressive or liberal at heart, but a New England conservative, the same as Calvin Coolidge."[104] His public retaliation was to ignore Wheeler when he passed through Montana in October. The omission was significant, since it broke his rule of never taking sides in state disputes within the party. At Fort Peck Dam, Montana, he mentioned Senator James Murray and Congressmen James O'Conner and Jerry O'Connell as being responsible for its construction, implying that Wheeler had had nothing to do with it. Since Jerry O'Connell had already announced that he would oppose Wheeler for his Senate seat in the 1940 primaries, Roosevelt appeared to be subtly endorsing the Senator's opponent.[105]

Nor did Wheeler's stand for the Supreme Court win him a great host of friends in the conservative camp. Although he was nominally the leader of the opposition to the Court plan, it was not really the case for the simple reason that the conservatives could not trust him. At several meetings of the steering committee he precipitated angry exchanges by urging compromise with the Administration. The belief was that he wanted to avoid being on the losing side at all costs and was, therefore, badly frightened until the battle was won.[106] Thus in 1937, however it may have appeared to outsiders, Senator Wheeler was the darkest of dark horses for the 1940 nomination.

The other presidential hopefuls could be divided between those who leaned gingerly to one side or the other in the party split and those who took an uncompromising stand in dead center. The more liberal candidates, whose chances for the presidency depended to a great extent on Roosevelt's good will, tended to support the Administration unquestioningly. Henry Wallace, for example, with the aid of four collaborators, got out a three-hundred-page book, *Whose Constitution?*, in defense of the President's Court plan,[107] and Harry Hopkins, though he was not a member of the New Deal steering committee on the bill, was informed of developments by Tom Corcoran and did make a radio address in defense of it.[108] Governor George Earle of Pennsylvania was quick to attack Governor Herbert Lehman of New York when he criticized the bill,[109] and Paul McNutt, who was safely off the firing line in the Philippines, nevertheless contributed support to the Administration indirectly through his successor, Governor Clifford Townsend of Indiana. Townsend announced from the steps of the White House that conservative Senator Frederick Van Nuys, who was one of the leaders of the opposition, would not be renominated in 1938 because of his critical attitude.[110] He told McNutt's campaign manager, Frank McHale, that he knew the High Commissioner would want to "beat Van Nuys," and the President had urged him to do something to reinstill the original fervor of four or five "weak sisters" in the Indiana congressional delegation.[111] The drum beating for McNutt as Roosevelt's logical liberal successor had already been begun by New Deal Senator Sherman Minton of Indiana, who described his Hoosier colleague as "a natural." "His views," said Minton, "are substantially the views of the New Deal."[112]

Perhaps the man in the most difficult position was Jim Farley, who was loyal to the President but at the same time unfriendly to the Court plan.[113] He solved his problem and roused the wrath of the New Deal general staff by racing around the country repeating over and over that the victory was "in the bag," but not lifting a finger to apply any real pressure.[114] People like Jesse Jones and Cordell Hull, on the other hand, were able to ignore the issues tearing the Democratic party apart—publicly at least—and go on quietly about their business.

The year 1937 marked the end of the President's unquestioned authority over the Democratic party. The ideological lines were already drawn for the party convention which was still three years away, with each side trying to save the nation from the other and with a number of candidates willing to try to save the nation and party from both. All agreed that 1938, with its congressional elections, would be crucial.

CHAPTER III

THE REBELLION GROWS, 1938

For a number of reasons there was apprehension in the Democratic party as the new year began. The third session of the Seventy-Fifth Congress was expected to be a showdown in regard to both future party policy and effective party control. Moreover, the mid-term party primaries and November elections were expected to give some indication as to whether the nation was drifting toward conservatism or liberalism; they would also eliminate some presidential hopefuls while spurring others toward the top of the heap. The problem of finding and agreeing on a successor for Roosevelt was crucial for the liberals; no New Dealer could hope to win the party's nomination without a considerable build-up which would have to include the backing of the President. On the other hand, the conservatives and party regulars could be fairly certain that without such a unified, Roosevelt-backed drive the nomination would go to one of their own simply because they and their followers formed the great bulk of the party.

It is sometimes said that Roosevelt made his own third term inevitable when he did not allow anyone else in the party to achieve sufficient prominence as a presidential possibility. By overshadowing everyone in his party and destroying anyone who appeared to be a potential rival, he made sure that he was the only possible nominee in 1940 with a chance of winning.[1] Roosevelt may, indeed, have been the only Democrat who could have won in 1940, but the evidence is that this was hardly his fault. By 1938 he realized that a build-up would have to begin for his successor at once to prepare him for party and national acceptance. The problem was to find a liberal who had the political potential to be President and the political sense and power to develop his potentiality. Ultimately, the year 1938 proved that no one but the President could get his foot in the glass slipper, but not before a number of other hopefuls were given the opportunity for a fitting.

The Search for a Liberal Candidate

Whatever Roosevelt may have thought of Jim Farley's chances as a presidential candidate, he gave him every encouragement to prepare himself for the job by running for Governor of New York in 1938. Herbert Lehman was proclaiming by late 1937 that he would not run for re-election, and Roosevelt strongly urged Farley himself to run. "You could become a very positive governor," he suggested, "and get the proper background for 1940." When Farley replied that he was not interested in 1940, the President bluntly and accurately pointed out that other people were interested in him and that without a deeper background in government than he had acquired as Postmaster General and Chairman of the Democratic National Committee he could scarcely expect the nomination or election as President.[2] Farley—or Mrs. Farley—refused the opportunity and with it the chance of being considered seriously by Roosevelt as a possible successor or even vice-presidential candidate. It was a mistake, the President told Ed Flynn, for Farley to aspire to either job without creating any background of statesmanship. His public image was that of a political boss and a patronage dispenser, neither a favorite type with American voters.[3] That Farley did nothing to change the image was certainly not Roosevelt's fault, and Garner's remark that it looked as if Roosevelt was trying to get Farley out of the way for 1940 was patently absurd.[4] The governorship of New York is not usually regarded as a political backwater from which no one ever reemerged into national prominence. Obviously whoever succeeded Lehman to the governorship was one huge step up on everyone else in either party for consideration in 1940.

Roosevelt's second choice for that crucial position was Robert Jackson, the brilliant head of the antitrust division of the Justice Department and a former upstate New York banker and corporation lawyer. Jackson correctly divined that law rather than politics was his strong point, and he was rather reluctant to enter the fight.[5] He did, nevertheless, on January 8, when he told reporters, "I am not a candidate, but if I am nominated, I will run."[6] Despite Roosevelt's thinly veiled backing and his own best efforts to gain support among the state party leaders, however, it became evident very soon that he was not going to be nominated. Roosevelt had given him the impression that Farley had been approached in regard to his candidacy and had approved of it, but that was not the case. Neither Farley nor Senator Robert Wagner approved, and without their support Jackson had no chance whatever. Whether his candidacy represented a threat to Farley's 1940 ambitions or whether the Chairman simply did not think Jackson was well enough known to win, which is the reason he gives for his opposition,[7] his attitude was known widely enough that state party bosses wanted no part of a Jackson-for-governor movement.[8] On January 21 he was appointed Solicitor General to replace Stanley Reed, who had just been elevated to the Supreme Court. The move was at first interpreted as an effort by Roosevelt to enhance Jackson's gubernatorial chances by increasing his prestige,[9] but in fact his political efforts were over.

If Jackson did retain any presidential aspirations, they received a shot in the arm during the Senate discussion of his appointment. Said Senator George Norris:

> He is one of the ablest, most competent men
> ever appointed by the President for the office. I am
> sorry we are not confirming him as justice of the

Supreme Court. Maybe, however, this office will place
him as a candidate for a much higher office. And I'd
be delighted to see him in the White House as President of the United States.[10]

Senator Robert Wagner, who was still interested in heading off
Jackson's gubernatorial ambitions, was inclined to think he was a
good man for Solicitor General and should concentrate on it. "I
am ready to subscribe to what the Senator from Nebraska has said,"
he observed cautiously. "I am not nominating Mr. Jackson for any
office. . . . Mr. Jackson has nothing else in mind except to serve
his country in this capacity."[11] This may have been wishful thinking, but, at any rate, by late May, Jackson was no longer being
mentioned as one of the prominent candidates for governor. Like
the other New Dealers, he was severely handicapped by his in-
ability to count on political control of his own state.

Having failed to start Jackson up the political ladder, Roosevelt next turned to his friend and confidant, W.P.A. Administrator
Harry Hopkins. According to his biographer, Robert Sherwood,
Hopkins was invited to the White House sometime in April and
told by the President that he was his choice as successor. Roosevelt
realized, he told Hopkins, that there were certain handicaps that
would have to be faced. Hopkins had had cancer and he was di-
vorced. To balance that, the doctors at Mayo Clinic had assured
him the odds against a recurrence of the cancer were two to one,
and Hopkins' second marriage, though a happy one, had had a
tragic ending with the death of his wife in the summer of 1937.
Perhaps a greater handicap than either of those, however, was his
exposed position as administrator of the relief program. Roosevelt
also proposed to eliminate that by elevating him to Dan Roper's
post as Secretary of Commerce later in the year.[12]

Raymond Moley has stated categorically that Roosevelt knew
and Hopkins should have known that the whole idea was pre-
posterous. The President was merely indulging in "friendly daw-
dling" with a close friend and had no intention of seeing anyone
but himself nominated for the presidency in 1940.[13] The idea may
have appeared ludicrous to Moley, especially with eleven years of
hindsight at Hopkins' ill health and a chronic suspicion of every
Roosevelt motive, but the indications are that neither Roosevelt

nor the other New Dealers thought so at the time. By May rumors were circulating in New York and Washington that the New Dealers, having failed to obtain the New York gubernatorial nomination for Jackson, were feeling out members of the American Labor Party and some key Democrats in behalf of Hopkins.[14] It was also reported that Jim Farley had turned thumbs down on the proposal, and very soon all rumors of a Hopkins-for-governor movement ceased. Nevertheless, the boom for Hopkins continued. As Sherwood has pointed out, Roosevelt made every effort to build him up as his right-hand man throughout 1938, and he had Hopkins photographed at his elbow on every opportunity.[15] In October Arthur Krock spent an entire column grumbling about Hopkins' rising star. "If he was No. 1 in June, 1937," groaned Krock, "he is No. 1-A now."[16] So evident was Hopkins' rather sudden growth in prominence that conservative members of Congress began to see a need to head off a possible presidential drive even in early spring. Representative Arthur Lamneck, a Democrat from Ohio, made it clear during the debate on the reorganization bill that he was opposed to the establishing of a Department of Public Welfare because Harry Hopkins would head it "and perhaps become the next President." The "octopuslike" welfare machine would become permanent and "the most potent force in the United States for many years to come." He further warned:

> "Who knows," say members of the Hopkins tub-thumpers, "it might make Harry President." There is no question but that he is the man whom the Administration would like to see the next President of the United States.
>
> He is the fair-haired boy of the Administration. What he wants, he gets. The reason is he thinks right and he spends right—and left. He also has that desirable ability of making votes in the name of federal relief.[17]

Several days later Congressman Malcolm Tarver of Georgia expressed the same objection. He was generally favorable to the reorganization bill except the part about a Department of Public Welfare, which was sure to be headed by Harry Hopkins. If that were included, he would vote against the whole bill.[18] Thus, by late spring it was becoming increasingly clear to friend and foe alike that Hopkins was the man most likely to receive all-out Administration support for the 1940 nomination.

The late winter and early spring also saw stepped-up activities by two other reputed liberals who were neither connected with the Administration nor very likely to receive any support from it. Paul McNutt had been in the Philippines for nearly a year and apparently felt it was time to place his name before the public again. Although one feature article in the *Saturday Evening Post* pictured him as the number one threat for the 1940 nomination against all Democrats, pro- or anti-New Deal,[19] there were also reports that his Indiana machine was in a state of chaos as a result of the impending purge of Senator Van Nuys, who was threatening to run independently, thus assuring a Republican victory.[20]

In early February the McNutt publicity campaign began to move into high gear. It was first announced that the High Commissioner would return to Washington to make a report to the President. It was then reported that he had made a mysterious aerial inspection of a small Japanese colony on one of the islands, that he had dashed mysteriously off to Shanghai to see Admiral Yarnell, that he was making the trip to San Francisco by fast clipper—which clipper was surrounded by an armed and menacing detachment of marines for days before the trip—and then that he was flying across the country by fast army plane.[21] His immediate destination: a banquet in Indianapolis given by the Indiana Democratic Editorial Association. McNutt spoke on the evils of Fascism, Nazism, and Communism. The editors spoke in general resolution on McNutt for President.[22] From there it was on to Washington for a reception which astounded even blasé Washington newspaper correspondents. Hosted by Senator Sherman Minton, the party was attended by some four thousand guests who consumed an estimated $6000 worth of food and drinks in honor of the High Commissioner.[23] It was also noted, however, that Jim Farley left for Florida the day McNutt arrived in Washington.[24]

The High Commissioner remained in the capital for several weeks. Although he made the customary denial that he was a candidate, a "spokesman" for him told a reporter the McNutt followers had word that the President had no intention of seeking a third term and had no objection to a campaign for McNutt.[25] A major threat, however, was developing in Senator Van Nuys. McNutt had no sooner returned to the Philippines than the Indiana Senator announced that he would run for re-election in the fall as an independent. What was more, he promised a vigorous campaign against the "State House machine." He was opposed to the Two Percent Club, and he intended to expose "the office furniture racket, the gadget racket, the potato racket, and the prostitution of local government and law enforcement through the granting of beer privileges." He had, he warned, copies of tax returns showing increases in the incomes of a number of prominent individuals from a few thousand dollars before the Democrats took office in 1933 to as much as $140,000 by 1937. He intended to name names and "let the chips fall where they may."[26] If he could and did carry out that threat, it was obvious that McNutt's presidential aspirations would be finished by the fall.

The drums for McNutt had no sooner quieted down after his return to the Philippines than a new liberal figure charged into the spotlight, only this time outside the Democratic ranks. After a series of four radio talks blasting the New Deal in April, Governor Philip La Follette of Wisconsin announced the formation of a new national party. At a meeting in the University of Wisconsin stock pavilion in Madison the new National Progressive Party came on the scene as Governor La Follette told an audience of 3500 that progressives had given up trying to make the party of the Hagues, the Kellys, the Pendergasts, and the Tammanys a vehicle of reform. Standing alone on a stark stage, backed by the party's symbol, a red, white and blue cross in a circle, he stated, "As certain as the sun rises, we are launching the party of our time."[27]

Philip La Follette was a genuine enough liberal to have been strongly backed by George Norris in 1937 for the Supreme Court seat eventually given to Hugo Black.[28] He had come to the conclusion that inasmuch as Roosevelt seemed to be losing his grip on his party and Congress, the Democratic nominee in 1940 would not be dictated from the White House. There was a good chance that there would be no liberal at all in the 1940 race unless a third party was begun early enough to organize effectively. Despite La Follette's blistering attack on the New Deal, the National Progressive Party was predicated on the notion that Roosevelt would not run for a third term.[29]

Although the response from other independent progressives throughout the country and particularly the East was not encouraging,[30] Roosevelt was concerned about the new group. He had warned Garner in a Cabinet meeting in late March that if a new third party arose from discontent with Democratic foot dragging, it would mean the Republicans would win the 1940 election beyond any doubt.[31] He had been hopeful of keeping the La Follettes in check, even suggesting to Hopkins that isolationist Robert La Follette be made his secretary of state in 1941.[32] Roosevelt's efforts had been in vain, however, and he characteristically made the best of a bad situation, writing Ambassador William Phillips in Rome that the new symbol of the Progressive party would soon be reminding people of the swastika, and all that remained was for someone to adopt a new form of arm salute. He was in favor of raising both arms above the head, followed by a bow from the waist. It would be good for people's figures![33] If anyone had reason to fear the new party, however, it was the conservative Democrats, for it meant that if the Democratic party nominated a conservative candidate in 1940 the liberal wing of the party could desert to a ready-made haven *en masse*.

While McNutt and La Follette were dramatically enlivening the political scene, the boom for the whitest of white Democratic hopes, George Earle, was slowly turning into a dull thud. McNutt's Washington trip and its attendant publicity had moved him up to fifth place among Democrats-for-President on the list of the Gallup Poll, but Earle still led all generally acknowledged liberals.[34] Like McNutt, however, he faced tremendous difficulties in keeping his own state party in line and, in the end, was unable to do so.

The major problem was that both Pittsburgh boss David Lawrence and Lieutenant Governor Thomas Kennedy, who was also secretary-treasurer of the C.I.O. and backed by John L. Lewis, had ambitions to succeed Earle as governor in 1938 when he gave up the governorship to run for the Senate. A showdown of sorts developed at the state convention, where, under the whip of Earle and Lawrence, Charles A. Jones, a relatively unknown Pittsburgh lawyer, was chosen to be the party's official candidate in the primaries instead of either of the others. The Labor wing of the party, however, would not abide by the decision, and a split developed, with John L. Lewis and the C.I.O. throwing their support to Thomas Kennedy for governor and Samuel D. Wilson, Mayor of Philadelphia, for the Senate. Senator Joseph Guffey, who had been responsible for Earle's election as governor in the first place, abandoned his former protégé and threw his support to Kennedy.[35] The situation degenerated with ghastly speed, as mud flew in all directions. Mayor Wilson, in one campaign speech, asked Earle if it was true that he had borrowed $30,000 from Democratic contractor Matthew McCloskey, and how many millions of dollars in government contracts had been awarded McCloskey. To everyone's astonishment, the multimillionaire Earle admitted that he had borrowed $26,500 from McCloskey and that McCloskey had been awarded some $10,000,000 in state contracts. There was, he said, nothing improper in that![36] Worse still, Attorney General Charles J. Margiotti entered the primary race as an independent, charging that state and party officials—most notably Earle's principal backers, David Lawrence and Matthew McCloskey—had taken large bribes to obtain favorable legislation for brewing and motion-picture interests and that some $2,000,000 had been obtained in kickbacks from state employees.[37]

The President by this time had come to the conclusion that Earle simply did not measure up,[38] but he was also well aware that Pennsylvania was too valuable to be handed back to the Republicans because of senseless factional fighting. On the very eve of the primaries he asked Jim Farley to suggest that all factions unite behind Earle for Senator and Kennedy for Governor. Although Farley's motives were of the purest, his efforts were met by a storm of abuse from Democrats over all the state and particularly from Governor George Earle, who regretted that "Mr. Farley has unwisely seen fit to come in at the eleventh hour and interfere in a purely local primary."[39]

Earle and his running mate, Charles Jones, won the primary by a fairly comfortable margin, which was regarded as a victory for the party conservatives, for, as Turner Catledge remarked, "Earle's break with Guffey and Lewis and his repudiation of Farley's support had put him outside 'the New Deal corral'!"[40] Said

Senator Carter Glass, "It's none of my business, but I think it's glorious," and Senator Royal Copeland claimed it was "a great victory for the American form of government."[41] Roosevelt himself told Farley angrily that Earle had killed his chances for the presidency unless he came to the Senate and made such a reputation that it nullified the memory of the primary battle of 1938.[42]

Earle never got the chance. The political situation sank deeper and deeper into the mire as Margiotti took his charges of graft and corruption against the Earle Administration to Carl B. Shelley, Republican District Attorney of Dauphin County, who was delighted to begin a grand-jury investigation. Earle indignantly demanded that the Pennsylvania Supreme Court call an immediate halt to what he regarded as an obvious political maneuver, and when the Court (six-to-one Republican) refused, he called the legislature into special session to "repel an unprecedented judicial invasion."[43] Although the heavily Democratic legislature effectively cancelled the grand jury hearings and transferred the investigation to a relatively safe legislative committee for the time being,[44] the result was that Earle, who had been crown prince of the New Deal only a brief year before, was now no more than an even bet to defeat Senator James J. (Puddler Jim) Davis in the Senate race.[45] He was not out of the presidential race yet, but neither was he very far in.

In the meantime all had not been sweetness and light between President Roosevelt and the third session of the Seventy-Fifth Congress. By the time of adjournment tempers were frayed, and the party was split wider apart than ever. With primaries approaching in a number of states and several of his key opponents up for re-election, Roosevelt determined to attack his opposition within the party directly. On his success hung his chances of naming his successor or even vetoing the choice of the party regulars.

The Seventy-Fifth Congress and the Congressional Campaign of 1938

The so-called purge campaigns of 1938 were originally products of the President's pique over the defeat of his Court plan and the defeat of his entire program during the special session of Congress,[46] although the final decision to mount an offensive was not made until after the third session of the Seventy-Fifth Congress. A group of New Dealers nicknamed the "elimination committee" had been pressing the President since the previous winter to cleanse the party of reactionaries and create a new and genuine liberal-conservative political alignment. Formed at a meeting at the home of Harry Hopkins, they included Ickes, Robert Jackson, Assistant Attorney General Joseph Keenan, Assistant W.P.A. Administrator David K. Niles, James Roosevelt, Tom Corcoran, and Ben Cohen.[47] Their reasoning was perfectly logical. If a New Dealer was to succeed Roosevelt to the presidency in 1940, the party must be firmly committed to the ideals of the New Deal. Quite obviously some of the most powerful "barons" in the party were bluntly opposed to New Deal liberalism and prepared to exclude any liberal from consideration for the nomination. To retain control of the party it was absolutely necessary to demonstrate to all Democrats that the people were behind the New Deal, not merely behind individual politicians or machines. The primaries of 1938 were obvious opportunities for a show of force. Further, victories for party factions friendly to the Administration in 1938 would mean friendly delegations to the national convention in 1940.[48] Significantly, only one New Deal presidential hopeful, Henry Wallace, was not a member of the elimination committee.

By the time Congress was nearing adjournment in July all signs indicated that a purge would be a smashing success and, indeed, almost a necessity if the President's second-term drive for the lowest third of the nation was not to bog down hopelessly. What he had expected from Congress in 1938 was not very different from what it had refused him in 1937. Steadily dropping farm prices emphasized the need for something to replace the A.A.A.; a wages and hours bill, a bill for the reorganization of the executive branch of the government, a new tax schedule, regional planning for new T.V.A.s, and the retention of work relief even at the cost of an unbalanced budget were "must" proposals of a more controversial nature.[49] As the recession deepened, the President abandoned his efforts for economy and budget balancing, accepted for a time at least the Keynesian proposals of Marriner Eccles and other New

Dealers, and requested a huge new pump-priming expenditure and a thorough investigation of monopolies in business.[50]

Congressional reaction to the tall order was variously described as a major offensive against the New Deal[51] and a desire to postpone any further controversial legislation until the elections were safely out of the way.[52] There was some evidence to support the first contention. To be sure, the President got his pump-priming bill passed, a second A.A.A., the Temporary National Economic Committee to study business conditions, and, after a hard tussle, the Wages and Hours Act. The Administration was dealt a bitter defeat on the reorganization bill, however, when 108 Democrats joined the opposition to vote it down in the House.[53] That staggering reprimand was followed almost immediately by another in the form of the Revenue Act of 1938, which virtually eliminated the Keynesian undistributed profits tax and capital gains tax except for a small amount left to satisfy the President that the principle was still being followed.[54] Rather than veto the bill, Roosevelt allowed it to become law without his signature, though not without sharp criticism. An angry defense of the bill was supplied in the Senate by Pat Harrison, who made it perfectly clear that he felt the President was completely in error on the tax question.[55] What is significant is not so much the hard feelings over the taxing principle, which was nothing new, but, as Basil Rauch has pointed out, the New Deal appeared to be in retreat. This was the first Administration measure under the heading of reform to be repealed.[56] Further, Congress did not even consider the seven regional T.V.A.s the Administration was proposing.

One congressional action which suggested to some observers that conservatives within the party were out to get rid of New Deal Administrators as well as New Deal laws was the creation of the Dies Committee to investigate and publicize un-American totalitarian movements in the United States. Rumors immediately began to circulate in Washington that the committee was a "Southern plot" to discredit the left wing of the New Deal, head off a possible third term for the President, and expose the Communist backbone of the C.I.O.[57] A "Southern plot" has never been proven, but the committee did very quickly establish itself as a sounding board for wild-eyed attacks on the New Dealers, with Martin Dies himself leading the pack. After a particularly spirited exchange in the fall of the year in which Harold Ickes referred to Dies as "the outstanding zany of our political history,"[58] Dies replied with a diatribe which probably reflected fairly well the attitude of the more extreme Southern conservatives toward the New Dealers. Said he:

> The Secretary literally reeks with the venom of hatred. It flows from him as naturally and freely as water from a spring. . . . I am sure that the resignation of Ickes, Perkins, and Hopkins, together with their army of satellites, would do more to restore normal conditions than any other single act.
>
> It is a consummation devoutly desired by the overwhelming majority of Democrats. Such resignations would restore peace and harmony in the Democratic party and, what is more, confidence in the government.[59]

Of course all of that, as well as the noteworthy part the committee played in the elections of 1938, were in the future when Congress approved the committee, but Dies' attitude was no secret even in May. Consciously or not, the conservatives were providing themselves with a mouthpiece for those periods when Congress was not in session and the President usually had the limelight all to himself. Dies was prepared to compete with Roosevelt for publicity, and as often as not he came out on top.

There were indications during the first half of 1938, however, that the nation was still solidly behind Roosevelt and might very well follow his voting recommendations. In January, for instance, Senator Lister Hill, one of the very small group of Southerners who were even then behind the Administration's wages and hours bill,[60] won renomination in the Alabama primary over the anti-New Deal reactionary Thomas Heflin. Hill was greatly aided, it was thought, by being allowed to appear with the President on a train ride through Alabama and because it was known that he was a New Dealer.[61]

An even more dramatic demonstration of the power of Administration approval in a primary campaign and the direct effect it could have on legislation pending in Washington was provided by Senator Claude Pepper's overwhelming victory. In February,

James Roosevelt, then vacationing in Florida, announced that "we" wanted Pepper returned to the Senate. Pepper's principal opponent in the primary was Congressman J. Mark Wilcox, who opposed the wages and hours bill and the reorganization plan.[62] The President did not openly add or subtract anything from what his son had said. When asked if James' statement accurately reflected his views, he dodged, "I only know what I read in the newspapers. I do not know whether he was even accurately quoted."[63] Nevertheless, he and the elimination committee could not help but be gratified by Pepper's solid victory and his proud announcement, "The people of Florida want you to know that this is their response to your recent patriotic appeal to the United States to unite behind your leadership to bring back a speedy recovery and better living and working conditions to the people of America. . . ."[64]

The New Dealers could be even more gratified by the obvious effects the election had on the progress of the wages and hours bill. Up to that time it had been bottled up in the House Rules Committee, which was presided over by conservative John O'Connor of New York. The House leadership had been working diligently to get the necessary number of signatures for a discharge petition, but progress had been discouragingly slow. Then, on May 3 came Pepper's renomination. Governor Fred Cone of Florida wired Roosevelt, "Senator Pepper assured majority over all opponents in first primary. Fight was made on your principles and you have been vindicated by the people of Florida. Please accept my congratulations and best personal regards."[65] An unspoken message was received by the House as well. The discharge petition obtained the necessary 218 signatures in record time three days later, and the bill passed the House on May 24 by a 314 to 97 margin.[66] In its final form it reached the President on June 25, 1938.

The New Dealers were further encouraged in their belief that the voters would support their efforts to create a new Democratic party by a poll made by the American Institute of Public Opinion in April. This poll indicated that in the event that there were only two parties—one liberal and the other conservative—72 per cent of those asked would join the liberal party. Moreover, if the President were not a candidate in 1940, 63 per cent of the Democrats stated they would favor a New Dealer to follow him, although with Hull, Farley, and Garner leading the poll there appeared to be some confusion over the definition of a New Dealer.[67] Still another hopeful harbinger of success was provided by the Oregon primary. There Governor Charles H. Martin—formerly a Republican, formerly a New Deal Congressman, and now at sword's point with Ickes, the National Labor Relations Board, and "that miserable Secretary Perkins"—was running for renomination against Henry Hess, an avowed New Dealer. Both Ickes and Senator George Norris supported Hess, and their letters of endorsement were considered decisive in his victory in late May.[68]

The elimination committee next turned to Iowa, but here it foundered. Iowa was a crucial state for a number of reasons. Most important of all was that it was the home state of both Secretary of Agriculture Henry A. Wallace and of W.P.A. Administrator Harry Hopkins, both of whom had ambitions of occupying the White House in 1941. Wallace was slowly and painstakingly building his hopes on the basis of friendship with the political leaders of his own home state. Hopkins, on the other hand, appeared ready to bypass the local machine and demonstrate his power with the Iowa voters by appealing directly to them against Senator Guy Gillette. The strategy was a disaster from everyone's point of view.

The fact was that until the purge Gillette was a relatively strong New Dealer, having gone "off the reservation" only on the Court reform bill and the Wages and Hours Act.[69] It appeared that what the New Dealers were aiming at was not necessarily so much a liberal bloc as an obedient bloc. Apparently Tom Corcoran was the architect of the policy. When a group of reporters asked Hopkins, who was born and raised in Iowa, to comment on the Iowa primary, he at first refused, but later, under the prodding of Corcoran, he arranged to make a brief statement to Richard Wilson of the Des Moines *Register and Tribune*. Of the young New Deal congressman who had been chosen to oppose Gillette he said, "If I were voting in Iowa I would vote for Otha D. Wearin on the basis of his record."[70] It was a badly miscalculatd move, not only as far as the purge was concerned but also as far as Harry Hopkins personally was concerned.

In the first place, Hopkins, as head of an organization for the unemployed, appeared to be playing politics with federal relief.

In the second place, Gillette, with a united state party behind him, was almost unbeatable anyway. Party regulars were furious. Senate debate on a relief bill was broken off abruptly when someone showed Senator Burton K. Wheeler a newspaper account of the Hopkins' statement. The Senator rose in a fury and was soon joined in his denunciations of Hopkins by Senators Pat McCarran and Hiram Johnson.[71] Eventually the debate returned to its original topic, but later in the morning Wheeler, who was obviously upset by the development, again interrupted to read a telegram just off the wire from the liberal Governor of Iowa, Nelson Kraschel. Said Kraschel:

> As a friend of all candidates in the Democratic primary, I resent the attempted influence of non-resident federal appointees. It has been the hope of all Iowa Democrats that selection of candidates would be made without dictation by pseudo leaders. If I have been willing to withhold my personal influence from a contest that designates my running mate, I feel justified in expecting out-of-state Washington appointees to do as much. It is regrettable that Hopkins is the first to violate his declared policy of keeping the W.P.A. out of politics.[72]

With that paralyzing repudiation the battle was on between the elimination committee and Iowa party leaders. Besides Kraschel, Gillette could also count on the support of Senator Clyde Herring, the A. F. of L., and the Catholics of Iowa.[73] So powerful did he appear before the Hopkins comment, in fact, that he had not even intended to return to Iowa to campaign. Once challenged by Hopkins and James Roosevelt, who added to the furor by writing a friend in the state and referring to "my friend, Otha Wearin," Gillette entered upon a vigorous campaign. Charging up and down the state, he repeatedly denounced "this gang of political termites . . . boring from within . . . planning on taking over, if possible, the Democratic party organization in 1940."[74] He was careful, however, to distinguish between President Roosevelt, who, he maintained, had nothing to do with the purge, and the evil radicals who were advising him. What made this strategy possible was not only the fact that Roosevelt did not openly back Wearin but that

Henry Wallace had also pointedly refused to say anything one way or the other, thus making it difficult for Otha Wearin to claim that the Administration in Washington was one hundred per cent behind him. Every time he claimed to have New Deal backing, Gillette simply challenged him to show any support from Roosevelt, Jim Farley, or Henry Wallace. Had he been able to do so, Gillette might have been in grave trouble indeed.[75]

The result was to generate intense resentment in Washington on both sides of the questions, as every effort was made by the elimination committee to "smoke out" the Secretary of Agriculture. The "smoking out process" was carried on chiefly by the Washington columnists, but the strategy was fairly transparent.[76] Jay Franklin, for instance, who was reputedly the voice of Tom Corcoran in print,[77] wrote that the defeat of Governor Martin in the Oregon primary increased considerably the heat on Wallace to declare himself in Iowa. Ickes had supported Martin's opponent, Henry Hess, had won, and was, therefore, in the process of capturing the leadership of the progressive wing of the party from Wallace. Hopkins was moving up in the race by his support of Otha Wearin. Since Roosevelt's attitude on the Iowa primary was fairly well known, Wallace simply could not afford any fence-sitting if he had any hopes at all for 1940.[78] The logic might appear strained, but everyone recognized the message.

Wallace, however, preferred to gamble on Gillette and said nothing publicly. Privately he let it be known that he was furious with those applying the pressure, and he twice went to the White House to warn the President he was making a mistake, which pleased neither Roosevelt nor the elimination committee.[79] He was, commented mild-mannered Ben Cohen, somewhat unpopular with the other New Dealers because he did not seem to be interested in anything but his own particular affairs,[80] in this case his own political future. Ickes noted characteristically in his diary:

> . . . I share the view that Tom Corcoran, Harry Hopkins and others have, that Henry Wallace is a selfish and not too forthright individual who is so consumed with his political ambition that there isn't anything he won't do to advance himself, even at the cost of injury to someone else. . . .[81]

The feeling was entirely mutual. Wallace was making a strong effort at the same time to form a cabal in the Cabinet to force the ouster of Ickes because he leaked Cabinet secrets to his favorite newspapermen. Harry Hopkins, however, tipped Ickes off, and the effort was in vain.[82] One thing was clear about the struggle, and that was that both Hopkins and Wallace were gambling heavily on the outcome of the Iowa primary and election. The primary was a clear-cut victory for Wallace. The purge policy suffered its first serious setback when Gillette won by a lopsided two-to-one margin.[83]

At this point the President decided to follow the advice of the elimination committee and place himself at the head of the purge campaign openly. In a Fireside Chat on June 24 he told the nation that as head of the Democratic party with a definite liberal platform to fulfill he intended to speak out against the "Copperheads" of the party who were demanding peace at any price. "I have every right to speak," he said, ". . . where there may be a clear issue between candidates for a Democratic nomination involving . . . pirnciples, or . . . a clear misuse of my own name."[84] With that he began a cross-country speaking tour, reassuring his friends and throwing fear into his enemies.

For the most part the campaign against those Democrats said by Josephus Daniels to be "seeking to lay the foundations for a National Convention in 1940 that will give us as a nominee a John W. Davis or Alton B. Parker model"[85] was an egregious error largely engineered at the last minute by and for political amateurs. The tremendous New Deal handicap of political inexperience and naïvete was never more evident. Not one of the conservative Senators Roosevelt attempted to defeat—Ed Smith of South Carolina, Walter George of Georgia, or Millard Tydings of Maryland—was defeated, though the Chairman of the House Rules Committee, John O'Connor, was unseated by the very professional Ed Flynn at Roosevelt's request.[86]

Undoubtedly some good may have resulted from supporting New Deal incumbents like Alben Barkley, Elbert Thomas, and Hattie Caraway, but it appeared to be offset by the bitterness and open divisions created within the party which were paving the way for a Republican comeback. Wrote one loyal party member to Jim Farley, "President Roosevelt's purge is one of the most despicable things that has ever occurred in United States history. I have been a believer in liberal democratic government, but when liberalism takes the form of dictatorship even I bristle."[87]

In direct contrast to the sloppy, inefficient, and bungling methods used in Pennsylvania by Governor Earle and in Iowa and elsewhere by the New Dealers, Paul McNutt and his Indiana machine hurdled the Van Nuys' purge problem with grace and verve, if not do-or-die courage. Faced with Van Nuys as a potential independent candidate capable of ruining the McNutt campaign and the Democratic party in Indiana on the one hand, and a pledge made to Roosevelt to get rid of him on the other, Governor Clifford Townsend hastily urged the Senator to accept the Democratic nomination for another term just one week before the state convention met. The two men who had previously announced themselves as available to fill Van Nuys' Senate seat, Samuel D. Jackson of Fort Wayne and Lieutenant Governor Henry F. Schricker, both expressed themselves as delighted with the Governor's action.[88] The convention joyfully welcomed the Senator back to the fold by acclamation and enthusiastically endorsed McNutt for the presidency.[89] It was, wrote McNutt gratefully to his campaign manager, Frank McHale, the best solution to "the most desperate situation in the history of Indiana politics."[90] There was some danger that the elimination committee in Washington might see a "double cross" in the arrangement or that Van Nuys might embarrass the Indiana machine by continuing his vendetta against the Administration once he was safely back in office for another six years. "Some of the President's immediate advisers may not like what happened," observed the High Commissioner philosophically, "but all the practical politicians will." Nevertheless, he was hoping fervently "that Fred will not disappoint us again."[91]

It was, indeed, a smooth and intelligent solution to a knotty problem, and there was some evidence that the fact had not been lost on other Democrats. The Gallup Poll for August showed McNutt replacing Earle in fourth place among Democratic hopefuls, right behind the "big three," Farley, Garner, and Hull. That was exactly where he wanted to be, not close enough to the top to be a target as yet and not so close that he could not still make impressive gains without arousing antagonism.[92] As the progress of the purge went from bad to worse in other states, he looked even better. One McNutt supporter noted that the President's defeats were solid blows to any third-term hopes he might have held, and that meant a boost to McNutt. "It seems to me you will come nearer to satisfying all the elements of the party than any other candidate."[93] Certainly McNutt seemed to be one of the best bets to survive politically until 1940.

If the primaries were a setback for the New Dealers, the 1938 elections proved to be a staggering blow to the presidential aspirations of nearly every liberal hopeful. Almost none escaped with prestige fully intact, and at least two were annihilated. Perhaps most seriously damaged of all was the image of President Roosevelt as the political magician. In his efforts to attack conservatism in the party he early made it clear that he favored liberals regardless to which party they belonged. Asked if he intended to help Governor Frank Murphy in his campaign for re-election in Michigan, he replied:

> I will probably do the same thing about him as I
> will do for various other liberals in the United States.
> I am in favor of liberals. I am not taking part in party
> politics in the election. If there is a good liberal run-
> ning on the Republican ticket, I would not have the
> slightest objection to his election.[94]

That was not calculated to please any regular Democrats, and the results of the presidential aid were not calculated to reassure any liberals. Roosevelt rushed to the defense of Governor Murphy when he was smeared by witnesses before the Dies' Committee in regard to Communism and the sit-down strikes just before the elections.[95] He sent letters into Pennsylvania supporting Earle's bespattered slate there, to Wisconsin for Senator Ryan Duffy, and to California for the Olson-Downey slate. He also indicated that he was certainly not hostile to Governor Benson's Farmer-Labor government in Minnesota.[96] In every case except California his writing was in vain.

For George Earle of Pennsylvania it was the end of a very bumpy political line. The Republicans swept his state, and the

Governor, the prime candidate for the presidency only a year before, was retired to private life. Frank Murphy of Michigan, too,
was defeated, but his record of cooperation with the Administration was somewhat better than Earle's and his reputation as a liberal
somewhat brighter. He had every reason to expect that the President would not allow him to be retired to private life. In Wisconsin
both presidential aspirant Philip La Follette and his National Progressive Party received their coup de grace from resurgent bi-
partisan conservatism. Rather than let La Follette win again in a
three-cornered race, the regular Democratic nominee, Robert K.
Henry, also ran in the Republican primary, stating that if he won
both he would run for the party from which he received the most
votes. When he failed to win the Republican nomination, he withdrew entirely from the race in favor of Julius P. Heil, the millionaire businessman whom the Republicans had nominated. The
Democrats hastily called a special caucus to nominate state senator
Harry Bolens to run for governor, but it was a half-hearted effort.[97]
and when the votes were counted, it was found that Heil had won
by an almost five to three margin over La Follette and that the Progressive Party had been rather thoroughly repudiated. It retained
only two of its seven seats in the national House of Representatives,
and in the state legislature its representation dropped from forty-
nine to thirty-two in the assembly and eighteen to eleven in the
state senate. Affiliate groups in Iowa and California were smashed
even worse.[98]

Nor could Administration New Dealers Harry Hopkins and
Henry Wallace take much comfort in the outcome. To be sure,
Wallace's silent support of Senator Gillette appeared very wise
when the Senator won re-election without serious difficulty. On
the other hand, his closest friend and ally in the state, Governor
Nelson Kraschel, was defeated. Moreover, the uprising of Republican strength throughout the farm belt appeared to reflect a good
deal of farm discontent with Wallace's efforts in the Agriculture
Department.[99] This factor was particularly emphasized by local
Democratic leaders from farm states who wrote National Chairman Jim Farley to explain their losses. Over and over came the
comment that the causes of the reverses were farmer dissatisfac-
tion with Washington bureaucracy and the low price of wheat

and corn, blamed—logically or not—on Wallace.[100] There were other factors mentioned, but none so frequently and unanimously as these.

Even more unpopular with local party leaders were Harry Hopkins and his W.P.A. organization. During the primary campaign in Kentucky, Scripps-Howard reporter Thomas Stokes had uncovered evidence of great political pressure being exerted by local W.P.A. officials in behalf of Alben Barkley.[101] A great hue and cry against federal relief in politics went up, and public disapproval tended to focus on Administrator Hopkins. Letters from party leaders, however, indicate that the Kentucky incident had been relatively isolated, too isolated. From almost every state came complaints that the W.P.A. was controlled by Republicans and that no pressure at all was put on the rank and file to support the Democratic ticket.[102] Wrote one irate local boss from New Jersey:

> The results of this last election show that the way Mr. Harry Hopkins handles the WPA politically is too easy, especially in Ocean County where we have to fight State and County Road Funds. Letters were sent to all WPA employees telling them not to play politics and vote to suite [sic] themselves and (I) believe they took advantage of it. It is the sentiment in this locality that the WPA should be national patronage.[103]

In many areas W.P.A. officials had leaned over so far backward to avoid discriminating against Republicans that Democrats were penalized.[104] That left Hopkins under fire from all sides. The general public was outraged at the political chicanery practiced by the W.P.A. in Kentucky and several other states, the party regulars were furious over his attempt to use his influence as relief administrator in the Gillette purge, and the local party bosses indicated rather strongly that they thought he was a bumbling incompetent when it came to making relief rolls pay off politically. "... I can tell you that we did suffer setbacks last November," he wrote grimly to a friend. "However . . . I do not despair about 1940. It will be up to us then to stake out the fight on whether we are to go forward in a progressive manner or turn back to the reactionary ways of the '20's."[105] At least one Democratic senator agreed that the party could win with a progressive candidate in 1940—as long as it was not Harry Hopkins, who did not "meet the specifications." But, said Senator Guy Gillette, should Henry Wallace become a candidate, "he will have my hearty support."[106] Before the year was out, however, the President had taken one of the heaviest of political millstones off of Hopkins' back. On December 23 it was announced that he had been appointed Secretary of Commerce to replace Dan Roper.[107] He would have two years to build a public image as a friend of the businessman and lose the image of the tough-talking federal relief administrator who reputedly wanted to "tax and tax, and spend and spend, and elect and elect."[108] Said conservative Democratic Senator William King, "I regret very much that the President has seen fit to name him to this important post."[109]

Nor had the elections and their aftermath been particularly kind to the ambitions of High Commissioner McNutt, though there was no visible sign of discouragement in the McNutt camp. A Democratic sweep of Indiana would have been a most impressive demonstration of his ability to deliver the vote. Indiana was in the path of Republican resurgence, however, and the Democrats lost six House seats to the Republicans. In addition, Senator Van Nuys was barely able to defeat Raymond E. Willis, a relatively unknown country editor. New York *Times* pundit Arthur Krock figuratively closed the book on the McNutt boom, commenting that it had collapsed with the McNutt state ticket.[110] McNutt did, indeed, drop from fourth to sixth on the Gallop Poll after the election, and there were rumors of suspicion and friction with New Dealers in the Administration, if not with President Roosevelt himself.[111] Nevertheless, on November 23, Frank McHale proudly and formally announced McNutt's candidacy for the presidency.[112] The announcement was couched in terms which suggested that he and his leader had interpreted the election returns as marking a trend away from Roosevelt and the New Deal. McNutt was described by his manager as a "middle-of-the-road candidate, a Jeffersonian Democrat with progressive tendencies." McHale predicted cautiously that "the nation in 1940 will want a middle-of-the-road candidate who will guarantee the great advances in social progress already won while keeping out of untried and dangerous experiments."[113]

To be sure, McNutt had no intention of breaking with the Administration, though he was not altogether positive that the Administration was not ready to break with him. Rumors had reached his ears that unnamed New Dealers were telling the President that he intended to break with the Administration on the question of Philippine independence when called to testify before a House Committee on the subject, since he had stated in March that he was opposed to it.[114] What was not generally known was that President Manuel Quezon shared his belief that the islands were not economically ready and able to be cut adrift. McNutt had presented his case to the President in a secret conference already, but Roosevelt merely remarked, "If that is what the Filipinos want, let them say so."[115] Quezon, of course, could not say so without bringing the wrath of the islands' nationalists down on his head. McNutt said so, but his views were chalked up to old-fashioned imperialism or disloyalty to Roosevelt.[116] To answer the latter charge and guard his political rear, McNutt dispatched a lengthy memorandum to the President, explaining his point of view and expressing his complete loyalty to whatever course of action the Administration might decide upon.[117] His protestations were apparently accepted at face value.

Of all the liberals and middle-of-the-roaders, probably only Senator Burton K. Wheeler came out of the 1938 elections with stronger political potentialities than he had gone in with. Not only had he maintained his popularity with party regulars, such as it was, by his unmeasured condemnation of the purge but also he had secured the base of his power in Montana by his own private purge of Congressman Jerry O'Connell, a liberal who had already announced his intention of seeking Wheeler's seat in 1940. Working behind the scenes and through his lieutenants, Wheeler backed Republican Jacob Thorkelson, who went on to defeat O'Connell by a narrow margin.[118]

Thus 1938 saw a depletion in the ranks of the liberal presidential possibilities. Effectively and completely eliminated from the competition were Governors La Follette of Wisconsin and Earle of Pennsylvania. Badly damaged but not completely dead was

Governor Frank Murphy of Michigan. Injured in varying degrees but still hopeful were Harry Hopkins, Henry Wallace, and Paul McNutt. Quietly minding their own business as much as possible and remaining relatively unhurt were Senators Alben Barkley, a very dark horse who maintained his seventh-place position on the Gallup Poll before and after the elections, and Burton Wheeler. It is noteworthy that in no case did President Roosevelt fail to do what he could to aid any of these men when requested to do so, and certainly there is no evidence that he did anything to injure any of them. They had been able to manage that themselves.

Presidential Prospects for 1940: The Conservatives

With Democratic members of Congress still showing strong tendencies toward independence in 1938 and with the markedly conservative trend in the 1938 primaries and elections, the prospects of the would-be conservative presidential nominees appeared to be growing better all the time. There was, of course, some difference of opinion over exactly what the elections proved. Governor Frank Murphy, for instance, philosophically chalked his defeat up to the recession and a combination of habit and tradition.[119] The President himself insisted the outcome was merely the result of local situations. Oddly enough, he even expected less trouble from the Seventy-Sixth Congress than he got from the Seventy-Fifth, since the party regulars, now confident that they would control the convention in 1940 and nominate their own man, would realize that they could not win the election without the support of his Administration, "and I am sufficiently honest to decline to support any conservative Democrat."[120]

The conservatives, on the other hand, believed that the country was finally beginning to see things their way, and the knowledge filled them with new militancy. Senator Wheeler, who was rightly regarded as sympathetic to conservative Senators because of the purge, was asked whether the opposition group in the Senate might retaliate against the President by fashioning a purge of Majority Leader Alben Barkley. There would not be much point in that, argued Wheeler cheerfully. "He leads only Minton and

Schwellenbach. We have the votes to remove him if we like, but we have nothing to gain." "Who," snapped liberal Senator William Smathers angrily, "does he mean by 'We'—the Republicans and who else?"[121] The answer to that was at least partly provided one day in the Senate cloakroom when "Cotton Ed" Smith observed that President Roosevelt was his own worst enemy. Replied Walter George fervently, "Not as long as I am alive."[122]

Letters to Farley from Democrats in the hinterland also indicated a trend away from liberalism. Congressman Harry B. Coffee, a conservative winner from Nebraska, observed that the election demonstrated that "the sentiment in Nebraska strongly favors a swing to the right in the next Congress," and Senator Gillette, now thoroughly disillusioned with the New Deal, blamed the party's defeats on "the Administration's attitude toward sit-down strikes, the Supreme Court Reorganization proposal, the attempted purge, . . . excessive spending with no apparent end in sight . . . and particularly the fear of the drift of our party toward an extreme left-wing position of radicalism."[123] What made these responses significant was that they were fairly typical.

Even the liberals, however much they might claim that the election returns were being misinterpreted, realized they would be hard pressed to head off the conservative surge. "We may expect," Josephus Daniels warned the President, "the reactionary Senators to start a movement 'back to Conservatism' with another John Davis as the 1940 nominee."[124] A frequent liberal critic of some New Deal legislation, Professor Paul Douglas of the University of Chicago, probably expressed the feeling of a good many other liberals when he wrote Abraham Epstein of the American Association for Social Security that in view of the rising reactionary tide they would do well to modify their criticism of the Roosevelt Administration somewhat, demonstrating sympathy and friendliness rather than antagonism in their suggestions. "In short," he added, "I think it is necessary that spiritually and emotionally we should close our ranks within the liberal fold in order to avert the danger of reaction."[125]

Surprisingly enough, the Democrat who probably gained the most in power and influence as a result of the heavy conservative vote was Jim Farley, whom Roosevelt was rapidly coming to regard as the most dangerous "conservative."[126] Ill feeling had been growing between Farley and the White House inner circle throughout the summer as a result of Farley's marked hostility to all purge efforts. In the Oregon race he sent a letter of commendation to Governor Charles Martin, marked for purging by Ickes. He had made no secret of the fact that he favored Senator Gillette in Iowa. By June there were rumors of a growing rift between Farley and the elimination committee, with the New Dealers reportedly fearful of Farley's tremendous influence at the grass-roots level of the party and resentful of his veto of the gubernatorial ambitions of Robert Jackson and Harry Hopkins.[127] In July there were more rumors and denials of disagreements between Farley and the Administration,[128] and in August the President took the trouble to tell reporters that there had been "complete agreement as usual" after a conference with his Postmaster General.[129]

These reports had an element of accuracy about them. The fact was that Farley was furious with the New Deal political amateurs for splitting his beloved Democratic party and for inspiring stories of a split between himself and the President by the Washington columnists.[130] Further, he not only pointedly refused to assist in the purge but he also showed far greater independence than at any previous time in his support of party regulars against non-Democratic liberals in direct opposition to Roosevelt's announced position. In Minnesota, for instance, he urged Democrats to stand up for "your own ticket and especially Thomas Gallagher, your able nominee for governor,"[131] although Roosevelt had already taken the trouble to write a letter indicating that he was not opposed to Governor Benson's Farmer-Laborite Administration.

The outcome of the elections appeared to be a solid vindication of the Farley policies, and his practice of writing each local Democratic leader to ask his opinion of the cause for the outcome of the elections brought a heart-warming response. Whatever the local politicos may have had to say about Roosevelt and the New Dealers, almost without exception they told the National Chairman that they were very flattered to be asked, and they were behind him one hundred per cent.[132] Reading through hundreds of such letters, Farley would have been less than human if he did not begin to wonder if he himself did not carry more weight with the rank and file of the party than the President. The New Dealers, according to Joseph Alsop and Robert Kintner, had been worrying about the same thing for six months,[133] especially in view of the rumors already beginning to circulate in the summer of 1938 that Farley was becoming more active in quietly promoting his own 1940 candidacy.[134] Their problem was to undercut Farley's power; his, of course, was to maintain and expand it. The next year and a half was to see a good deal of heat generated from the resulting friction of cross purposes.

Although Farley may have been considered the most dangerous outsider by the New Dealers, it was Vice President Garner who was furnishing the rallying point for the conservatives just as he had in 1937, and in that position his power appeared to be expanding. While Congress was in session, he was reputedly furnishing strong opposition to the President's spending program. At a Cabinet meeting in late March he told Roosevelt that he was ruining the party as well as the nation with his pump-priming bill.[135] The President thought enough of his influence to quickly deny that the incident ever took place when news of it was leaked out to the press.[136] Relations between the two were still publicly cordial when Congress adjourned, but Garner had departed for Uvalde only a short time when unnamed conservative Senators reported that he had stated quite emphatically that he would not be a candidate for a third term as Vice President.[137] The implication was that a similar disavowal would be welcome from the President.

During the late summer and early fall, as the Roosevelt purge blundered toward ignominious defeat and failure, the Garner-for-President movement began to pick up momentum. In early August the Texas State Democratic Executive Committee adopted a resolution endorsing the Vice President for the presidency in 1940 and urging the active support of all party members.[138] Several days later, Senator Edward Burke of Nebraska, about to sail for the Inter-Parliamentary Congress at The Hague, repeated his 1937 endorsement of Garner, "Progressive, forward-looking, and has both feet on the ground all the time."[139] Said an unimpressed Lewis Schwellenbach, "You can put me down as opposite to everything Burke says and save a lot of time."[140] The Texas state Democratic convention in September also endorsed Garner.[141]

Following the November elections, with their promise of better things for conservatives, the Garner-for-President drums began beating in earnest. Engineered by Roy Miller, a wealthy lobbyist for the Texas Gulf Sulphur Company, the first official Garner-for-President Club was established at Detroit, Texas, site of the log cabin where both Garner and his mother had been born. The crowd at the ceremony, according to the press release, was made of "aging but sturdy pioneer residents of the county, some of whom played baseball and poker with Mr. Garner." In the keynote address Miller described Garner as a liberal "without a tinge or taint of radicalism," and a firm believer in "pay-as-you-go" government.[142]

Rumors of personal hard feelings between the President and Vice President circulated freely as members of the Seventy-Sixth Congress began drifting into Washington in December for the opening of the first session. Washington columnists reported that friends of Garner were indignant at the whispered New Deal charges that Garner was the brains behind the Dies Committee and its attacks on the New Deal. Considering the brains shown by the Dies Committee, they maintained, the charge was virtual slander.[143] An effort was made by outgoing Secretary of Commerce, Dan Roper, to get the two men together at Warm Springs to reconstitute the Democratic caucus in Congress for greater legislative efficiency. Replied Garner, "I have no invitation from the President to visit Warm Springs, and I hope he don't [sic] take up your suggestion and call me over there, since I want to stay down here in the woods until after Christmas. . . . I am willing to make any sacrifice, however, for the benefit of the country."[144] The supreme sacrifice of coming out of the woods, however, was not exacted. Instead, Roosevelt asked Garner to come to Washington early to discuss the legislative program for the coming year.[145] Conferences were, indeed, held, but by the end of the month relations between President and Vice President were reported to be as bad as ever, and Farley was telling friends that Garner was not interested in being President—he merely wanted to determine who would be.[146]

The three men who headed every Gallup Poll taken in 1938 on the most likely successor to President Roosevelt were Garner, Farley, and Hull, with Garner's lead over the other two gradually increasing as the year wore on. The third member of the "big three," Cordell Hull, retained his popularity despite the fact that he said absolutely nothing of a political nature throughout the year and his name was linked with no group or faction. Despite his silence, however, there were liberals who worried about a future boom for him. Except for his age—he would be sixty-nine in 1940— he had all the marks of an ideal candidate. Neither New Dealers nor conservatives could find fault with him, and Roosevelt could scarcely refuse to support one of his own loyal Cabinet members. Yet everyone knew that if Hull were elected, the New Deal would be quickly liquidated. The problem that worried the liberals was, what would or could Roosevelt do about it?[147] The answer in 1938 was, obviously, nothing.

Interest in Jesse Jones still existed as well, hovering like a very small cloud on the horizon. Roosevelt was certainly aware of it. When Farley suggested Jones as a possible successor to Dan Roper in the Commerce Department, he rejected the idea at once. Jones, he explained, would immediately want to use his Cabinet office as a springboard to the presidency. "And he would make a bad President, Jim; he's too old and in bad health."[148] Others were also aware of Jones' potentialities and thought better of them than Roosevelt. Wrote Governor Carl Bailey of Arkansas:

> It is generally conceded that you are the only out-standing member of the Democratic Party who has the balance born of the proper respect for sound fundamental economics plus the vision necessary to prevent the accumulation of social problems which would prove disastrous.[149]

The trouble was that friendly endorsements of this sort came almost exclusively from the southwestern part of the country and were chiefly made by bankers and businessmen, essentially the same group which was backing Vice President Garner. What gave Jones some reason to hope was the report that Garner did not want the presidency for himself, but he was determined to see some "safe" candidate chosen in 1940. If Garner had anything even approaching a determining voice in the national convention, Jesse Jones' stock would be very near the top indeed, since the Vice President thought very highly of him. Garner confided to Bascom Timmons that he would rather see Jones considered for the presidency than himself. "He has a head full of sense and the confidence of the country," said Garner. "I think he would pull more independent votes than any other candidate we could nominate."[150]

The November elections not only dampened liberal hopes of continuing to control the party but also produced a brilliant new star among the conservative presidential hopefuls. As a result of his landslide victories in both the party primary and the election itself, Senator Bennett Champ Clark of Missouri appeared to be a real possibility. From nowhere at all before the elections he suddenly appeared in fourth place on the Gallup Poll, right behind conservatives Garner, Hull, and Farley.[151] It was thought by some that he might make an ideal compromise candidate.[152] His distinguished family political background and his generally orthodox voting record were expected to smooth over Administration pique at his opposition to the Court reform bill and other recent peccadilloes. His record of party regularity and his relatively conservative economic theories certainly would make him acceptable to the right wing. Vice President Garner was quoted as saying of Clark, "If I were going to rob a train, and I had to choose an accomplice from the United States Senate, I would pick Bennett Clark."[153] Many, in fact, felt that Garner was serving as a stalking horse for Clark rather than Jones.

The notion that Clark would be acceptable to the New Dealers or liberals in general was illusory, of course. Joseph T. Davis, Clark's reluctant opponent in the Missouri primary, warned the President that Clark's strong backing from Republicans as well as conservative Democrats was a concerted effort to force a compromise candidate and a compromise platform on the party in 1940. "I admire you for the position you have more recently taken against the reactionary Senators and Representatives," he wrote. "If you compromise now you will be forced to do the same during the next two years, and all liberal Democrats will be forced to compromise in 1940."[154] The New Dealers could not have agreed more, and they certainly had no intention of compromising on Bennett Clark in 1940. When Davis informed Tom Corcoran that Secretary of War Harry Woodring was planning to speak at the opening of the Clark campaign in Sedalia in early October, Corcoran fired off a telegram to Steve Early protesting that it would look like official Administration support of Clark. He backed Davis' suggestion that Woodring have business elsewhere than in Sedalia that night.[155] Woodring spoke, but his topic was "the cool mind and skilled, sure fingers of Franklin D. Roosevelt in crises," rather than the glories of Bennett Champ Clark.[156] Clark won by a landslide anyway.

Thus, if one could believe the Gallup Poll, by December of 1938 the top four prospective successors of President Roosevelt in the Democratic party were all conservatives, and one had to look all the way down in ninth place to find Harry Hopkins, the highest-ranking Administration liberal.[157] One factor, however, hung like the sword of Damocles over the heads of all the hopefuls —the possibility of a third term for Roosevelt.

The Third-Term Issue in 1938

Relatively little was heard of the third-term issue in the first half of the year, though the United Mine Workers' Convention in January gave every indication of being strongly in favor of it. It appeared that it was only with some difficulty that John L. Lewis shrewdly managed to postpone efforts to pass resolutions favoring a third term until the 1940 convention.[158] It was another union group, the Colorado Fuel and Iron Corporation Steel Workers Club, which presented the President with the first formal petition by any organized group that he run for a third term. This occurred in Pueblo, Colorado, in July. The President made no comment, but reporters said he looked pleased.[159]

Others were also beginning to see a third term as the only possible way to continue the New Deal. As Robert Jackson fell by the wayside in New York, George Earle disappeared in the mud of his campaign in Pennsylvania, Harry Hopkins aroused the anger of all regular Democrats by his interference in Iowa, and Henry Wallace gained the hatred of the elimination committee by his failure to interfere in Iowa, it began to look more and more as though there was no one left but the President to maintain liberalism in the government. Columnists Alsop and Kintner felt that none of the many eager but inept candidates could win, and "no one but Ickes cares a rap for perpetuating the New Deal,"[160] which meant that no one but Ickes was for a third term. By a curious coincidence Ickes was telling people the same thing, though he was at first a voice in the wilderness. "I was the only one in the Cabinet for Roosevelt," he later told Robert Sherwood. "Most of the others were candidates themselves—Hopkins, Hull, Farley, Wallace, Garner—you couldn't throw a brick in any direction without hitting a candidate."[161] It was about the middle of July, according to the pugnacious Secretary of Interior, that he and Corcoran both became convinced that Roosevelt must run again, though his reason for thinking so had nothing to do with the New Deal. Ickes had recently returned from Europe, where he had found everyone believing that war was inevitable. Under the circumstances he felt Roosevelt would be the only man qualified to handle the emergency.[162]

Ickes, however, was the only New Dealer thinking in terms of the international crisis as a reason for a third term. Others saw it as a necessity for preserving what had been gained. Roosevelt, wrote liberal journalist Paul Anderson, would not run for a third term if he could name his own successor. But the man he wanted would have to (1) be able to get the nomination, (2) be able to win the election, (3) be a proven New Dealer. Ickes, Jackson, Wallace, or even La Guardia might fulfill the last two provisions, but their nomination was out of the question. Therefore, Roosevelt would probably have to run again.[163] This was essentially the reasoning followed by more and more liberals as the year wore on.

Endorsements for the third term, though generally expressed in guarded terms, became more frequent once the Colorado steel workers had reopened the question. Two weeks after their petition was handed to the President, Governor Frank Murphy told an audience of northern Michigan Democrats that "the New Deal must go on, and we may have to draft the President for four more years of leadership."[164] The next day in a national radio address Ickes warned:

> If the reactionaries in the Democratic party
> want a real test of President Roosevelt's strength with

the people, I suggest that they continue to work for a situation that will result in the people being given an opportunity to vote directly on the proposition of whether or not they are for President Roosevelt and his policies.[165]

Asked by reporters if the President had had anything to do with the implied third-term threat, Ickes admitted, "Nope, I thought it up all myself. I didn't ask papa."[166]

As the situation in the liberal camp grew worse, the appeals for a third term grew stronger. Senator Guffey, whose breach with the faltering Governor Earle had been somewhat healed after the Pennsylvania primary, remarked cautiously in September that it would be up to the people to decide whether a third term would be necessary in 1940.[167] In December, after the overwhelming Republican victory in Pennsylvania, he announced that Pennsylvania wanted Roosevelt as the Democratic standard bearer in 1940. With obvious reference to the opening of the McNutt campaign, Guffey warned, "Pennsylvania does not want and will have nothing to do with any so-called 'middle-of-the-road' candidates." All of its seventy-two votes, he claimed, would be cast for Roosevelt in the Democratic convention.[168] Since the almost total defeat of the Earle machine had left Guffey the only important Democratic office holder, his statement was no mere idle threat.

Ickes, the leader of the movement, also stepped up his campaign. Asked about the 1940 candidate in a press conference in October, he merely said, "It's in the lap of the gods. I think President Roosevelt would carry the United States if he ran again and he might have to run. But for his sake, I hope he doesn't."[169] After the elections, however, he commented that inasmuch as the President was "the liberal leader in the country," he had long thought it might be necessary to draft him for a third term.[170] This drew an interesting rejoinder from Secretary of Agriculture Henry Wallace, whose own campaign was far from dead. Snapped Wallace, "I think it is altogether outside the province of any Cabinet member to express an opinion on that subject."[171]

Other expressions of support, however, continued to come in. Wrote Texas Congressman Wright Patman, "I still believe that you are the only one to be considered for the presidential nomination in 1940. The people are with you and should be. Your program is too big to leave it incomplete. You may be assured of my continued cooperation."[172] On December 13, Senator Wheeler's colleague, Senator James Murray of Montana, joined the other "third termites," as they were nicknamed, in finding a third term necessary because of "the danger of emasculation of Roosevelt reforms."[173]

After the election, however, there was considerable doubt that even Roosevelt had enough power to secure the nomination, much less the election. Raymond Clapper conceded that a grave emergency might make a third term feasible, but otherwise "the election shows clearly, I think, that President Roosevelt could not run for a third term even if he so desired."[174] Dr. George Gallup of the Institute of Public Opinion told the Insurance Advertising Convention in December that two out of every three Americans opposed a third term for Roosevelt, but he admitted that probably forty per cent would vote for him.[175]

Among the local Democratic leaders who wrote Farley on the causes of the Democratic defeats in 1938, approximately four times as many found the third-term issue a handicap as expressed themselves in favor of it. Typical was the comment of David H. Mc-Clugage, Mayor of Peoria, Illinois, who wrote:

> I do not know whether the President desires to be a candidate for a third term;—sincerely hope not. With all his popularity, the ordinary chap on the street does not like the third term for any of our Presidents, and with the press playing it up as they would, I'm afraid it would result badly for our party.[176]

Political writer G. Gould Lincoln found on a tour through eighteen northern and western states during the 1938 campaign that the vast majority of Democrats not only opposed any renomination but did not believe the President would enter any contest for a third term. Roosevelt might possibly win renomination after a hard fight, Gould continued, but that would split the party and preclude his election.[177]

Roosevelt maintained his usual silence on the question, except on one occasion when John Winant, Director of the International Labor Organization, stopped in to see him while on a visit from Geneva. At the urging of some of the New Dealers, Winant brought up the question of the third term, strongly suggesting that Roosevelt should consider it his duty to run. The President answered in cold anger that he had done his part to further liberalism, and it was time for others to "share the burden of carrying forward the things we professed to believe."[178]

The year 1938, however, had failed to produce a single likely replacement for Roosevelt through no fault of his. Indeed, so disastrous had the political developments been that there was now some question whether he would even have a great deal to say about his successor at the convention. Further, there was almost no likelihood that he would be able to recoup his losses in popularity and prestige through dramatic, new liberal legislation as he had in the past. The unpurged Seventy-Sixth Congress was not likely to be sympathetic to any New Deal proposals. Thus, 1938 had solved nothing for the liberals and had deepened a good many existing problems. Only the conservatives and party regulars could look forward to 1939 with soaring hopes for better things to come.

CHAPTER IV

THE TURNING POINT, 1939

The battle for control of the Democratic party in 1939 fell into two more or less recognizable periods. The first, lasting for perhaps six months, or the duration of the first session of the Seventy-Sixth Congress, saw the conservatives taking the offensive on all fronts and the liberals clearly on the defensive. The second period was marked to a certain extent by a closing of ranks behind the President with a resulting increase in his effective leadership and popularity and a decrease in the prestige of his conservative opponents. Whether the change was the result of a war-inspired agreement on foreign policy or a belated recognition of the still great political power of the President brought on by the first flexing of its political muscles by the White House inner circle is a moot point. In any case, the political mood within the party appears to have altered sharply after the adjournment of Congress in August.

It was obvious from the beginning that the Seventy-Sixth Congress was under conservative control and would be the occasion for a strong conservative propaganda drive. Despite the President's Jackson Day warning that "if we Democrats lay for each other now, we can be sure that 1940 will be the corner where the American people will be laying for all of us,"[1] Congress and he were at one another's throats almost at once, with the President usually coming out second best. Although Roosevelt did not challenge the conservatives with any requests for vast domestic reforms in his annual message, he did goad them into a fury by his appointments during the first month or two Congress was in session. The elevation of Harry Hopkins to Secretary of Commerce was only the first in a series to set conservative teeth on edge. The day Governor Frank Murphy of Michigan retired from that office, he was appointed Attorney General to succeed Homer Cummings, and other appointments of the same sort followed in a steady procession. Roosevelt's intention was probably not so much to irritate the conservatives as to find jobs for the host of loyal New Dealers who had gone down to defeat in the 1938 elections, but the effect was the same. There was, as Josephus Daniels remarked, "not a little growling among the anti-New Dealers,"[2] while the liberals, who had been fearful that the Administration might be prepared to bow to the rising conservative tide for the sake of cooperation in foreign policy, were jubilant. Oswald Garrison Villard of the *Nation* believed it meant that Roosevelt was recovering "some of the fighting spirit of the first years of his administration."[3]

Not only did the President succor defeated liberals by appointments, but he also attacked conservatives by the same means, most notably in his appointment of Floyd H. Roberts to be justice in the Second Judicial District of western Virginia. The selection of Roberts, with the cooperation of Governor James Price and Congressman John W. Flanagan, both strong New Dealers, represented a direct frontal assault on the Glass-Byrd machine in Virginia.[4]

It was small wonder, then, that the President suffered some stinging rebuffs from the conservative-directed Congress, now acutely aware of its new-found popularity with the voters. Though almost all Democrats were willing to allow the President to choose his own advisers and voted, however reluctantly, for most of his selections, at least two of them represented challenges too direct to be ignored. In the case of the appointment to the Interstate Commerce Commission of Thomas Amlie, a lame-duck Progressive from Wisconsin who was on record as advocating government ownership of railroads, banks, businesses, industry, and manufacturing,[5] the hue and cry reached such a pitch that Roosevelt eventually withdrew the nomination at Amlie's request.[6] The attack on the Glass-Byrd machine, too, was repulsed by an 81 to 9 margin in the Senate.[7] A House caucus called in the middle of February by Congressional leaders, alarmed at the anti-Administration bitterness in the party, failed to smooth over anything. Word leaked out of anti-Administration leader Eugene Cox of Georgia warning the caucus that Congress should not be asked to do all the cooperating and "we do not want to be treated like wooden men to be pushed over at the will and whim of the President."[8]

With each successive week the gap widened further, so that by adjournment time the Administration had lost all semblance of control in either house. During the last two weeks of the session the Administration-inspired neutrality law revision was turned down in both houses; the Senate passed the Hatch Act as an almost open slap at the President; 104 Democrats, of whom 72 were from the South, joined the Republicans in voting a sweeping House investigation of the administration of the Wagner Act; and the House, by fairly wide margins, refused to even consider Administration requests for housing and spending-lending bills.[9] "If the Democrats throughout the country are as badly divided as are the Democrats in the Senate and House," moaned Senator Jimmy Byrnes, "it is a waste of time to discuss who will be nominated by the Democrats, for the party will certainly be defeated."[10] Senator Claude Pepper, an ardent New Dealer, vented his disgust with the session on the last day with a blast that Senator Josiah Bailey, presuming that reference was being made to his associates and himself, immediately labeled "cowardly and mendacious."[11] Pepper's philippic was, indeed, harsh. Said he:

> Mr. President: I am unwilling to let this session of Congress end without lifting my voice to decry the unrighteous partnership of those who have been willing to scuttle the American Government and the

American people and jeopardize the peace of the
world because they hate Roosevelt and what Roosevelt stands for. I accuse that alliance of putting personal grudge and party feeling above the welfare and
safety of the American people.

. . . .

I accuse them of having prostituted their
power to serve the United States Chamber of Commerce, the Manufacturer's Association, and the
beneficiaries of special privilege, who hate in their
hearts the man who has tried to lighten the burden
of toil on the back of labor. . . .[12]

Up in the press gallery reporter Ulric Bell of the Louisville *Courier-
Journal* murmured what a good many others were thinking, "There
goes the Democratic party."[13]

The party regulars, however, could not have agreed less. The
scene merely pointed up one of the more painful aspects of the
end of any administration, the changing of the guard. Waiting in
the wings to pick up the pieces of the apparently shattered party
was the reputed engineer of the Congressional revolt, Vice President John Nance Garner. Many of the successes and failures of the
first session of the Seventy-Sixth Congress can be understood only
in terms of his ambitions and those of others for the presidency.
What the entire session seemed to point to was a conservative in
the White House in 1940.

The Candidates Move Right

Beyond any doubt, John Nance Garner, despite his advanced
age and six years of almost perfect public silence, appeared to be
well out in front of all other rivals for the presidency as the year
began. His build-up over the previous two years had marked him
clearly as the man who personified the anti-New Deal and antithird-term movement in the Democratic party, and, perhaps because no one else was so expendable, the man who had been chosen
to bell the third-term cat. Behind him were lining up most of those

in favor of balancing the budget, putting labor in its place, reassuring business, and getting rid of radicals in the government. He led the Gallup Poll and, if one could believe the newspaper accounts, held Congress in the palm of his hand. A columnist as friendly to the New Deal as Raymond Clapper reported that new members of Congress were being told by the veterans that they could ignore the President because Garner was the real boss anyway. The first question Congressmen were to ask themselves was, "What would Jack Garner want me to do?"[14] On that point, at least, anti-New Deal columnist Frank Kent was in complete agreement. Although Barkley was the majority leader, Kent observed, the real powers were Garner and Pat Harrison, neither of whom cared much for New Deal domestic policies. Roosevelt, therefore, would get out of Congress just what Garner and Harrison decided to give him. That might be quite a bit, since they wanted to heal the split enough that the President would have no legitimate excuse for refusing to support a conservative ticket in 1940.[15]

This testimony appeared to be borne out at the onset when Garner saluted Frank Murphy, Roosevelt's controversial new Attorney General, as "one of the finest men in American public life," thereby refuting the New Dealers' whispered accusation that he had been behind the pre-election attack on Murphy by the Dies Committee.[16] As Congress met to be sworn in, it was noticed that there was a constant trek of members of both parties to the rooms of Vice President Garner—for advice, it was suggested, on the "Garner Plan" for cutting federal spending.[17] It was also noted that he was consulted on the same day by both Harry Hopkins and Henry Wallace.[18] Small wonder that Elliott Roosevelt, broadcasting from one of his Texas radio stations, indicated he thought Garner would be the next President—and that it would be a good thing.[19]

The good feelings—what there were of them—between the Vice President and the Administration lasted only until the President's first request for more money for relief. He wanted a $875,-000,000 deficiency bill to carry the W.P.A. to the end of the fiscal year. The House revolted to the extent that it decided that the sum was exactly $150,000,000 too much. It voted $725,000,000 and sent the bill on to the Senate,[20] where it became the symbol of the split in the party and the first real show of strength. Though he said nothing about it openly, Garner was reported to be the backbone behind the conservative drive to maintain the House cut. His office was pictured in the press as the nerve center of the economy bloc from which the doughty old warrior sent floor leaders Alva Adams and Jimmy Byrnes to do battle against the spenders. Garner himself reportedly was marching up and down, telling his lieutenants angrily, "We've got to economize and we've got to start now."[21] It was said that Senator William Smathers, a warm supporter of the bill, had prepared a speech in which he stated, "During my campaign I pledged myself to adhere to the leadership of the President, not the Vice President," but Majority Leader Barkley talked him out of giving it in the interest of party harmony.[22] When the economy bloc won the issue, Garner emerged, at least in the newspapers, as the strong man in the government.[23] That image was further strengthened by the passage of a new tax schedule, removing—against the President's wishes—the last vestiges of the undistributed profits tax;[24] by the reorganization act, which was credited to Congressman Lindsey Warren and the "Garner moderates" rather than the Administration;[25] and especially by the passage of the Hatch Act, which forbade any political activities by nonpolicy-making federal employees, thus supposedly neutralizing Roosevelt's chief source of support within the party. Certainly Garner appeared to be the most effective lobbyist for the latter act.[26] When it passed, Senators poured into the Vice President's office to congratulate him as much as Senator Hatch.[27] It was, according to one Roosevelt lieutenant in the Senate, one part of a double-barreled agreement engineered by Garner between conservative Democrats and Republicans to include the defeat of the President's spending-lending recommendation.[28]

With the newspapers creating the impression of tremendous Garner power, prestige, and popularity with the leaders of both parties in Congress, his appeal to politicians and voters outside of Congress rose precipitantly. In the December 1938 Gallup Poll, he had led all other Democratic hopefuls except Roosevelt, who was not taken into consideration, with 20 per cent of those questioned supporting him. His nearest rival was Cordell Hull with 11 per cent support. By March 1939, Garner's popularity had shot up to 42 per cent, while Hull and Farley, his nearest rivals, each showed 10 per cent support.[29] By May, Garner was favored by 50 per cent, and the margin remained in that vicinity as long as Congress was in session.[30] During the late spring and early summer something resembling a Garner bandwagon seemed to be developing. In March former governors Joseph Ely of Massachusetts and George Hodges of Kansas announced for him, and Henry Ford surprised many by commenting, "Jack Garner would make a mighty fine president."[31] It was reported that he already had two hundred delegates pledged to him, and Raymond Clapper felt that there might still be time to stop him, but not much. He had the same kind of momentum that had won the Republican nomination for Alf Landon in 1936.[32] Emil Hurja, whose political soundings for the Democratic National Committee in the 1932 and 1936 elections were said to account for much of Jim Farley's success as a prophet, pointed out that no candidate in history had got so far ahead of the field as Garner was and failed to win the nomination. Intelligent politicians simply did not care to oppose their party's leading contender, so they usually sought the safety of the bandwagon.[33] Hurja proved his own point by going to work for the Garner forces.

By May the Garner-for-President Club had set up its headquarters in Dallas. Its official leaders were Eugene B. Germany, chairman of the Texas State Democratic Executive Committee, and Clara Driscoll, the Texas National Committeewoman.[34] It was immediately evident that the Garner campaign would not be hard pressed for finances. Germany, who was mayor of a wealthy suburb of Dallas, had struck oil in the 1920's and by 1939 owned wells in three states,[35] and Clara Driscoll had inherited an estate of $10,000,000, including a bank and a ranch bordering on King Ranch.[36] There were also twenty-six regional campaign managers, chiefly businessmen and chiefly millionaires.[37] Behind it all was the slightly sinister figure of Roy Miller of the Texas Gulf Sulphur Company, who had originated the movement and had harbored its headquarters in his hotel room in Washington until more appropriate quarters could be arranged in Dallas. There were reports in June, however, that he had been ordered to keep in the background and make no more speeches for Garner in an effort to soothe labor hostility.[38] Who gave the orders was not made clear.

Although the Garner bandwagon made the most noise and

attracted the most attention in the first half of 1939, the drive for the third term, originating largely from offices in the new Department of Interior Building, was quietly picking up momentum as more and more liberals realized that Roosevelt was the only dependable champion of their cause left in the running. With the exception of Harry Hopkins, who was a very serious candidate in his own right, what had been the elimination committee during the purge of the previous year now regrouped itself under the leadership of Secretary of Interior Ickes; Tom Corcoran, whose adroit hand could be seen in a number of newspaper "leaks" and endorsements for the third term; Ben Cohen, whose offices served as a convenient, if informal, gathering place;[39] Solicitor General Robert Jackson, by no means entirely out of the political picture himself; and Attorney General Frank Murphy.

Soon after the Vice President was reported to have led the fight against the W.P.A. deficiency bill in late January 1939, this New Deal inner circle began to show concern at the growing Garner strength. An assault on Garner, headed by Drew Pearson, was soon begun by sympathetic Washington columnists.[40] In a tone that suggested an indictment would soon be forthcoming, Pearson and Robert Allen reported that Roy Miller was under investigation by the Temporary National Economic Committee.[41] Later, they also reported that Garner had failed to attend the Marian Anderson concert at the Lincoln Memorial, which Secretary of Interior Ickes had arranged when the D.A.R. refused the use of its concert hall for that purpose. To avoid offending Negro voters, Garner was denying that he had received an invitation from Ickes. That, said Pearson and Allen, was only technically correct, since the records clearly proved that an invitation had been sent by Oscar Chapman, Ickes' assistant, and a Western Union receipt showed that it had been received six days before the concert.[42] At least there was not much doubt about where they were receiving their ammunition. Ickes himself came out openly on the subject in a June issue of *Look Magazine* when he wrote:

> This is no time for a candidate whose "qualifications" are the fact that he has been chirruping weak opposition to everything the world's greatest democratic leader has done, or a candidate whose claim to

office consists of the traitorous knifing in the back of
the commander in chief to whom he has sworn fealty,
or whose "strength" is that of knowing nothing,
doing nothing.[43]

Further New Deal sniping came from Garner's home state
of Texas, where the irrepressible Maury Maverick had been elected
mayor of San Antonio. From that eminence he proceeded to call
for a third term and issue some withering blasts at the Garner
candidacy. "Sure I'm for Garner for President," he told reporters,
"I'm for Garner for President of the Pecan Growers' Association.
. . . Garner is a myth. He has never said anything or done anything
except keep quiet and get elected to office. He's been a deaf and
dumb politician all his life."[44]

All of this was music to the ears of the New Dealers, but it
had no appreciable effect on the Garner campaign. Because he
was not affiliated with the Democratic party, Ickes' views counted
for less than nothing, and Maverick's influence was considered to
be slight indeed after his 1938 defeat. Clearly, if the Garner boom
was to be stopped at all, a gun of a much heavier caliber would
have to be brought to bear, and soon. To the delight and relief
of the New Dealers, the big gun made its appearance at an otherwise rather dull session of the House Labor Committee. To a
stunned audience John L. Lewis, President of the C.I.O., with fists
banging and voice bellowing, stated:

> Now, turning [from the House of Representatives]
> to the other end of the Capitol, we find the United
> States Senate headed by a poker-playing, whiskey-
> drinking, evil old man who would destroy labor.
>   Some gentlemen may rise in horror and say,
> "Why Mr. Lewis has made a personal attack on Mr.
> Garner." Yes, I make a personal attack on Mr. Garner
> for what he is doing, because Garner's knife is search-
> ing for the quivering, pulsating heart of labor. And I
> am against him. I am against him officially, individ-
> ually, personally, concretely, and in the abstract,
> when his knife searches for the heart of my people.
>   I am against him in 1939 and I will be against
> him in 1940 when he seeks the Presidency of the

United States. And I say to Mr. Garner and I say to
the people of the United States that he will never
achieve the Presidency of this Republic by baiting
labor and seeking to debase Americans.[45]

Congress went into an uproar over the attack, and Senator William
King probably spoke the mind of two-thirds of the members as
well as conservatives throughout the United States when he said,
"Mr. Lewis' statement . . . will probably add to Mr. Garner's
strength, probably will give him the nomination."[46] Others suggested that Lewis' words were better than "Rum, Romanism, and
Rebellion" of a previous election. Liberal commentators did not
agree. As one remarked, few people could visualize torch-light
processions in which the marchers carried banners reading, "Vote
for the labor-baiting, poker-playing, whiskey-drinking, evil old
man."[47]

Counterattacks were, of course, made by the Garner forces,
but it was evident that overt labor hostility would badly injure
their man. On the brighter side, Garner supporters appeared somewhat surprised and entirely delighted when the liberal House Majority Leader, Sam Rayburn, stated, "I am for that outstanding
Texan and liberal Democrat, John Nance Garner, for the presidential nomination in 1940, believing that if elected he will make
the country a great President."[48] Rayburn owed Garner the favor,
since the latter had supported him "two hundred per cent" in his
bid for majority leadership against John O'Connor in 1937,[49] and
there was also the necessity of keeping his own fences mended in
Texas. In any event, the announcement merely reinforced the impression that at the end of the first session of the Seventy-Sixth
Congress, despite some rather telling blows the New Dealers had
been able to land, Garner was still very much in the front-runner's
saddle, still the man to beat. Danger signs, however, were not lacking for those who had eyes for them. Clearly three segments of
the great Roosevelt coalition—labor, Negroes, and the unemployed
—would cut themselves adrift if Garner were nominated. Very few
professional politicians were willing to trade blocs of voters of
that size for the luxury of having a conservative leading the party
once again.

In the meantime, the New Dealers, in addition to their attacks on Garner, were anxiously pressing forward a positive campaign for a third term. By late May it was reported that the inner circle had not only picked Roosevelt for a third term but had decided on Frank Murphy to be his Vice President as well.[50] Murphy gave every impression that he might be preparing himself for such a role as he dashed from city to city with F.B.I. Director J. Edgar Hoover, breathing threats against corrupt political machines, threats that were by no means empty.[51] It appeared that he intended to compete for headlines as a racket-buster with the glamorous Republican hopeful, District Attorney Thomas Dewey. Roosevelt himself probably agreed with Cardinal Mundelein that no Catholic could become President by "the back door,"[52] but he did tell one caller proudly that when Murphy was finished Dewey's achievements would look like "pretty small potatoes."[53]

Even among liberals there was no unanimous agreement on the desirability of breaking the third-term tradition. The *New Republic*, for instance, gave every indication of being prepared to ignore the contrary tradition,[54] whereas Oswald Garrison Villard and the *Nation* would have preferred to accept Bennett Clark, Lloyd Stark, Cordell Hull, or, presumably, any one of a host of others.[55] With Ickes' June article in *Look Magazine* the battle increased in volume and virulence. He was immediately answered in a radio address by Senator Ed Burke of Nebraska.[56] Throughout June and July other New Dealers lined up behind Ickes. On June 17 Harry Hopkins gave up the ghost of his own campaign by stating, "First, last and all the time, my choice for President in 1940 is Franklin D. Roosevelt, and I believe that a great mass of the people agree with me."[57] On June 21 Robert Jackson, in a speech to a convention of American Business Clubs, argued that there should be no talk of a third term since the first term had been cancelled by the courts. The implication was that Roosevelt would really only be running for a second term.[58] The next day Senators William Smathers of New Jersey and James Hughes of Delaware climbed on the bandwagon, although their statements were matched by those of Senators Pat McCarran of Nevada and Alva Adams of Colorado for the opposition.[59] Senator Joseph Guffey of Pennsylvania made an all-out appeal for a third term in a radio address on July 3,[60] and on July 14 Frank Murphy devoted part of his press conference to expressing the hope that "the President can and will continue his leadership of the nation."[61] At the same time the Attorney General was pulling some highly important strings behind the scences. At his insistence the Wayne County Democratic Committee of Detroit adopted a third-term draft resolution and appropriated funds for a third-term headquarters. Inasmuch as the committee represented all the surviving Michigan Democratic office holders and forty per cent of the Michigan Democratic vote, it was clear to the insiders that its delegation to the national convention would be as safely in the third-term column as that of Pennsylvania.[62]

The opposition, besides continuing the Garner build up, answered the third-term challenge as best they could, usually basing their opposition on the belief that no one should run for a third term under any circumstances. Senator Frederick Van Nuys, for instance, stated that he would not support Roosevelt or anyone else for a third term,[63] and Senator Guy Gillette, while expressing his "deepest admiration for the President" and his approval of all the goals for which he worked, stated that he would not vote for his own father for a third term.[64] More effective as a vote of "no confidence," however, was the battering the Administration forces took during the last weeks of the first session of the Seventy-Sixth Congress.[65] Many thought that the chief reason the neutrality legislation was defeated was the fear harbored by some Congressmen and Senators that Roosevelt might control the destinies of the nation for another four years.[66] The removal of federal office holders, who had made up half of the delegates to the 1936 Democratic National Convention,[67] from the political scene by the Hatch Act was considered the most open attempt to pull some presidential political teeth. Since there was no similar ban on state employees, it appeared that tremendous power had been released into the hands of state party bosses, who, presumably, would tend to support favorite sons or fall very much under the influence of Jim Farley. Said *Time*'s political reporter, "If ever there were a juncture when Franklin Roosevelt needed to talk to Jim Farley, this was it."[68]

Farley's status in the Administration as well as his intentions for 1940, however, were something of an enigma to all political observers. As a member of the President's Cabinet and as the party's National Chairman, he could not openly run for office, but by April his friends were claiming he could count on 265 delegates to the National Convention to Garner's 200.[69] The crucial question was what was his standing with the President and what was he prepared to do about the third-term drive. At the beginning of the year Farley believed that Roosevelt would not run again and that his first three choices for his successor would be Hopkins, Jackson, and Murphy in that order; if he were forced to choose one of the three leading party regulars, it would be Cordell Hull.[70] It was about this time that rumors began to circulate that Farley's ambitions went no higher than second place on a ticket with Hull. (It is Farley's contention that that is all he was ever interested in.)[71] This in a quiet way presented the third-term clique with a far more serious problem than the Garner campaign. Their solution to it, with Roosevelt's active cooperation, was to undercut Farley's power over party patronage by not consulting him before appointments were made or openly ignoring his recommendations. When the job of United States Attorney for the Southern District of New York became vacant, for example, Farley was openly humiliated when the two men he had recommended for the post were passed over for John T. Cahill, who was known to be Tom Corcoran's choice.[72] By July it was evident to reporters that Farley was not being consulted on a number of political matters, and it was a common rumor that he had told friends in the Senate that he was opposed to a third term.[73] William Cardinal Mundelein, who was somewhat apprehensive of another 1928 debacle, approached him early in July with the request that he not consider running for the presidency—and was curtly refused.[74] Finally, toward the end of the month Farley met Roosevelt at Hyde Park for something of a showdown conference, during which Roosevelt bluntly assured him that he would not seek a third term. He indicated that he would withdraw his name from consideration at the time of the North Dakota primary, and "the thing for us to do now is to get friendly delegations." When Farley wanted to know for or against whom the delegations were supposed to be friendly, Roosevelt merely said he wanted someone sympathetic to his administration who would continue his policies.[75] With the third-term threat thus apparently eliminated, the road was open for Farley to continue his drive for delegates and to hope he was demonstrating adequate sympathy for and desire to carry on the policies of the New Deal. That he was only seeking second place on a ticket with Hull made his task considerably easier. A secret poll of Democrats in the House of Representatives in April showed that 90 per cent of them favored Hull, with Farley a weak second.[76]

Hull, to be sure, continued to make not the faintest sign that the presidency interested him in the least. His replies to letters urging his candidacy were totally noncommital.[77] More important to him than the presidency itself was the renewal of the power to make reciprocal trade agreements, which would also have to be decided on in 1940. With even New Dealers in the farm states pledged to end it, he wanted to generate as little political opposition as possible.[78] Except for the brief announcement "I hope to see this great Tennessean become the next President of the United States" by Governor Prentice Cooper at the New York World's Fair in July,[79] there was no sign of a Hull boom during the first half of 1939.

Undoubtedly, the 1938 elections, the success of the Garner drive, and the conservative revolt in Congress encouraged the candidacies of several "moderate" Democratic hopefuls. The nation was obviously swinging in a rightward direction, and so, quite naturally, were the presidential aspirants. Even Harry Hopkins, the President's heir apparent, began trending to the right, perhaps partially because he realized that strong conservative opposition could block his nomination and partially because he was getting much of his political advice from conservative Bernard Baruch.[80]

A major hurdle to be faced right at the beginning of the year was obtaining confirmation of his appointment as Secretary of Commerce from a Senate whose members were still furious over his political manipulations of the previous year. Some indication of what was in store for him was given two days after Congress met for the first time when Senator Styles Bridges, apropos of nothing, made a speech in the Senate attacking Hopkins and his alleged "spend and spend and tax and tax and elect and elect" statement. Senator Tom Connally protested that the appointment would be debated in due time when the committee reported on it. "Why," he asked plaintively, "does the Senator want to break in on this otherwise peaceful and inconspicuous morning by 'jumping the gun' and beating all the other Senators who want to kick Mr. Hopkins around? Is it simply because the Senator wants to be the first to hit Mr. Hopkins?"[81] Whatever the reason, it was evident that the line of Senators behind Bridges was a long one. As the committee hearings began, Senator Arthur Vandenburg parodied Roosevelt's comment to Walter George during the purge of the previous year with, "God bless you, Harry. Let's always be friends."[82]

When the committee, nevertheless, reported his appointment favorably to the Senate, the resulting debate was without precedent in the Roosevelt Administration.[83] Led by Carter Glass, Rush Holt, and Millard Tydings, the opposition concentrated a blistering fire on Hopkins' meddling in politics, the purge, and his general unfitness for office.[84] There was, however, no great danger of his being rejected, especially since even Senator Guy Gillette said he would vote for him on the grounds that the President should have the right to choose his own adviser.[85] In the end the vote was fifty-eight to twenty-seven, with eleven not voting. Only five Democrats—all staunch conservatives—voted against approval, but a long list of other conservatives abstained. Carter Glass probably spoke the mind of all of them when he said he could neither vote against a Cabinet appointment nor for Harry Hopkins.[86]

Hopkins' first major effort to lose his reputation as a dangerous radical and gain one as a friend of business was a statement of his policies and beliefs in a speech at Des Moines, Iowa. The effort to identify himself as an Iowan and the frankly friendly sentiments toward business expressed in the speech led Farley to call it "Hopkins' acceptance speech."[87] Normally it might have widely been interpreted as a political effort, but by coincidence it came only the day after Secretary of Treasury Henry Morganthau stated in a press conference that he would like to see Congress re-examine the tax structure to see if there were any "deterrents to business" in it that might be removed, and only a week after Roosevelt himself had stated that business and industry need fear no new taxes.[88] In his own speech, which was to a great extent the product of recommendations made by the Business Advisory Council, a group of businessmen brought together by Dan Roper, Hopkins had suggested that taxes "which tend to freeze the necessary flow of capital" be amended.[89] The result was that instead of being accepted as a statement of his own probusiness sentiments, the Des Moines' effort was largely viewed as part of an Administration drive to gain business confidence.[90] *Time*, in fact, reported that State Democratic Chairman Ed Birmingham had nearly ruined the whole thing by giving the impression that the Iowa delegation was being lined up for Hopkins next year.[91] If some effort to line it up for Hopkins was not being made, the trip to Iowa had been a waste of time indeed.

Whether he had planned it or not, Hopkins' statement on the tax program had put him squarely on the side of Henry Morgenthau and the Treasury Department in an intra-Administration battle that raged throughout the spring of the year. On the other side of the issue were Hopkins' former close collaborators Marriner Eccles, Leon Henderson, Tom Corcoran, Ben Cohen, and the whole third-term clique, who regarded the drive against "business deterrents," which chiefly meant the remains of the undistributed profits tax, as an attack on the Keynesian principles of economy as well as progressive taxing principles.[92] The inner circle naturally resented Hopkins' apostasy, and there were soon reports circulating that the New Dealers were blasting him as a traitor to the cause and taunting the President with "surrendering to business."[93] Marriner Eccles complained that he could not get much cooperation from the President's close associates in taking the Administration's case for spending to the country because "Presidential bees had begun to buzz at this time. . . . His associates were running up neutral flags."[94] Robert Jackson, deeply disturbed by the apparent split in the ranks, wrote Hopkins toward the end of March to suggest that the opposition was playing the New Dealers off against one another with vicious falsehoods and conflicting leads. It was time for friends of the Administration to mobilize before it was too late. "Perhaps I see more than you," he wrote gloomily, "the disorganization, the lack of understanding of objectives, and the conflicting plans and purposes of those who are perfectly willing to cooperate and to follow a leader." Some of the leadership, he suggested, should come from Hopkins. The delegates for 1940 were already being lined up and there was not a minute to lose. What he had in mind was a small steering committee, under the direction of the President, which could best determine liberal policy at any given time and build up political power for the future.[95] But Hopkins, like Farley, was apparently suspicious about for or against whom the political power was supposed to be friendly and if this invitation to return to the fold had any effect on him, there was no evidence of it at the time.

The Secretary of Commerce was going ahead in a workman-like way with his plans for obtaining the nomination. Since Farley could obviously block him in New York, it was absolutely neces-sary to wrest control of the Iowa delegation from the none-too-solid grasp of Henry Wallace. While he was in Des Moines in February, Hopkins had made a side trip to his old home town of Grinnell, where he had attended a reception at the Methodist Church, met his old Sunday School teacher, and watched a basket-ball game at his Alma Mater, Grinnell College. Said the lover of fast horses and faster Long Island society, "My home isn't New York or Washington or wherever I happen to have a house to live in. This is my home."[96] These touching sentiments were enlarged upon in April, when he announced that he had established his legal residence in Grinnell so that his little daughter could have a home and a permanent circle of friends. "There is," he announced blandly, "no political significance whatever in my decision to make my legal residence in Iowa."[97]

That, however, was as far as his candidacy got. While making the trip to Grinnell, he became extremely ill, and from that time on his political career was virtually over.[98] Reports were already cir-culating in May that his candidacy would seriously be handicapped by his illness, and by June he was sufficiently aware of it himself to join the clamor for a third term for Roosevelt.[99] Friends of Hop-kins told Robert Sherwood that he had begun angling for the vice presidency, but there was no evidence that he ever really went after it.[100] He eventually checked into Mayo Clinic in late August and was virtually given up for dead by the doctors there as a result of a severe gastro-intestinal impairment. Although he was able to return to his Georgetown home and do some of his office work there late in the year, it was nearly eight months before he was able to leave his house.[101] So ended the hopes of another Democratic liberal.

The ambitions of his chief rival in the Administration, Henry Wallace, also appeared to be somewhat less likely of fulfillment in 1939. *Newsweek* commented in January that his stock was at an all-time six-year low as a result of his evident lack of prestige with the farmers during the elections and another year of huge farm surpluses in prospect. It added, however, that because of his attitude toward the purges the previous summer and his many favors to Congressmen from agricultural states, he still rated considerably higher with the conservative group in Congress than any of his New Deal colleagues.[102] The analysis was a fair one. His name did not appear among the ten leaders on the Gallup Poll until May, when it edged weakly into a tie for last place. Nevertheless, he was not prepared to hand over the Iowa delegation to Harry Hopkins without a struggle, and there were reports that his followers were furious over the invasion. Hopkins no sooner announced his intention of setting up legal residence in the state than Wallace told reporters his family would move back to Des Moines for the summer.[103]

In Iowa as elsewhere, however, any candidate aiming at controlling the state delegation, even as a favorite son, faced a stiff battle from the liberal faction favoring the third term. Wallace stood a better chance of succeeding than many other contenders because he had backed the successful Senatorial clique in the 1938 struggle, but by the same token he had created some very bitter enemies. Chief among these, of course, was Otha Wearin and the New Dealers who had backed him against Gillette in 1938 and who were now facing a conservative counterpurge. The battle began when Wearin, who was slated to be appointed National Director of the Rural Electrification Administration, heard rumors from his friends in Congress that his appointment would be resisted and defeated by Wallace and the two Iowa Senators, while at the same time he would be offered a minor place in the Surplus Commodities Corporation. Angrily he made a public statement in Iowa that he would not accept the post with the Rural Electrification Administration if it was offered because he was not in sympathy with the program of Secretary Wallace. "In my opinion," he said, "Wallace is a bungler and I wouldn't want to be connected with his department." He added that Wallace was also guilty of having presidential aspirations and had begun a "premature" campaign for delegates to the National Convention.[104] Edward Eicher, a member of the Securities and Exchange Commission and, like Wearin, a defeated New Deal Iowa Congressman, had been working desperately for Wearin and his faction. Prior to Wearin's blast he suggested to Roosevelt that failure to appoint the former Congressman would be "disastrous to the morale of our fighting friends in Iowa," and he added, "I know that Harry Hopkins thoroughly agrees with me. . . . Unfortunately, the Secretary's [Wallace's] perhaps unconscious ambitions still blind him (as they did during the Primary last year) to the fact that there can be no such thing as a 'No Man's Land' in the approaching Armageddon."[105] Once Wearin spoke out, Eicher made a last try for him, pleading that failure to appoint him would leave control of the state delegation wholly in the hands of Senators Gillette and Herring. "The average Democrat," he pointed out, "could reach no other conclusion than that he has everything to gain and nothing to lose by following the leadership of our Senators and Secretary Wallace."[106]

Roosevelt, however, was unwilling to undercut his Secretary of Agriculture by appointing Wearin to any position after his open attack. Moreover, as a member of the President's Cabinet and a liberal, Wallace was in no position to head a hostile Iowa delegation to the National Convention even if he was so minded. Smoked out somewhat on the third-term issue by Ickes' June magazine article, he grudgingly allowed that "I'm sure all members of the Cabinet . . . are completely loyal to President Roosevelt."[107] By July his worries with one of the worst crop surpluses to that time were such that *Time* noted he "must have forgotten all about 1940."[108] As far as the presidency was concerned, he might as well have. President Roosevelt and Jim Farley were not agreeing on a great deal that summer, but they did agree that Wallace did not have "IT."[109]

If the so-called liberal candidates were finding it prudent to sound more conservative during the first half of 1939, it was only natural that conservative and middle-of-the-road hopefuls should press on with increasing optimism. Jesse Jones in particular appeared to be increasing his availability by emphasizing his conservatism and fiscal responsibility in contrast to the wild-eyed New

Dealers. In February, when the conservatives were taking the offensive, he told a Senate committee, "I would rather take my cue from men who have done a thing than from men who only know how it ought to be done. They are very worthy gentlemen, but they are scholars."[110] In August he told a Los Angeles crowd, "American citizens in 1940 must make the most critical decision in all the nation's history, with the people forced to determine whether business shall be swept permanently under the wing of government control or whether economic life can be turned back to the forces of free enterprise system."[111] There was not much question about which path he favored. Jones further angered the New Dealers by his testimony in "favor" of the President's lending-spending bill, during which he appeared to some to lack conviction.[112] "Some of the inner circle," he complained to Hopkins, "give me credit for damning it [the bill] with faint praise, which, of course, is silly. Sam's [Rayburn's] explanation is that seventy Democrats were absent when the motion to re-commit was made."[113] During the summer newspapers from widely divergent areas appeared to be discovering his political potentialities for the first time. Said the Minneapolis *Tribune*, ". . . Mr. Jones is, in many respects, the ideal compromise candidate and in the matter of sheer competence, stands head and shoulders over the others mentioned."[114] the Boston *Observer* found Jones "the one gigantic figure whose conduct of public affairs during a period of huge and careless expenditure of public money stands out like a beacon of hope. . . ."[115]

Two other conservatives also announced their candidacies in August. Millard Tydings of Maryland, who had survived an attempted Administration purge in 1938, threw his hat into the ring as a favorite son, and Speaker of the House William Bankhead of Alabama expressed his willingness to accept the support of the state delegation "if a majority of the voters in the primary sincerely favor my nomination."[116] Neither had a very good chance of even emerging as a dark horse, but they were fairly certain to control their states' delegations and perhaps to be able to head off a third-term draft.

One indication of the tremendous influence Roosevelt still had over party leaders and voters alike, however, was the meteoric rise in the political fortunes of Paul McNutt during the summer of 1939. Any conservative aiming at receiving the nomination in spite of the President could have seen the handwriting on the wall had he analyzed the McNutt boom carefully. Prior to July, while McNutt was still in the Philippines, a low-key drive, directed from a three-room suite in the Claypool Hotel in Indianapolis, was aimed at local party leaders, often asking only for consideration for second choice.[117] The responses did not indicate an overwhelming ground swell for McNutt, but there were occasional expressions of good will. The pace quickened in early June with the news that he was returning to the United States to resign as High Commissioner. A tremendously flattering send-off by Filipino officials and American businessmen alike, despite the fact that he had been the first High Commissioner to openly favor retention of the islands in many years, was considered in this country an indication of a job remarkably well done.[118] Even while he was flying back, his chief supporters, Frank McHale and Senator Sherman Minton, announced that he would be a candidate only if Roosevelt did not seek a third term,[119] and McNutt reiterated the point during a stopover in Hawaii, thus making it evident that he would be no part of a conservative "stop Roosevelt" movement.[120]

To the great astonishment of most observers, he had scarcely returned when Roosevelt appointed him Federal Security Administrator,[121] a position newly created under the Reorganization Act to control the Social Security Commission, the National Youth Administration, the Federal Public Health Service, the Office of Education, the U. S. Employment Service, and the Civilian Conservation Corps. Speculation over the meaning of the appointment was extensive, since Roosevelt had not even consulted any of the New Dealers before making it. He denied that it had any political significance, pointing out that McNutt was an extremely able administrator and that he would not be pushing his own candidacy any more than "ten, twelve or fifteen" others in the federal government.[122] Some suggested the President had done it to humiliate Jim Farley, who was known to be still bitter against "that platinum-haired so-and-so";[123] Farley himself, as well as Raymond Moley, immediately interpreted it as an effort to silence the McNutt campaign or at least keep it under presidential control;[124] still others saw it as a sign Roosevelt was grooming McNutt for the presidency or at least giving him the opportunity to demonstrate his capacities.[125] By and large, both friends and foes tended to accept the latter explanation. The Washington correspondent for the *New Republic* only a short time before had written contemptuously, "From Mr. Roosevelt down to the lowliest aspirant—for example, High Commissioner Paul V. McNutt...."[126] He now wrote gloomily, "If Mr. Roosevelt does not wish to be the candidate himself, the 1940 Democratic nomination belongs to Mr. McNutt. No other interpretation of the situation is possible."[127] From the Military Adviser of the Philippine Army, Douglas MacArthur, came warm congratulations "from one rooting in the bleachers in response to his favorite's good play."[128] Perhaps most important of all was the reaction of potential Democratic voters to the appointment. In June, McNutt had been a weak fifth on the Gallup Poll. By August he had whipped past Hopkins, Hull, and Farley into second place, and by September he was receiving the support of twenty-one per cent of those polled—seven times as much as in June and nearly half of the Garner strength. Clearly his appointment was widely regarded as a vote of approval by Roosevelt.

By August the situation looked bleak indeed for the New Deal forces. The Democratic Congress was out of control, and the majority of its members appeared to be clearly hostile to a continuation of the Roosevelt Administration after 1941. The Gallup Polls were indicating that a conservative was almost sure to be the next Democratic nominee, and the liberal who was probably best qualified to fight for the nomination had been eliminated by illness. A third-term bid was gaining some ground, but few believed it could roll over all-out conservative opposition or that Roosevelt would even accept a third nomination if it were offered. The party regulars, on the other hand, also had reason for worry. One man, whose political appeal was still obviously tremendous, had called the great coalition of 1936 into being, and it seemed likely it could be kept in being only by his active support if not his nomination. However much they might have preferred a John Garner, a Jim Farley, or a Cordell Hull, it was clear that the nomination of any one of them might result in the loss of a sizable bloc of the vote.

Although it is usually assumed that the watershed of third-term popularity was the outbreak of World War II on September 1, 1939, there are indications that President Roosevelt never totally lost the support of the majority of local party leaders, and there might quite possibly have been a third-term draft whether the war broke out or not. The continuing power of the Roosevelt magic was becoming evident almost as soon as Congress adjourned and a month before the Panzer divisions began their awesome destruction of Poland's defenses. It is true that the war tended to overshadow all other considerations during the fall and was undoubtedly responsible for some of the tremendous jump in presidential popularity that was noted by the poll takers.[129] Nevertheless, its influence on domestic politics can be exaggerated. Many party conservatives who had been at odds with the Administration the previous three years forgot their differences over domestic problems to join the President in his effort to alter neutrality legislation, and many liberals were opposed to the Administration's foreign policy, but there is no evidence that the outbreak of the war changed any political leader's mind in 1939 about the necessity for a third term.

"Roosevelt or Ruin"

Throughout the latter part of the summer it was obvious that antithird-term sentiment was declining among the party's rank-and-file, the hard-bitten professionals who wanted and needed a winner regardless of who it was. Senator George Norris observed that most of the opposition to Roosevelt within the party came from his colleagues in Congress whose hatred for Roosevelt was largely personal and whose motives "can never be defended upon any ground of justice or patriotism."[130] His harsh judgment perhaps reflected his own personal bias, but it was evident that the President's popularity among Democrats in the hinterland was considerably greater than with those in Congress. A private poll of the delegates to the 1936 convention taken in July of 1939 by George E. Allen indicated that Roosevelt was still the choice of half of them and he would have won the delegations of thirty-eight states. Garner, his closest rival, received half as many delegate votes and would have controlled only four states.[131] Another Allen poll, this time of Democratic County Chairmen, was completed by the middle of September. The results were approximately the same: as many supporting Roosevelt as all the others combined.[132] The Gallup Poll also shows that the greatest jump in public approval of a third term took place between May and August, when it rose from 33 per cent to 40 per cent. Between August and October it rose only another 3 per cent.[133] What this suggests is not that the war was not significant but that it was far from essential in explaining the success of the third-term drive. The failure of any other liberal champion to "take hold" and the tremendous Administration power and urge to self-perpetuation are adequate explanations for that.

During the spring of 1939 President Roosevelt himself demonstrated that he intended to be in a position at the National Convention to accept or reject a draft or impose his own candidate and platform on the convention. When asked by the Georgia Democratic State Committee Chairman, James Gilles, for instructions for 1940, Roosevelt indicated he wanted an uninstructed but friendly delegation. Under Georgia law this could be insured quite easily by having the state committee name the delegation rather than calling a primary, thus freezing out presumably strong Garner opposition.[134] At about the same time he was consulting with former Governor Max Gardner of North Carolina about "breaking up" a rapidly developing antithird-term movement in that state.[135]

The cooperation of the President eased considerably the task of the inner circle third-term cabal, since it meant that there was little danger they would be repudiated. Evidence of their success and the impression it was making on the party regulars could be seen at the Young Democrats' Convention in Pittsburgh in August, where, thanks to heavy pressure on the leaders of the organization the previous March, almost every speaker was a prothird-term New Dealer.[136] Even more impressive was the enthusiasm of the delegates, which at times appeared to be almost out of hand. Senator Josh Lee of Oklahoma nearly brought the theater seats out by the roots when he thundered, "Now is the time to unleash the devil dogs of democracy and send them baying on the trail of the wolf of Wall Street! ... Now is the time to raise the banner of Roosevelt for 1940!"[137] Roosevelt himself added to the delirium of the liberals by telling the convention bluntly:

> If we nominate conservative candidates, or lip service candidates on a straddlebug platform, I personally, for my own self respect and because of my long service to and belief in, liberal democracy, will find it impossible to have any active part in such an unfortunate suicide of the old Democratic party.[138]

Clearly he intended to be the candidate, name the candidate, or "take a walk." In addition to amateur enthusiasm such coolly realistic practitioners of politics as Mayor Ed Kelly of Chicago and Mayor Frank Hague of Jersey City made it clear that they also were one hundred per cent behind the third term.[139]

When the war did break out in September, the President's attention was centered almost entirely on obtaining a revision of the neutrality legislation which would allow the United States to furnish military supplies to the Allies. Anxious to head off merely partisan political opposition, he called for a political truce in the interest of the national welfare and did his best to silence any further third-term talk.[140] The result was a special session of Congress in which he received the support and wholehearted cooperation of many Senators for the first time since the second term began. Lined up solidly behind Roosevelt were such rebels as Walter George—whose crucial adverse vote on the neutrality legislation the previous July was attributed largely to personal hatred for Roosevelt[141]—Carter Glass, Millard Tydings, Harry Byrd, Edward Burke, and Frederick Van Nuys. The opposition was largely from the western states, and it too tended to cross liberal-conservative lines, including such anti-Roosevelt men as Bennett Clark, Worth Clark of Idaho, Pat McCarran, and David I. Walsh, as well as such generally liberal figures as Burton Wheeler, Henrik Shipstead, Ernest Lundeen, and Robert La Follette.[142] Clearly if foreign policy was to be the most significant factor in determining the 1940 Democratic nominee, many western liberals should have been cooling perceptibly toward Roosevelt, while the bulk of the conservatives should have become less virulent in their attacks. This was, indeed, exactly what one prominent news analyst predicted.[143]

That such was not the case in 1939 was evident during and after the special session of Congress. Henry Wallace, apparently convinced at last that the safest place for any liberal candidate for the presidency was aboard the third-term bandwagon, ignored the President's truce to announce his belief that the war situation made a third term necessary.[144] Steve Early indicated White House displeasure the next day with the comment, "It would have been kind and polite of the speaker to have consulted the victim before he spoke."[145] The damage, however, had been done. Roosevelt's conservative allies were furious. Most refused to be quoted, but Alva Adams probably spoke for them when he snapped, "I don't think the war has anything to do with domestic politics."[146] Once the special session was over and the truce ended, conservative attacks resumed. Senator Van Nuys told reporters that the President had an obligation to tell the nation what he intended to do, and he himself would never support any man for a third term. Senator Wheeler chimed in to say hopefully that the President was too smart a politician to try for another term.[147] "Cotton Ed" Smith, Carter Glass, and Al Smith were other supporters of the President's foreign policy who quickly joined the conservative chorus against the third term.[148]

Senator Van Nuys' demand that the President inform the nation of his intentions pointed up the most difficult problem all aspirants to the White House faced, the wall of silence around Roosevelt's intentions. It forced other members of the Administration into silence or to face the charge of disloyalty; indeed, no federal office holder could safely speak out for another candidate if he had any desire for job security. When word reached the President via Governor Lloyd Stark that the state census supervisor of Missouri was working to line up the state delegation for Bennett Clark, the White House arranged to let the guilty party know that "a Census job should require most of a man's time—the fulfilling of which should have been his purpose of acceptance!"[149] The warning was justified, but one may well wonder whether anyone would have bothered giving it to a supervisor in favor of the third term.

Throughout the spring and early summer, stories continued

to appear to the effect that the President had been so badly battered in the previous year's elections that he would not even consider running again[150] or that he intended to retire to write a history of the New Deal.[151] Quite probably in 1939 Roosevelt was not even considering—one way or the other—running for a third term. In a letter to his wife in August he said, "In other words, any discussion of a third term would hamper my efficiency as the existing President of the United States and I, therefore, consider then any discussion would be contrary to the public interest."[152]

It was during this summer of 1939 and not throughout his second term, as James McGregor Burns rather implies,[153] that the President, with Hopkins completely out of the picture, began encouraging a host of rival candidates, thus insuring scattered and divided resistance to a third-term bid. It is unlikely that the policy was deliberate; a host of politicians wanted to be President, and Roosevelt, characteristically, would not tell any of them to his face that he did not consider him presidential timber. Thus, he told Farley that Wheeler was out,[154] and he told Wheeler that Farley would not do.[155] The result, in any case, was to prevent a unified antithird-term movement and enable the inner circle to attack and destroy opposition candidates one at a time.

In late October, however, the advance plans of the third-term campaigners suffered a seemingly staggering blow, not from conservatives but from former ally John L. Lewis. The previous summer Howard Costigan, leader of the Washington Commonwealth Federation, and Norman Littell, Assistant Attorney General, had planned a conference of western progressives to be called in the fall with the view of extending it into a permanent third-term organization in eleven states.[156] Littell brought the idea up with Roosevelt at the Little Cabinet Dinner on June 20, and ten days later submitted a detailed memorandum on the groups that might attend. He had, he said, discussed the matter with Mrs. Roosevelt, John and Anna Boettiger, Tom Corcoran, and Ben Cohen, all of whom appreciated the fact that such groups "could become a vital factor in 1940."[157] Replied Roosevelt, "I think it is a good idea to have liberal organizations meet in the western states—better within the next three or four months than later on."[158] Clearly the conference, as it was suggested to Roosevelt, was aimed at political ends, though not necessarily a third term; it fitted in well enough with his own policy of insuring friendly delegations to the convention. By the fall the inner circle had enthusiastically embraced the plan and was going ahead—secretly—making arrangements for it.

In the meantime, John L. Lewis, whose political arm, Labor's Nonpartisan League, was expected to form a large part of the conference but who had not been let in on the plans, had become furious with the Administration. He believed the Democratic party would revert to conservatism in 1940 and that the time was right for a new third party. For this purpose he wanted to organize the W.P.A., but Hopkins was vehemently opposed and Roosevelt followed his advice and turned Lewis down.[159] The result was that the labor leader, already angry over presidential rebuffs suffered during the Little Steel strikes of 1937, was in no mood to support any third-term movements, particularly when they arrogantly presumed on his support without bothering to inform him of their plans. Characteristically, he exploded violently into print. In a letter to Governor Culbert Olson of California Lewis stated that the conference, which had been organized by two members of the Administration, Littell and Marshall Dimock of the Labor Department (thereby violating the Hatch Act), was for the purpose of engineering a third term for Roosevelt. What appeared to anger him the most was that Senator Wheeler had not been invited to attend and was to be excluded from the conference. He would under no circumstances allow Labor's Nonpartisan League to have any part in the affair.[160]

The New Dealers who had been planning the conference were rather badly shaken by the blast. Not only did Lewis virtually torpedo their plans but he also sounded ominously as though he had found his own candidate in Senator Wheeler and intended to oppose the third term.[161] The following day Roosevelt hastened to wash his hands of the whole affair, saying that he had been told the conference had been planned as a nonpartisan gathering to discuss such progressive ideas as special welfare and old-age pensions. The idea that it was for the purpose of furthering a third term was someone's invention.[162] Although Ickes later tried to resurrect the plan,[163] Lewis had, for all practical purposes, destroyed it as a potential third-term platform.

The inner circle was further tormented by the rapidly growing boom for Security Administrator Paul McNutt, whose supporters were easily the most active and noisy group in the race for the nomination. McNutt himself appeared to be doing an excellent job as Security Administrator, keeping his expenses down to develop a reputation as a New Dealer who was efficient and budget conscious.[164] His speeches, of which there were a goodly number, were nonpolitical in content and increasingly liberal, one indication that his middle-of-the-road position had been abandoned and every effort was being made, apparently with considerable success, to give the impression that there had been a "laying on of hands" and at the proper moment Roosevelt would step aside for him. By late November his managers were claiming—with considerable exaggeration—to have 100 of the 350 eastern seaboard delegates pledged to their man on the first ballot,[165] and there were alarmed reports from third-term backers of promises of second-vote support from all over the country.[166] Ickes, whose diary begins to indicate at this time his strong yearning to be Vice President (an ambition which, though not admitted openly even to himself, was fairly obvious to his associates),[167] began to see two years of hard labor going down the drain. The other New Dealers, too, began to worry about McNutt's increasing popularity. They regarded him as merely an ambitious, somewhat shallow man who wanted to be President—despite the efforts of his speech writers to give him an ideology somewhere to the left of the New Deal—and they were resentful of his pressing his own candidacy while they were working so hard in Roosevelt's behalf.[168] Then, too, there were their jobs to consider. They were not sure at all that Roosevelt did not really favor him,[169] but they were determined to make an effort to head off the boom before it was too late. Thus McNutt was introduced to the trials of being a front runner.

The introduction took place at an Ickes' press conference in early December. Columnist Robert Kintner, thoroughly prepared ahead of time by Tom Corcoran, proceeded to "grill" the "reluctant" Secretary of Interior on the authenticity of the reports that the President was supporting McNutt. Ickes admitted that he did not think the President had told anyone he favored McNutt and he doubted that he did. Moreover, even if he did, Ickes and progressives of both parties would not feel bound to follow his lead.[170] The following day, in a further effort to banish the Hoosier's long shadow, Ickes had lunch with Jim Farley to urge the National Chairman to use all his influence to keep McNutt out of the vice presidency as well as the presidency. It would be, he warned, "the worst thing in the world that could happen to the country." Obviously it would also be the worst thing that could happen to Ickes' ambitions for the vice presidency. He noted with satisfaction that Farley appeared ready to leave no stone unturned to keep McNutt entirely off the ticket,[171] apparently still unaware that Farley had designs on the vice presidency himself and needed no urging to head off McNutt—and everyone else—from that honor.

If the victim expected any sympathy or kind words from Roosevelt, he was disappointed. The President refused to comment at all on the ground that it would soon lead to more questions about this man or that until his plans were revealed by a process of elimination.[172] In a speech to the Indiana University Football Banquet McNutt complained, "You don't know whether the quarterback wants you to carry the ball or run interference. Sometimes the whole team wants to call the signals." As for Ickes and Farley, said he bitterly, "My office is only an epithet away from the Interior Department and a stone's throw from the Post Office Department."[173]

Another inner circle worry about which very little could be done as yet was the subdued campaign under way for Senator Burton K. Wheeler of Montana. During the first session of the Seventy-Sixth Congress not an anti-Roosevelt diatribe was heard from him; he spent his time working quietly and earnestly on railroad legislation.[174] On June 28 it was reported that a source close to the President had suggested—admittedly without the President's knowledge—that Wheeler's candidacy for the vice presidency would be acceptable to Administration supporters and perhaps even the President himself. Wheeler immediately let it be known he was not interested in the vice presidency,[175] but when several days later Senator Edwin Johnson of Colorado made a lengthy formal statement to the effect that only the nomination of Wheeler for President in 1940 could heal the breach in the party and bring victory over the Republicans, Wheeler remained modestly silent.[176] Observed Oswald Garrison Villard sagaciously, "Wheeler may be a candidate."[177]

Like McNutt, the Senator realized that his candidacy would have to have Roosevelt's approval and consequently followed the same policy of stating he would be a candidate only if the President did not want a third term, despite his 1937 statement that he would oppose a third term as a matter of principle.[178] By November Wheeler-for-President Clubs were operating in several states.[179] Although his own state of Montana had only eight delegates to the National Convention, it was clear that Wheeler would have considerable appeal to a number of groups. He was in the forefront of the isolationist group in the Senate, he was gaining popularity throughout the far western and agricultural states because he was hotly opposed to renewal of Hull's reciprocal trade agreements,[180] John L. Lewis was showing a friendly interest in him,[181] and he was, at the same time, making every effort to appear sympathetic to business. To a Congress of Industry, sponsored by the National Association of Manufacturers, he stated that it was time to "stop, look and listen" in the battle for economic reform. He favored modification of the national labor laws, a balanced budget, and the elimination of governmental waste and extravagance.[182] It all added up to an impressive number of friendly pressure groups—and the bitter enmity of Franklin D. Roosevelt, who told Farley in early 1940 that he would vote Republican if the Democrats nominated Wheeler.[183]

A third new possibility the New Dealers had to take into consideration—though in this case very friendly consideration—was not a candidate at all in any real sense, but had a whispering campaign carried on in his behalf throughout most of the year. William O. Douglas, the forty-year-old Justice of the Supreme Court and former head of the Securities and Exchange Commission, was spoken of as presidential material in some circles as early as March.[184] Although completely without a political following, he was not without advantages. His climb to the Supreme Court was a genuine "rags to riches" story in the best American tradition. Moreover, he would probably be acceptable to both factions of the party, since Wall Street had by and large been very satisfied with his chairmanship of the S.E.C.[185] By the fall there were persistent rumors that the President would shortly step aside and name Douglas his heir apparent.[186] In the middle of December, however, another story appeared to the effect that Douglas had been called to the White House and told solemnly that he would be Roosevelt's choice except that his election in 1940 would be an impractical dream.[187] There was at least this much truth to the reports: by late 1939 Roosevelt would have preferred Douglas to anyone else, but he fully recognized that his nomination—not to mention his election—would be a political impossibility.[188] It is not unlikely that he did tell Douglas that these were his feelings.

In the meantime the name of the conservative front runner, John Nance Garner, was appearing much less frequently in the newspapers during the latter half of 1939, and it appeared that some of the momentum had been lost from his drive. What was missing was both publicity and the support of political realists. Two elements had gone into the formation of the movement in the beginning: one was the cabal of the two dozen or so conservative-minded Democratic Senators—reputedly led by Walter George, John Bankhead, and Jimmy Byrnes[189]—which represented and spoke for conservatives and regulars shunted aside by New Dealers of various political hues; the other was a group of businessmen, largely from the southwestern United States, which was tired of six long years of business-baiting and harassment and, in addition, felt a certain local pride in Garner. It is probable, and it was presumed by many at the time, that prior to 1939 Garner had no interest in the presidency for himself and was merely allowing his name to be used to stop a third-term drive or in behalf of a conservative dark horse like Jesse Jones or Bennett Clark. This was in all probability also the motive of the Democratic Senatorial group behind him. It was a simple matter, as one observer noted, to build up an illusion of Garner strength. Hard-bitten legislative experts in the House and Senate slashed and battered the Roosevelt program to a shambles and then gave the credit for their victories to the man supposedly pulling the strings, Vice President Garner. Garner said nothing and was never directly quoted, but the reports carried by conservative Congressmen to their favorite reporters indicated there was a roaring lion inhabiting the Vice Presidential chambers.[190] The fact that Garner would be seventy-two in 1941 and had demonstrated only a knowledge of the mechanics of legislation rather than any statesmanlike profundity did not seem to affect the credibility of the build-up a whit.

The success of this conservative effort, however, was in some respects the cause of its own defeat. So flattered and astonished was the Vice President over the tremendous attention he received from the newspapers and the other indications of popularity that he began to think his nomination might be possible. As one commentator noted in April, having won every Gallup Poll for over a year by increasingly wider margins, "the old gentleman is understood to be taking his candidacy seriously."[191] The old gentleman was indeed. In an interview with a friendly reporter over a convivial bottle of bourbon, Garner crooked a finger in the direction of the White House and remarked, "I don't want to go down there. That place is a jail. The job's a four year prison sentence. But, if the people want me. . . ."[192] By June it was reported that his friends were saying he had decided to seek the presidency whether Roosevelt ran again or not.[193] What that meant, of course, was that Garner was committing himself to stay in the race, thus dimming the hopes of several more youthful challengers.

Late in the summer the blows began to fall on the Garner candidacy with considerably more force than the earlier sniping. Even as John L. Lewis was angrily blasting the Vice President's attitude toward labor, word leaked out of Capitol cloakrooms of a poll taken by conservative Senators in their own districts which indicated that Roosevelt could receive the nomination with no difficulty as far as local leaders were concerned. As a result, a number of Senators who had previously encouraged Garner were thereafter reported to be telling members of the inner circle that they were solidly for Roosevelt.[194] No names were mentioned, but it is obvious that Jimmy Byrnes leaped off the Garner bandwagon early enough to become Roosevelt's floor leader at the National Convention in 1940. In August Roosevelt indicated that he would refuse to support a conservative nominee, reinforcing the impression that he could and would stop the Garner drive if it came to showdown.[195]

With the outbreak of World War II on September 1 and the calling of the special session of Congress on September 21, Garner backers encountered new difficulties. The only issue before Congress was the neutrality policy, and the conservatives, including Garner, were largely in agreement with Roosevelt. The breach in the party appeared to be healed for the time being at least, or at any rate smoothed over by a political truce. The times Congress was in session, however, were the only ones when Garner could be built up as a Roosevelt rival, since he himself did nothing to further his own candidacy. The problems and strategy of the Garner campaigners were outlined in the following alleged statement of Roy Miller made late in 1939:

> I believe our time is right. We have started very early because we have to build the person from the ground. Garner has no color; he cannot speak; he is quite old and cannot be shown.

> We have to make an Andrew Jackson without Andrew Jackson's force; we have to depend upon what we believe the American people are ready to do.

> We believe the American people are tired and want to sit down. We feel that they want one of their own kind to sit in a rocking chair.

> Our man cannot talk so he will stay in his small town and only talk in simple sentences when the opposition gives him a chance, like the Lewis attack. We will have the same general troubles as the Coolidge backers for his popular elections.

> We believe the attacks on Garner's disloyalty can be overcome by Roosevelt's attack and threat to become disloyal to the Democratic Party. We will say "Who is God, and who made Caesar?"

> We will let him fish—all the fishermen will like that.

> They attack him for whiskey-drinking; all the whiskey-drinkers will have an excuse for their own weaknesses.

> He will be attacked as too old to be any good; every man and woman over sixty will resent that.

> He will be attacked as a Bourbon, and as too conservative;—every fellow that wants to sit down and is afraid to say he is a conservative will go ahead and vote for "Safe and Sane John."

The appeal to all of these minorities makes necessary a long, slow and non-vigorous build-up where the person of Garner is built beautifully by the attacks on him. The American sense of fair play always goes to the rescue of the weak, the helpless and the smiling. John will do and be all these, as the young and vigorous take after him with ridicule and whips.[196]

Whether Miller actually made this statement or not, it is a fair analysis of what Garner backers were up against, and of their method of meeting the challenge. Whatever were the chances of success of a Garner campaign in peacetime, the outbreak of World War II made it very evident to political realists that the times were not right for a leader who would be weak, helpless and smiling, or as Heywood Broun put it, "a Cactus Coolidge."[197]

Nevertheless, when the special session of Congress was over and the political truce ended, the campaign was pressed on. In November a biography of Garner by Marquis James appeared (*Mr. Garner of Texas*) as well as a catchy Jack Foy-Rex Lampman campaign song entitled "Cactus Jack."[198] Finally, down in Uvalde in mid-December Garner called together a few newspaper friends and stated formally:

I will accept the nomination for President. I will make no effort to control any delegates. The people should decide. The candidate should be accepted at primaries and conventions as provided by law, and I sincerely trust that all Democrats will participate in them.[199]

He then disappeared into the woods on a fishing trip. The guesswork was finally over, and the New Dealers faced an open challenge.

The year closed on a note of great scurrying for delegations and frequent endorsements and denunciations of the third term. Of these, only Ambassador Joseph Kennedy's statement favoring Roosevelt's nomination caused any raised eyebrows, since it was the only noticeable exception to the rule that liberals and city machines favored the third term and conservatives opposed it.[200]

Thus, the latter part of 1939 witnessed a rather remarkable reversal in political fortunes. That the war had a great deal to do with it is evident, but to say that the war was the only or, perhaps, even the most important cause of this reversal is to ignore the realities of election-year politics and the tremendous political power of the Administration forces. The trend was not noticeably in any ideological direction, from conservative to liberal or isolationist to internationalist. Rather, local, state, and even congressional figures in the party realigned themselves with powers emanating from the White House, rather than remaining attached to centers of opposition found in Congress and elsewhere. Secretary of Interior Ickes analyzed the situation at the year's end as accurately as anyone when he wrote, "I still believe that public pressure will force the President to run again next year, but if he does not run, I do not see anything on the democratic [sic] side that would encourage a liberal."[201] Once again liberals both in the government and out were agreeing that the next election would mean "Roosevelt or Ruin."

CHAPTER V

BY PROCESS OF ELIMINATION

The period from the fall of Poland, September 27, 1939, to the opening of the German offensive against Denmark and Norway in April was, except for the somewhat minor Russo-Finnish War, one of relative military quiet in Europe. Pictures appeared in American newspapers of British soldiers in France knitting sweaters for the folks back home and of French troops using antiaircraft guns to support clothes lines. There were still hopes in many circles that some sort of peace might be negotiated before the fighting was resumed in the spring.

In America the "sitzkrieg," or "phony war," relieved somewhat the feeling of danger and emergency which had been so obvious in the fall of 1939. The New York World Fair prepared to open again, bigger and better than the previous year, and unemployment was still the major concern of liberal crusaders. Nevertheless, no one was ignoring the crucial international situation.

One effect of the war on domestic politics became very evident early in 1940 with the President's annual message to Congress and his budget for fiscal 1941. The New Deal was, as far as he was concerned, essentially complete, and the old conservative-liberal alignments were no longer quite so pertinent. This is not to say that Roosevelt did not continue to favor liberals and liberalism over conservatives, but for the most part his interest was diverted by foreign affairs and his efforts in behalf of liberalism largely reduced to lip service. The irony of that was that his support for a third term was coming largely from liberals and progressives, many of whom were isolationist in sentiment. Only a handful of them, however, saw foreign policy as the major issue of the coming campaign, whereas it was very much on the minds of a good many rank-and-file Democrats. The result was a smoothing over of old animosities and a tremendous boost to Roosevelt's power over the Democratic party.

The Sphinx and His Rivals

The President's annual message to Congress and his annual budget message were shrewd gestures not only at uniting the nation and preparing it for war but also for extending the political truce of the previous fall. The only item slated for increased appropriations in the budget was national defense; practically all other expenses were to be reduced, although not enough to prevent another deficit—for the eleventh consecutive year.[1] There was, complained Ernest K. Lindley, some incongruity in the President's appeal for consideration of the problems of unemployment and idle youth and the cuts in the Civilian Conservation Corps and National Youth Administration. In checking the reactions of ten leading liberals in the Administration to the two messages, the most favorable comment he heard was, "They weren't quite as bad as I had expected."[2] John L. Lewis pointed out the trend of the Administration with considerably more asperity. The nation, he announced, "must decide whether it will listen to those who would divert attention from the difficulties of our internal problems and stake the Nation's future on the vagaries of wars abroad." He added that "labor believes that the American people will vigorously reiterate their conviction that America's problems must and will be solved in this country by American methods, that we must steadfastly turn aside from giddy dreams of foreign ventures."[3]

Nevertheless, most liberals realized by this time they had no place else to go and no other possible candidate to support, however much they might agree with Lewis' criticism. Wrote Sherwood Eddy, one of the more prominent radicals:

> We would be satisfied if one of his New Deal friends could get it, but as they have never won any election they cannot get either the nomination or the election. . . . If these cannot get it, I think Roosevelt would run for a third term to keep the election from going to a reactionary like Garner, McNutt, Hull, Clark, the Governor of Missouri, Farley, or any other politician in the Democratic camp. . . . [Reinhold] Niebuhr and many others feel the same way. [Harold] Laski urges all liberals to support Roosevelt in this crisis.[4]

Even Socialist candidate Norman Thomas commented, "I would rather see a good President in office for a third term than a bad one for a first term. I don't see anybody in the New Deal capable of succeeding President Roosevelt—and all the Republican candidates are so mediocre."[5] Counteracting Lewis' attack, Sidney Hillman, President of the Amalgamated Clothing Workers of America and Vice President of the C.I.O., told a convention of his union that though he could not speak officially for them, "as far as our membership is concerned, I am sure we will give Franklin D. Roosevelt greater support in 1940 than ever before."[6]

Two factors besides the President's generally noncontroversial legislative program probably kept conservative attacks to a minimum. One was the evidence of the rapidly rising popularity of the President, which boded ill for anyone directly opposed to him. The January *Fortune* survey staggered a good many third-term critics when it showed that Roosevelt had more support for a third term than the three leading Democratic and four leading Republican hopefuls combined had for a first.[7] The Gallup Poll for both January and February indicated that Roosevelt was favored by 78 per cent of the Democrats polled, with Garner, his leading rival, polling 13 per cent in January and 10 per cent in February.[8] On the other hand, the conservatives were encouraged by frequent newspaper reports from the White House in the early months of 1940 which implied or stated bluntly that the President would not allow himself to be drafted under any circumstances and that he felt that Cordell Hull would be the ideal compromise candidate and would support him.[9] Insiders knew that these news stories were not the usual political gossip which often seemed to originate in the imaginations of the Washington columnists.

Since late 1938 Roosevelt had been hinting to Hull that he would be his choice as successor,[10] and around December of 1939 he made it more explicit. Lisping excitedly, Hull told Jim Farley, "Cwist, Jim, Woosevelt told me he's for me." Said Farley with experienced cynicism, "Cordell, if he told me he was for me, I'd announce it right away from the front steps of the White House."[11] Hull, however, was unique as a presidential candidate inasmuch as he continued to believe that the enactment of his program, the renewal of reciprocal trade agreements, was more important to the nation's future than his own election as President. Rather than risk having the two issues confused with the possible loss of both, he continued to remain silent, depending entirely on Roosevelt's support for the presidency and strongly discouraging all political organizing in his own behalf.[12] To those writing him begging him to allow them to work for his nomination, the only encouragement he gave was the grudging comment that "Events are moving with such rapidity as to make the future utterly unpredictable, and accordingly it is easy to understand that a decision arrived at this moment might be subject to reversal or modification a few months hence."[13] To reporters who asked about his candidacy he stated briefly that he had commented on that all he intended to six to twelve months before when he stated in writing that he had no political interests.[14]

Perhaps partially to mollify left-wing outrage and partially to head off a Hull-Farley ticket, which he was sure could never win, the President invariably mentioned Robert Jackson for Vice President whenever he suggested Hull for President.[15] As Ickes quickly pointed out to him, however, Farley would undoubtedly

throw his weight behind Hull with the expectation of being nominated Vice President. Whether Farley received it or not, there was
little likelihood that either he or Hull would stand for a New
Dealer's nomination, and there would be nothing Roosevelt could
do about it once he had given his support to Hull for the presidency.[16]

The President was careful, on the other hand, to leave his
position completely flexible. Privately he was mentioning Hull,
but publicly he was saying nothing, much to the anguish of the
other candidates in and out of the Administration who were severely handicapped in their struggle to acquire delegate votes.
He told Farley the previous August that he would withdraw from
the race when it became necessary to file for the primaries. In late
January he told Ickes that the situation had changed so radically
because of the war that he not only would not remove his name
from contention but was already arranging not to be even asked
whether he wanted his name on any primary ballot or not.[17]
Indeed, he made it clear to reporters that he did not care to be
asked anything at all about his candidacy. The final decision would
be announced at a time of his own choosing, he warned sharply,
and not that of the newspaper editors.[18] His silence and apparent
lack of interest in politics, however, did not prevent him from
arranging to have the convention in Chicago so that Mayor Ed
Kelly could control the galleries.[19] In March he wrote Governor
Henry Horner of Illinois to deprecate the notion that his own
renomination was necessary but at the same time to warn that they
must nominate a candidate who would be liberal and who could
win in November.[20] According to Rex Tugwell that stand was a
virtual announcement of his own candidacy, since no one else
could possibly meet both qualifications,[21] but this does not take
into account the fact that Roosevelt was willing to throw the
mantle of liberalism over Cordell Hull.

The great third-term enigma, as the newspapers were grandi-
osely calling the President's silence, caused considerable strain on
the nerves of both wings of the party. Even the inner circle was
baffled about the President's intentions. Although Tom Corcoran
was reported (falsely on at least one occasion)[22] to be applying
heavy pressure in a number of states for third-term delegations to

the convention, there was growing doubt that the President would accept the draft. Robert Jackson wrote in February that he thought the President would run if it were clearly "the desirable course," but he admitted gloomily that it was impossible to get his permission or approval for any organized movement in the direction of a third term.[23] By March almost all of the inner circle had virtually given up hope except Ickes, though they could not see how he could back out of the situation gracefully.[24] Harry Hopkins had recovered his strength sufficiently by early 1940 to re-enter the fray by forming his own pressure group for the third term. Senator Claude Pepper, Mayor Ed Kelly of Chicago, and Mayor Frank Hague of Jersey City were called together for a meeting at the Mayflower Hotel. "Gentlemen," said Hopkins dramatically, "this may well be a historic meeting. This group will be the nucleus of a movement that will force President Roosevelt to run again."[25] Though the members of this clique lacked the high idealism and broad social objectives of the White House inner circle, they more than made up for it in sheer political power and experience. How successful their efforts to bring pressure to bear on Roosevelt were was evident from the many noisy demands for a third term from one city machine after another. Wrote an amazed Josephus Daniels, "It is a strange thing that the city bosses who were strongly against Roosevelt in 1932 are now crying out, 'Save us, Franklin, or we sink.' "[26] Ickes and the inner circle continued to function by attacking and doing all they could to eliminate all Democratic opposition wherever it might arise. Nevertheless, Roosevelt insisted that he wanted no headquarters and no manager. He would not, he said, be pressured into revealing his intentions until he was ready. In the meantime, everyone else would have a full opportunity to develop his strength or weakness.[27]

As long as the possibility existed that Roosevelt might want the support of the state party leaders, of course, there was no real possibility that anyone could build up much support, and the growling among the supporters of would-be candidates grew louder by the day. The thunderclap of opposition to this policy eventually broke forth in late January, though not from the right wing, but from the left. The Burton K. Wheeler-John L. Lewis alliance was clearly setting itself to "smoke out" the President on his intentions. As the United Mine Workers prepared to celebrate their Fiftieth Anniversary Convention, Lewis issued an invitation to Wheeler to be the featured speaker, "recognizing you as one of the most eminent of our contemporary statesmen,"[28] and New Dealer David K. Niles reported privately to Roosevelt that the convention would adopt a resolution endorsing Wheeler as its candidate.[29]

Something went awry, however, and the convention was something less than a triumph for either Lewis or Wheeler. The Senator was, indeed, cheered to the rafters when he called unemployment the nation's number one problem and pledged "never to vote to send an American boy across the water to fight on foreign soil,"[30] but Lewis' speech was bitterly aggressive and drew little applause from the stunned delegates. He advised the miners to withhold their endorsement from any candidate and added pointedly:

> I am one who believes that President Roosevelt will not be a candidate for re-election. Conceding that the Democratic National Convention could be coerced or dragooned into renominating him, I am convinced that, with the conditions now confronting the nation and the dissatisfaction now permeating the minds of the people, his candidacy would result in ignominious defeat. . . ."

There was, it was reported, hardly a handclap when he left the platform.[31] From the reactions of his own miners and other labor leaders throughout the country, it was evident that Lewis had struck anything but a responsive chord with his anti-Roosevelt comments. The following day, Sidney Hillman, speaking at Lewis' invitation, received an ovation when he told the miners that no man in public life was more deserving of labor's confidence than Roosevelt.[32] William Green of the A. F. of L. called Lewis a "singer of a song of hate" and an arch ingrate, and he pledged all-out A. F. of L. support to Roosevelt.[33] Said David Dubinsky of the International Ladies Garment Workers' Union, "Lewis is counting his labor votes before they are hatched. On the whole the American laboring masses whose economic standards and social security have been materially improved in the last seven years . . . have better memories and are not as ungrateful as some of their leaders."[34] Although some forty-seven resolutions had been presented by U.M.W. locals in favor of the third term, Lewis was able to prevail to the extent that the convention formally empowered him and the executive board to formulate policy in the presidential campaign. In their speeches from the floor, however, members made it plain that if Roosevelt were nominated and the executive board did not support him, "we shall have to make a split and go down for Roosevelt."[35] There was no mention of a Wheeler-for-President endorsement.

Despite the shaky support Lewis was receiving from his own union, the New Dealers were worried. That same week Senator Norris announced that if Roosevelt did not run, Wheeler would be his choice for the nominee.[36] Ickes was told by Robert Kintner that Wheeler would definitely receive the support of Lewis, which would amount to at least a million dollars. In addition, the railroad brotherhoods were about to declare for him, and Dan Tobin of the Teamsters would eventually come out for him as well.[37] Kintner's information was almost entirely wrong, but at the time the development looked ominous indeed to those in favor of a third term. Wheeler's credentials as a liberal, as Senator Norris pointed out, were unimpeachable; his only serious pending difference of opinion with the Administration was foreign policy, and in this area many liberals agreed with the Senator. If the war did not take a serious turn by convention time, Wheeler appeared to stand a good chance of being a left-wing threat. The lobbyists for the railroad brotherhoods were reportedly busy in his behalf in Congress,[38] and Progressives in Wisconsin were buzzing over rumors that a coalition ticket was being quietly planned in case he was able to win the nomination, with Philip La Follette being named as his vice presidential running mate and Robert becoming a candidate for the Senate on the Democratic ticket.[39] There was even a threat by early April that John L. Lewis might form a third party for him consisting of organized labor, the American Youth Congress, the N.A.A.C.P., the American Negro Congress, the liberal agricultural organizations, and the Townsend Old-Age Pension groups unless the Democratic party adopted a platform and ticket acceptable to labor.[40]

Roosevelt's silence, however, continued to make it next to impossible for the Montana Senator to gather any strong support among the liberals, and all efforts to pry some encouragement or commitment out of him proved futile. In the middle of February Senator Edwin Johnson of Colorado, Wheeler's staunchest backer, called on the President to make public his intentions and denounced the manipulation of delegates by the New Dealers.[41] He pointed out quite accurately that if the President wanted a draft, silence was the way to get it. "If, on the other hand, the President has no intention of accepting the nomination, his continued silence is terrible and he must accept full responsibility for demoralizing and disrupting the Democratic party."[42] Within the next four days he was seconded by Senators Pat McCarran of Nevada and John Bankhead of Alabama—in vain.[43]

Wheeler's enemies, on the other hand, had by no means been totally idle. His colleague in the Senate, James Murray, whose election he had opposed in 1936, secretly but firmly pledged one-hundred-per-cent support to Paul McNutt should Roosevelt not desire a third term, and McNutt backers were quietly making heavy inroads in western states most observers presumed would be in the Wheeler column.[44] The New Dealers, through columnists Drew Pearson and Robert Allen, attacked with a heavy hand, reporting on one occasion that Mrs. Wheeler, who was regarded in New Deal circles as being overly ambitious, was called and asked to allow her name to be used as sponsor for a Negro concert in Washington. "Don't you know better than to ask a thing like that in an election year?" she reportedly snapped and hung up.[45] In an essay in *Current History* Allen reported that Wheeler had destroyed his chances of success by "playing politics" with the Supreme Court issue in 1937 and not remaining true to the liberal cause. Had he supported the fight, said Allen, he would today "be either a member of the Supreme Court or the undeniable successor to Franklin D. Roosevelt." As it was, he was suspected and distrusted by both liberals and conservatives.[46] Allen's article reflected the real cause for much of the hatred of Wheeler in Administration circles as well as the lightness with which many liberals tended to ignore the differences in foreign policy between Wheeler and the Administration.

While the Wheeler campaign appeared to be picking up momentum, that of Security Administrator Paul McNutt ran into a major road block in the late winter and early spring of 1940. Early in January the Washington correspondent for the *New Republic* reported that the influential New Dealers were becoming mysteriously and grimly silent about his candidacy and that there was reason to believe they expected it to come to an immediate and unhappy end.[47] A short time later the reason for their optimism became apparent. Treasury agents, it was revealed, were investigating his income-tax statements and the activities of the Indiana Two Percent Club, and they were doing so none too quietly. Every organization before which McNutt had spoken was asked if McNutt had been paid for his speech and if so, how much, leaving the impression that he was under strong suspicion.[48] Although the investigation was supposed to be secret, Pearson and Allen reported its progress on at least three occasions with lurid suggestions that the agents expected to find a secret "slush fund" set up by gamblers in gratitude for McNutt's policy of regarding gambling as a local affair when he was Governor and similar equally pleasant possibilities.[49]

In addition, a storm of insults and ridicule from all directions appeared to be aimed at finishing off any part of the McNutt reputation the Treasury Department left intact. John L. Lewis made his position clear to the Mine Workers when he called the Security Administrator a "political adventurer who likes to pretend that he was a soldier, who was accompanied by a motley crew of Two Percent bagmen which he hoped would be able to buy enough votes to make him President . . . so that he would have more soldiers to play with."[50] William Allen White referred to him as "merely Garner in a high hat, a white vest, a pongee silk scarf, pumps and the glamour of a movie hero." He was a Fascist who was planning to come to power—like Mussolini and Hitler—by trying to appear liberal.[51] Equally harsh evaluations appeared in the *Nation* and the *New Republic*,[52] though they were mild compared to Alva Johnston's feature story in the *Saturday Evening Post*, which, despite pleas to the editor for mercy by one of McNutt's campaign managers,[53] could only leave the reader with the impression that McNutt was an amoral egomaniac whose only desire was to be President regardless of what he had to do to achieve it.[54] On a smaller scale the Communist-led Workers' Defense League was circulating a folder entitled "Keep Labor's Enemy Out of the White House."[55] Summing it all up, *Time* reported that "like a movie-serial heroine, he had been politically shot, stabbed, poisoned, garroted, sawed into short lengths, burned, decimated, smothered, bumped off, rubbed out. He has been 'given the business.' "[56]

Despite the rain of abuse McNutt's backers continued to hope that the campaign would be able to get into high gear again once the Treasury Department had finished its investigation and exonerated their candidate (even his enemies were admitting that there was not much likelihood that he himself had been guilty of any wrongdoing).[57] The difficulty was, however, that the Treasury Department agents simply did not call off their investigation or was any statement ever made by the government exonerating McNutt, despite the fact that the Indianapolis grand jury was dismissed in March.[58] McNutt's managers were told that Secretary of Treasury Morgenthau was furious over the accusations of some columnists that he was personally responsible for "knifing McNutt" and would, therefore, issue no statement exonerating him on the grounds that the law forbade him to give out information about taxpayers' affairs.[59] The Administration, as reporter Ludwell Denny remarked, would neither give McNutt a clean bill of health nor prosecute him. It merely perpetuated an innuendo which assassinated his candidacy.[60] To add insult to injury, the *New Republic*'s Washington observer asserted that although it might look like outright persecution inasmuch as a New Dealer was running the Bureau of Internal Revenue (Guy T. Helvering), actually the Treasury agents had discovered a great deal which the New Dealers were graciously keeping quiet until after the convention to spare McNutt's feelings![61] Even McNutt's old enemy, Jim Farley, was moved to remark in a press conference—off the record—that he did not favor such long-drawn-out investigations which created periods of distrust and suspicion.[62] Certainly this one created tremendous problems for the McNutt campaign. Even in January one associate chairman reported being swamped with letters and calls asking if the candidacy was folding up or if McNutt contemplated withdrawal from the race.[63]

Although it might have appeared that he might as well have withdrawn, the campaign went on, chiefly because both he and his advisers recognized that, in the last analysis, Roosevelt would probably decide who the candidate would be, and they still had high hopes of winning his approval. When to this end McNutt did begin active campaigning in late April, his speeches were more liberal than ever, and, in addition, a manuscript for a campaign book to present his ideas on government, which was ghost written by his administrative assistant, Fowler Harper, and economist David Coyle, argued that he believed in extending the New Deal in all areas.[64] Indeed, so far to the left did he appear to be swinging that his eastern manager, Oscar Ewing, argued bitterly to Fowler Harper that even Roosevelt had refused to have anything to do with some of the things to which he was committed.[65] Harper's argument was that Roosevelt liked the book, and that was the important thing.[66] The rather pathetic aspect of this debate as well as McNutts' feverish swing through the Midwest and Southwest was that it never had a chance of success. Roosevelt did not consider McNutt a real liberal[67] and was apparently genuinely concerned lest his Two Percent Club be a real source of scandal for the Administration. When Henry Wallace suggested that Claude Wickard of Indiana be appointed Under Secretary of Agriculture, Roosevelt's first question was, "Has Wickard had anything to do with the Two Percent Club?"[68] He had not even bothered to read McNutt's book, but had passed it on to Steve Early with the request that he read a chapter or two and send McNutt a nice note over his signature.[69] Nevertheless, despite the threat of a major exposé constantly hanging over his head and the storm of abuse from the press, McNutt made real progress throughout the spring and early summer as the convention was to prove. He was, as Roosevelt remarked, a very attractive figure and a good campaigner.[70]

The state of the Garner campaign, on the other hand, appeared to grow more woeful by the day despite the Vice President's apparent popularity in the January Gallup Poll.[71] The fact that Roosevelt seemed to favor Hull for the nomination and that he had practically ceased all attacks on the conservatives within the party went far toward cutting the ground out from under the Garner drive, and the rapid growth of third-term popularity went the rest of the way. By February Roy Miller was complaining that "some of the fellows who told me they were against a third term as a matter of principle seem to be rising above principle now. Between officeholders and people getting subsidies, there are not many people left to talk to."[72] It was an accurate summary. In almost every state conservative businessmen and old-guard politicians, long since pushed aside by New Deal Democrats, manned the Garner organization. The Senatorial group which had whipped up the Garner enthusiasm in the first place and had at one time numbered at least twenty-eight now almost entirely abandoned him with the exception of a few diehards like Walter George of Georgia and the Texas Senators, Tom Connally and Morris Sheppard.[73] Many were even afraid to be seen entering his office to "strike a blow for freedom."[74] It was, said one reporter, almost as if a smallpox sign had been hung on his door,[75] and the Vice President himself was reported glum and irritable.[76] Wrote Arthur Krock contemptuously of Garner's erstwhile friends:

> In his private rooms they have waxed brave and have uttered terrifying predictions of national doom if the two term tradition is broken. They have prophesied that Mr. Garner would find them right behind him . . . And are the cheerleaders behind him? They are, indeed. Silent and so far behind he can't even see them.[77]

Even William Randolph Hearst, who had virtually created the Garner candidacy in 1932, apparently decided the old man was a lost cause in 1940. In May, newspapers belonging to his chain broke forth in huge half-page editorials singing the praises of Jesse Jones and winding up with the comments:

> Mr. Jones refutes the erroneous impression that the New Deal has been entirely barren of good and sound American leadership. He most certainly

refutes the mistaken assumption that the Democratic
Party has no leader worthy and capable of succeeding
Mr. Roosevelt.[78]

Although Jones had been explaining to most of his admirers that
he had no interest in politics, his thank-you note to Hearst included no such information.[79] With the decline of Garner and the
lessened likelihood of the convention needing a compromise candidate, however, his chances for anything better than the vice presidency declined too. William Randolph Hearst was not the king-
maker in the Democratic party that he appeared to be in 1932.

The only other major worry the New Dealers faced was Jim
Farley, whose intentions were still obscure. It was known that he
wanted the vice presidency, but no one, probably not even Farley
himself, knew in early 1940 if he was willing to buck the third-
term drive to get it. His efforts to line up delegates to the convention were primarily in behalf of Cordell Hull, though he had also
ordered the William H. Rankin Advertising Company of New
York to do everything in its power to build up Jesse Jones as a dark
horse. He would be delighted, he said, to be the running mate of
either Hull or Jones.[80] The same week John L. Lewis had attacked
the third-term movement at the Mine Workers' Convention, Farley made headlines across the nation by a speech he gave at
Winston-Salem, North Carolina, before a nonpolitical Chamber of
Commerce dinner. Quite obviously it was an effort to define his
philosophy of government (and prove he had one) and was regarded as an opening bid for the presidential nomination by those
not aware of his vice-presidential ambitions.[81] The views expressed
were orthodox enough—cooperation between government and
business and a fair deal for the farmer—but there was an unmis-
takable hostility toward the antibusiness attitude of the New Dealers. Even more disquieting was his comment:

> I also want to make it clear that if at any time I am
> confronted with the issue of the welfare of my party,
> on the one hand, or the welfare of my country on the
> other, that that issue has already been decided. I love
> my country better than I love the Democratic
> Party.[82]

No one was sure to what he had reference, but some guessed that he might feel such a conflict of loyalties if there was a third-term nomination.

A few days later Farley asked Roosevelt's approval to enter the New Hampshire and Massachusetts primaries because "if a delegation is not filed, a half dozen sets of delegates would enter the primary and disturb the party's position in the November election."[83] His unexpressed reason was to see that the delegations were nailed down for Hull.[84] The inner circle understood at once what the move portended and reacted quickly. John L. Sullivan of the Treasury Department was dispatched to his home state of New Hampshire to inform the local politicos that Farley was not acting on Roosevelt's orders and that the delegation should be instructed to back the third term, orders that were promptly obeyed.[85] The Massachusetts leaders were similarly informed, and soon public statements were being made in that state that although the slate was pledged to Farley, if the President wanted a third term, "Farley and the Democratic Party as a whole will support his candidacy."[86] They were, observed Farley, in a panic to stay on good terms with both sides. Senator David I. Walsh, normally an anti-Roosevelt conservative and an isolationist as well, but facing re-election in 1940, announced that he would be party to no antithird-term movement,[87] and John McCormack, in accepting a place as delegate-at-large on the slate, issued a public statement that he would reserve to himself complete freedom of action to support Roosevelt for a third term if his name were submitted to the convention.[88] He was elected chairman of the delegation. Farley's tremendous popularity with New England Democrats had been somewhat neutralized, but not, it was thought adequately. Further, there was the likelihood that he would be able to capture a large part of the huge New York delegation.

To finish his candidacy off, Roosevelt and the New Dealers attempted to use the same heavy-handed newspaper tactics they were employing against McNutt and Wheeler and thus committed a blunder which probably insured Farley's bitter and unshakeable opposition to the third term. Ernest K. Lindley, a close friend of Roosevelt since his days as governor and his first biographer, published a newspaper article quoting an unnamed southern Congressman as reporting that Roosevelt had told him definitely that he would not run again, that he favored Cordell Hull for his successor, and that Jim Farley would not be acceptable as Vice President because "they'd say we were using Cordell Hull as a stalking horse for the Pope."[89] The following day Roosevelt was asked in his press conference if he would comment on the story, and although it had made the front page of the Washington *Post*, he merely said he had not seen it.[90]

Farley was furious at what he regarded an underhanded and unethical effort to sabotage his candidacy. Two weeks later he gave a radio address on the importance of tolerance in American life. Belatedly Roosevelt issued a denial of the Lindley story in his next press conference,[91] but it was not taken too seriously. In any event the damage was done. The next day Farley stated bluntly, "To clear up any misunderstanding, let me say that my name will be presented to the Democratic National Convention in Chicago and that's that. I am sure that anyone who has known me during my political career will know that I make that statement frankly without reservations."[92] In effect, he had uncompromisingly joined the antithird-term drive. Despite efforts by backers of the sagging Garner drive, however, Farley declined to enter any formal understandings with any of the other candidates.[93] And Roosevelt, rejecting Democratic publicity director Charles Michelson's cynical advice that he let Farley have the nomination so that the inevitable 1940 defeat would be blamed on his Catholic religion rather than the New Deal,[94] continued to do what he could to deny Farley delegate strength. His contribution in New York was to suggest to Ed Flynn and Herbert Lehman that the "right thing" for the New York delegation to do would be to support Lehman for at least one vote.[95]

Thus, by March the Roosevelt-Farley combination had at last publicly come to an end, and there were those who thought that Farley carried enough weight on his own to at least destroy the fiction of a spontaneous draft. Under the circumstances the necessity of winning all the primaries by convincing majorities was crucial to the New Dealers, since it would be necessary not only to have a bare majority of the convention votes but to actually stampede the convention to a unanimous or near-unanimous draft if the third-term drive was to have a chance of success in November. Indeed, not only would victories by heavy margins in the primaries be necessary but some favorite sons would have to be eliminated behind the scenes at state conventions as well. All the antithird-term Democrats had to do was demonstrate "substantial opposition" within the party, and the illusion of a near-unanimous draft would be exploded.

Gathering the Delegates

The opening gun of the vote-gathering campaign was the New Hampshire primary on March 11, 1940, the results of which were ambiguous enough to encourage everyone a little. Through the efforts of New Dealer John L. Sullivan the state organization put up a complete slate for the eight at-large places completely pledged to the third term. In addition, three unauthorized candidates pledged themselves to support Roosevelt, two were for Farley, one for Garner, and two were unpledged. The official party slate won, and the other three pro-Roosevelt delegates finished close behind.[96] Only 13,500 Democrats voted in the primary, however, as opposed to 40,000 Republicans, suggesting that Lewis might have been right in predicting ignominious defeat for a third-term effort. Further, the Garner and Farley delegates polled an average of between 3000 and 4000 votes each despite the fact that neither candidate had made any effort at all to win votes in New Hampshire. As a result, Garner backers were reported to be elatedly redoubling their efforts in other states.[97] With the exception of Massachusetts, whose delegation was at least nominally pledged to Farley, the other New England state party organizations quickly fell in line behind New Hampshire.[98] Farley sentiment was strong, however, and there was not much question of who would control the lion's share of their votes if the President should decline to use them.

The crucial contests were where Garner forces had organized and prepared for all-out campaigns against third-term delegations. There the New Dealers had to win and win impressively. Invariably the state leaders swung into line behind Roosevelt, but their unity in that respect often appeared more than balanced by their internecine hatreds for one another. The first and one of the fiercest of these campaigns occurred in Wisconsin, where Garner chances looked especially good because of a three-way split in the Democratic party there, two of the groups supporting Roosevelt and one Garner. The group headed by National Committeeman Charles Broughton, which consisted to a great extent of federal officeholders and, it was said, conservatives who had leaped on the bandwagon to protect their jobs,[99] controlled party patronage. Although they named their slate "The Official Roosevelt-Farley Delegates," it was emphasized that Farley's name was purely complimentary and it represented no second-choice commitment.[100] As a matter of fact, however, the National Committeeman was a close personal friend of Farley's and was prepared to support him all the way if Roosevelt declined the nomination.[101] The rebel group which also claimed to love Roosevelt was headed by Outgamie County Democratic Chairman Gustave Keller and called itself "The Liberal Democratic Party of Wisconsin." Its chief objection to Broughton was the matter of patronage, half of which was channeled to the Progressives,[102] but the two groups also differed on their second-choice candidate. Keller's faction was made up largely of McNutt backers.[103]

The third part of the party backed Garner and was headed by John Slocum, the Secretary of the State Central Committee, and William Callahan, son of John Callahan, who had been an Al Smith supporter in 1932 and candidate for the Senate in 1934, when Roosevelt had ignored him to back Robert La Follette.[104] Most of the Garner men and their entire slate of delegates were old-line Al Smith backers, chiefly Irishmen from the industrial part of the state who were long out of office and extremely conservative in outlook.[105] (Harry Bolens, their candidate for governor in 1938, was antilabor and anti-income tax.)[106] They expected to profit not only from the split in the pro-Roosevelt forces but also from the fact that great numbers of the liberals in the party had deserted to the Progressives during the 1930's. The Democratic vote in 1938 was only some 70,000 as opposed to 300,000 Progressives, and almost all the Democratic votes came from the Irish centers in the large cities where the Garnerites figured to be the strongest. The

Progressives, on the other hand, held no primary and were free to vote in either the Republican or Democratic primaries. The Garner forces were extremely fearful, with good reason, that they would reciprocate for the many patronage favors they had received and enter the Democratic primary. The Garnerites were further aided by large amounts of cash from Texas, almost twenty times as much as either third-term faction was able to muster.[107]

As in the case of New England, the New Dealers dispatched a henchman, Leo T. Crowley, head of the Federal Deposit Insurance Corporation and a native of Wisconsin, to unite the warring Roosevelt factions if possible or throw Administration support one way or the other to avoid an even split. Crowley found that personalities were involved to such an extent that no healing of the breach was possible.[108] He, therefore, wholeheartedly endorsed the Broughton faction.[109]

The results were a distinct shock to the New Dealers. They had been predicting a winning margin of at least five or six to one in spite of the split on the basis of Wisconsin's famed liberalism, but the margin was only three to one, and the Garner forces were able to win three of the twenty-four delegates, with the Broughton wing taking fourteen and the Keller group seven.[110]

The same day the Wisconsin primary was held, the Garner forces battled Tammany Hall in the New York City primary. Tammany wanted an uninstructed but prothird-term delegation and showed enough concern over the Garner threat to have the leading Garner candidates, John McNaboe, a state senator, and Al Smith, Jr., ruled off the ballot. McNaboe, it was said, had neglected to register as a Democrat the previous fall, and Smith did not live in the district in which he was running for office.[111] Less than a week before the elections the state Appellate Court overruled the Board of Elections and restored their names to the ballot.[112] The result was that though none of the Garner delegates was able to win, his forces did attract nearly a third of the vote from the Tammany machine.[113]

Garnerites in both Wisconsin and New York claimed a moral victory, and Garner's campaign managers, E. B. Germany and Mrs. Clara Driscoll, issued a statement that "Mr. Roosevelt could not be re-elected if nominated" on the basis of the vote, and they blamed Garner's defeat in Wisconsin on "an army of job-holders and check receivers" coupled with an invasion of the Democratic primary by Progressives.[114] Harold Ickes roared furiously that they were "talking like Republicans," and he doubted that they expressed the sentiments of Garner himself, or Sam Rayburn. He was not the only liberal shaken by the outcome; the *New Republic* suggested that supporters of Farley and McNutt had secretly drifted into the Garner ranks to head off the third term. The solution to that situation, it suggested, was to fire McNutt and Farley.[115] The inner circle was reportedly worried lest Roosevelt take the results too seriously and announce abruptly that he was not available.[116]

The glee of the conservatives and the discomfiture of the liberals was short-lived, however, and the remainder of the Garner campaign was sharply downhill. Manager Roy Miller had originally figured that the Illinois delegation would fall to Garner because of a state law that required the candidates to sign statements that they were candidates.[117] The rule was ignored, however, and the Kelly-Nash machine of Chicago joined with Governor Henry Horner's downstate machine on a harmony ticket for Roosevelt. Garner's forces were led by Julius F. Smietanka, a Chicago attorney and a former Collector of Internal Revenue under Woodrow Wilson, and Colonel William M. Bannon, a Chicago businessman.[118] The result was, predictably, a smashing defeat for the Garner forces by a six to one margin, the Roosevelt forces polling over a million votes to less than two hundred thousand for Garner.[119] The same day Roosevelt won the Nebraska primary unopposed, and, perhaps more significantly, his followers buried anti-New Deal Senator Edward Burke's bid for renomination.[120] The problem was, complained Burke, that the real Democrats had abandoned the party and left him to face the one-hundred-per cent New Dealers.[121]

The Garner forces still had some hopes of recouping their losses in California, where the Democratic party was even more splintered than in Wisconsin. Moreover, Garner had won the primary there in 1932. The two major factions were headed by Governor Culbert Olson and former Senator William Gibbs McAdoo, and both wanted to put pro-Roosevelt slates in the field.

Each bitterly hated the other, and the possibility of their cooperation seemed slight indeed. A third group, headed by Lieutenant Governor Ellis Patterson, consisted of the extreme left wing of the party and received its support largely from the C.I.O. and Labor's Nonpartisan League. It appeared to be ready to support the third term if necessary, but presumably would have preferred to cast its votes for Burton Wheeler. In addition, Senator Sheridan Downey, who was openly opposed to a third term,[122] entered a utopian "Ham and Eggs" slate of candidates. The Garner forces were headed by Zach Lamar Cobb, called by one California Congressman "a bag of hot air of the ultraconservative forces calling themselves Democrats," an acknowledged reactionary, anti-New Deal, antiprogressive, antiliberal. "Assuming that a Garner delegation just HAD to be formed," wrote Albert S. Brown, "we couldn't have ourselves picked for opposition a less potent leader."[123] Nevertheless, the Garner forces had money and were so active in their campaign that as shrewd an observer as Raymond Moley wrote that the Vice President "has a surprisingly good chance of getting a solid delegation" from California.[124]

What made the California split so extremely dangerous to the New Dealers was the California law which stated that when two delegations were entered in the primary favoring the same candidate, the candidate had to repudiate one or the other of them. Under the circumstances Roosevelt was forced at last to take an active if covert hand in the affair. Through Congressman Jerry Voorhis, Roosevelt indicated to Olson that he would not give his support to any other group,[125] but at the same time asked Ickes to fly out to California and arrange a coalition slate from among the warring factions.[126] To everyone's surprise, including his own, Ickes was able to get representatives of the various pro-Roosevelt groups together in his hotel room and hammer out an agreement on a list of delegates.[127] The peace, however, was short-lived. Ickes had hardly returned to Washington when the Patterson group bolted the ticket and entered one of their own in the race, and McAdoo, after sharp warnings from his doctor, also dropped off despite Ickes' anguished pleadings.[128]

The results, nevertheless, were everything the New Dealers could have wished. The third-term coalition ticket received

716,591 votes to Garner's 111,453, Downey's 88,178, and Patterson's 48,009.[129] It was the end of the trail for any serious Garner hopes. Wrote Ickes "sympathetically," "Poor Garner already had one foot in the grave and the other on a banana peel, and from this time on it is our duty to speak respectfully of him."[130]

The sympathy was of rather short duration, however, and it was not long before the New Dealers were plotting to administer the cruelest cut of all—taking Garner's own state of Texas away from him. Roosevelt himself was reluctant to enter any such fight, not so much because he objected to humiliating Garner, but because an open defeat, which he considered likely, would be a severe and probably unnecessary blow to his prestige.[131] Nevertheless, with his tacit consent an open attack was begun April 5 when Under Secretary of Interior Alvin Wirtz, a Texan himself, spoke at the dedication of a dam in Austin. He charged that Garner's backers were "trying to defeat President Roosevelt's chances for a third term even at the cost of a do-nothing Republican Administration."[132] The Garner forces retaliated with a news release in the Dallas *Morning News* to the effect that the third-term movement in Texas was being conducted against the wishes of the President.[133] The origin of the statement, it developed, was Jesse Jones,[134] and it momentarily threw the Texas third-term group off its stride. "We can and will win the fight," complained Mayor Tom Miller of Austin, "but are entitled to have the cooperation of the friends of the President in Washington, or at least they should put their numbers on their jersies so that we will know whom they are playing for and against."[135] Wirtz reacted quickly, stating to Ray Brooks of the Austin *American* that the report was simply anti-New Deal propaganda,[136] but at the same time he sent a hasty plea to Harry Hopkins to "let me know the score, please."[137] He returned to Washington somewhat confused by the conservative flank attack from Roosevelt's official family, but a week later, after a visit to the White House, he headed back to Texas expecting to "put in some licks for the third term,"[138] an ambition that was amply fulfilled.[139]

Though the Garner forces could probably have won the battle, Jesse Jones and Sam Rayburn asked for a compromise to avoid further strife in a hopeless cause. They agreed that twenty places, or a third of the state delegation, should go to Roosevelt backers, another third to the Garnerites, and the last third to moderates who did not feel too strongly either way. The first vote would be given to Garner as a favorite son, but thereafter the vote belonged to Roosevelt. The New Dealers, who did not believe they could defeat the Garner forces in an open battle in Texas, agreed on condition that a public statement of the compromise be issued from Washington by Sam Rayburn for the Garnerites and by Congressman Lyndon Johnson, who had been in the thick of the fight, for the New Dealers. Despite the humiliation Rayburn suffered from being put on even terms with a brash freshman Congressman like Johnson, the "treaty of Washington" was arranged.[140] In addition to surrendering the Garner candidacy, the compromise also called for the endorsement of the entire New Deal record: the handling of sit-down strikes, deficit spending, and all.[141] It was the first in a series of humiliations inflicted by the liberal wing of the party on the Democrats who had so successfully battled the New Deal throughout Roosevelt's second term.

The Oregon situation was somewhat touchy also. There the Garner forces were headed by former Governor Charles Martin, who had been purged in 1938 through the efforts of Ickes and Norris. The remainder of the party was in effect in two separate camps, the party regulars in one and the Oregon Commonwealth Federation, which was largely controlled by the C.I.O., in the other. The Garner forces, believing they could control a state party convention, tried to capture the state delegation by having the conservative legislature pass a law abolishing the direct primary,[142] but this strategy was foiled rather easily by obtaining enough names to a petition to make the bill a referendum and thus suspending its operation until the 1940 primary was held.[143] The Roosevelt forces appeared to suffer a setback, however, when the two factions supporting him for a third term split over his foreign policy. Willis Mahoney, head of the party regulars, completely repudiated the Commonwealth group when it attacked the President's defense program and attempted to pledge the Oregon delegation to Robert La Follette for Vice President.[144] The result, nevertheless, was another smashing victory for the third term, with Roosevelt polling over 100,000 votes to Garner's 15,000. Two

Commonwealth candidates were elected to the delegation, but they were virtually powerless.[145]

The almost total elimination of the Garner threat in the primaries by no means meant that the New Dealers could rest on their laurels. There was also the problem of a number of state conventions and primaries which might well be controlled by a favorite son. Since it was generally believed that the President would consent to a draft only if the convention overwhelmingly favored him, preferably by acclamation, it was evident that every vote counted, and every favorite son possible had to be eliminated.

Ohio was one case where a favorite son was absolutely necessary, since no one could be entered in the primary without his written consent. Originally it was planned that the state's fifty-two votes be pledged to popular Senator Vic Donahey and turned over to Roosevelt when needed, but the Senator upset the plans by announcing that he considered such a candidacy dishonest.[146] His remarks caused a certain amount of embarrassment, but his withdrawal did not affect matters in the least. The party merely substituted National Committeeman Charles Sawyer for him, with the clear understanding that the state's votes belonged to the President whenever he wanted them.[147]

In Iowa the problem was to choke off Henry Wallace's quiet drive for favorite-son support. As early as January it was rumored that Wallace was being asked to give up his candidacy in favor of an uninstructed delegation and that Roosevelt had told one of the Iowa Senators that Wallace lacked "IT."[148] By the first of May it was further reported that Wallace, the Iowa congressional leaders, and State Chairman Ed Birmingham had pretty well agreed that the convention should instruct first for Roosevelt and then for Wallace if Roosevelt chose not to run.[149] The local Iowa Democrats, however, either because they did not understand the need Roosevelt had for the first ballot votes or because they did understand and wished to withhold them, petitioned their congressional delegation to ask the President to approve publicly a first-ballot vote for Wallace on the same basis as the Garner compromise in Texas. Failure to so do, they suggested, would be construed as a repudiation of Wallace's farm policy and would seriously weaken the Democratic position in the farm states.[150] Roosevelt received the petition without any public comment.[151] Privately he had already told Wallace that he had no objection to his favorite-son candidacy,[152] but his silence in the face of a petition asking his public approval strongly indicated that the rug had been pulled out from under his Secretary of Agriculture. He also privately told the Iowa congressional delegation that Wallace was a nice fellow, but didn't have a chance.[153] Three days after the presentation of the petition, the Iowa convention instructed its twenty-two man delegation to vote for Roosevelt first and for Wallace only if the President were not a candidate.[154]

The elimination of rivals in the North was relatively easy, but in the South, where there was more genuine and open opposition to the New Deal and where conservatives more often controlled party machinery, it was otherwise. Maryland, for instance, instructed its delegation for archconservative Millard Tydings. The Virginia convention, despite a determined effort by the pro-New Deal forces of Governor Price, was largely in the hands of the Byrd-Glass machine, and the delegation elected appeared likely to support any conservative candidate who looked as if he might have a chance.[155] Alabama sent twenty-two delegates to the convention instructed for favorite son William Bankhead,[156] though many of them were Roosevelt men. In Missouri a fierce battle raged between the followers of Senator Bennett Champ Clark and New Deal-supporting Governor Lloyd Stark, with Clark, aided by the battered Pendergast machine, ruling the Missouri convention with an iron hand. The result was an uninstructed delegation which, presumably, would favor Clark's candidacy if he decided to put his name before the national convention.[157]

Elsewhere the New Dealers were more successful. In North Carolina Governor Clyde Hoey was originally expected to receive a favorite-son nomination, with the second vote going to Hull. As a third-term movement began to grow in the state, however, Hoey stated that he wished the first vote to go to Hull and predicted that the Secretary of State would receive the President's backing, thus rebuking those who were pushing hard for a delegation instructed to support the third-term drive.[158] The President and the inner circle, however, after first agreeing to a Hull slate, decided they could not spare the North Carolina votes on the first ballot, and state leaders were quietly told to halt instruction of the delegation.[159] The result was a "compromise" by which the delegation was instructed for Roosevelt if his name was presented but left free if he did not choose to be a candidate.[160]

An effort was made to support Hull's candidacy in Tennessee also, despite his own vigorous protests. When the Knoxville organization passed a resolution ordering its delegation to the state convention to support him, Hull quickly wrote its chairman to ask that his name "not be used in connection with any proposed political recognition, either conditional or unconditional."[161] Through his close friend, J. W. Gardenhiser, Hull informed the state convention that he wished it to proceed as though he "were not in existence." The state leaders, however, deemed it unthinkable to instruct for anyone as long as Hull had a chance, and, reported Gardenhiser, "your close friends, who had a right to speak for you . . . were shunted aside and the program went through like greased lightning."[162] It was clear, nevertheless, that if the President did not throw his weight to Hull, Tennessee would be in the Roosevelt column on the first ballot.

The going was somewhat easier in some of the other southern states. A potential favorite-son delegation for Pat Harrison from Mississippi was choked off in 1939 in a race for the governorship. Harrison's bitter enemy and staunch backer of the third term, Senator Theodore Bilbo, supported Paul Burney Johnson in the governorship race, while Harrison backed Michael Conner. The victory went to Johnson and with it control over much of the eighteen-man Mississippi delegation.[163]

Senators Walter George and Richard Russell were backing a potentially powerful Garner movement in Georgia, but were blocked by pro-New Deal Governor E. E. Rivers, who took advantage of a state law which permitted but did not require a primary to be held. Normally one was held, but Rivers, who controlled the party's executive committee, ignored a petition bearing 25,000 signatures and had the delegation named at a state convention instead. So completely did he control the convention that no one was even allowed to make a speech in favor of a primary from the floor, and a strongly pro-Roosevelt seventy-two man delegation, which included neither of the Senators, was chosen.[164]

In Florida, where the political picture was so confused that some one-hundred candidates were running for fourteen places on the delegation, Senator Pepper struck a bargain with the McNutt forces to support the same slate with the understanding that McNutt would get the delegation if Roosevelt did not want it.[165]

In South Carolina, where as in Georgia and Virginia, Roosevelt had been badly humiliated in 1938, Senator Jimmy Byrnes had nimbly switched sides again, and his support made a great deal of difference in the battle against conservative "Cotton Ed" Smith. After a sharp and bitter debate between Smith and Byrnes, the state convention voted by a two to one margin to instruct its delegation for a third term.[166]

Oklahoma was still another southern state where conservative strength, represented by Governor Leon Phillips, was thought to be strong enough in high places to cause considerable difficulty to the third-term drive,[167] and the McNutt group was also reportedly making heavy inroads in the party.[168] Thanks to a whirlwind campaign by Senator Josh Lee and his supporters, however, fifty-five of the state's seventy-seven counties instructed their delegates to the state convention for Roosevelt while the remainder favored an uninstructed delegation.[169] Another state was firmly in the Roosevelt column.

One after another, by conventions and primaries, the various state parties either instructed their delegations for Roosevelt "if he is a candidate" or left them uninstructed but friendly to a third term. As Farley told the President angrily in early July, they really had no other course open to them unless they wished to risk Administration wrath and punishment.[170] The best the other candidates could do was get promises for support in the unlikely event that Roosevelt would not take the draft. Although many of these commitments were secret, Farley forces claimed to have 482 such votes pledged.[171] Nevertheless, although the instinct for self-preservation on the part of local political machines made the inner circle's job easy, other events in the late spring of 1940 outside the realm of domestic politics were instrumental in widening considerably the demand for the third term and perhaps convincing the President himself that he had a duty to run again. Once again the shadow of Hitler and the European war loomed large across the American political scene.

The Blitzkrieg and the Third Term

The ninth of April, 1940, saw the great German war machine moving again, this time overrunning Denmark in a matter of hours and beginning a quick conquest of Norway. Within a month operations in the North had been successfully concluded, and on May 10 the drive through the low countries and around the French Maginot Line was begun. In five days Dutch resistance was virtually ended, and the Germans were fighting on French soil. Less than two weeks later the trapped and beaten British expeditionary forces were being sea-lifted off the beaches of Dunkerque and the French left to fight on as best they could. On June 10, despite frequent efforts by Roosevelt to forestall it, Mussolini entered the war, striking the French army from the rear. Eleven days later France signed an armistice.[172]

The effect of the lightning-like crushing of the supposedly powerful French army on Americans was for a time somewhat similar to a panic. Petitions from students in a number of colleges poured into Congress to demand that the United States keep out of the fray. The Gallup Poll showed that confidence in final Allied victory had dropped from 82 per cent to 55 per cent during May, and following the invasion of France, Governor E. E. Rivers of Georgia proclaimed a state of emergency and demanded that all aliens in the state be fingerprinted and registered at once. News of the Nazi use of paratroops in Holland brought out scores of volunteer organizations, many of them made up of middle-aged mothers, for target practice to "meet the invaders."[173]

Politically, the effect was to increase dramatically the President's popularity overnight. Between August of 1939 and April of 1940 the percentage of those polled who favored a third term had crept up from 40 per cent to 47 per cent, but between April and May it jumped to 57 per cent.[174] "The Democratic Convention," cracked Tom Corcoran confidently, "was held in Copenhagen."[175] That was a trifle premature. One might have said that the Democratic Convention was held in Paris, except that by May 10, when the Nazi drive through the low countries began, all of the more important primaries were over and the others foregone conclusions for the most part. On May 16 the President spoke to an anxious joint session of Congress to ask for $1,200,000,000 more for preparedness (which was quickly voted) and was cheered to the rafters. It was, said Harold Ickes, the warmest reception the President had received from Congress in five or six years.[176] From the frightened, doomed city of Paris Dorothy Thompson reversed herself on the third term late in May and voiced the feelings of many Americans when she wrote, "The fall of Roosevelt in America would be worse for the cause of democracy and freedom than Nazi occupation of Switzerland."[177]

As the crisis deepened, it appeared that the liberal-conservative split was more and more becoming blurred over in the interest of national unity. The President himself was in the forefront of the movement, despite his demand for the continuation of the New Deal in his Fireside Chat of May 26. "We have carried on an offensive on a broad front against social and economic inequalities and abuses which had made our society weak," he observed. "That offensive should not now be broken down by the pincers movement of those who would use the present needs of physical military defense to destroy it."[178]

To New Dealers, however, it appeared that he was doing just that when in the latter part of May he set up a new Advisory Commission for the Council of National Defense heavily weighted with businessmen and appointed James Forrestal, formerly head of the Wall Street banking firm of Dillon, Read and Company, to be one of his six administrative assistants. "Just how chummy can the New Deal be with Wall Street," asked one alarmed liberal, "and still continue to be the New Deal?"[179]

Although there was a great deal less evidence of liberals and conservatives being at one anothers' throats as the war news grew worse—especially after the utter demolition of the Garner forces in the primaries as an object lesson—the split between internationalists and isolationists within the party grew wider and more serious by the day, with the result that the John L. Lewis-sponsored campaign of Burton Wheeler leaped into the spotlight once again. In late April Wheeler announced his candidacy. He would withdraw from the race, he said, if the President was a candidate simply because he could take the nomination if he wanted it—"and [about that] there is no use kidding yourself"—but he doubted that Roosevelt would accept a third-term nomination. He is, repeated Wheeler over and over, "too smart of a politician and has too much regard for American tradition."[180] By the end of May, however, with the British army trapped on the beaches of Dunkerque and the French pleading for American aid, the Senator had changed his mind about Roosevelt's intentions. Paul McNutt, who had been campaigning vigorously through the West and Southwest until then, issued a statement that the welfare of the nation required Roosevelt's re-election and added, "It is my sincere hope that he will accept the renomination for the presidency." Snapped Wheeler angrily, "I don't think Mr. McNutt or anyone else needs to worry over whether Mr. Roosevelt will accept renomination. Every recent action has shown that he will."[181] It was no longer clear, however, what the Senator would do in that case. On June 13, two days after Roosevelt had dramatically condemned Mussolini's "stab in the back" of France, Wheeler announced in the Senate, "I want everyone who is interested in the matter to know that I am not going to support any candidate for President of the United States of America, no matter who he may be, who is going to try to get us into this war."[182] The statement was immediately interpreted as a threat to bolt the party if Roosevelt were renominated.

There was deep concern in inner-circle ranks over the liberal-isolationist threat throughout the spring and summer, particularly since New Dealers Ben Cohen and Senator Claude Pepper were spending much of each day together studying legal means of supplying Great Britain with the equipment she needed—especially fifty overage destroyers—to carry on the fight.[183] Wheeler's growing importance as the isolationist spokesman, evidenced by his appearance on the cover of *Time* in April and frequent journal articles written about him, was regarded as genuinely dangerous in a year when the issue of war and peace appeared to be rapidly overshadowing all others. One overeager Administration supporter attempted to head him off by again suggesting that he take the vice presidency. At a dinner at the home of newspaper columnist Robert Kintner, economist Leon Henderson told Wheeler bluntly that the convention would nominate him for the post and he would have to accept. Wheeler objected that he did not want the job and he doubted that Roosevelt wanted him anyway since he would not keep his views to himself the way Garner had. Replied Henderson, "Here's Bob Kintner, here's Ben Cohen, here's Ed Foley, and you know how we stand," implying that the offer for the vice presidency came directly from the White House.[184] Ben Cohen, who was squirming uneasily in his chair during the conversation, was well aware that Roosevelt had authorized no such offer and would have vetoed it at once. Although he felt it was not his place to contradict Henderson, he could not help feeling relieved when Wheeler showed no interest.[185]

Fortunately for the peace of mind of the inner circle, Wheeler's power was more apparent than real, and to his great humiliation he was able to secure a favorite-son endorsement from his own state of Montana only by subterfuge and steamroller tactics in the state convention. The majority of the delegates favored instructing for Roosevelt with the provision that Wheeler should have the votes if the President was not a candidate. To avoid an embarrassing floor fight which might split the party, they sent a committee to Wheeler's hotel room the night before the convention to make that offer. The Senator flew into a rage at the suggestion and stated that he would lose prestige all over the country if he could not control his own state's delegation. He had, he said, a telegram from Senator Murray which stated that Roosevelt would be satisfied to have the delegation pledged to Wheeler as long as the platform endorsed the New Deal (which, it was reported afterward by Senator Murray's son, was not quite the truth). "If Roosevelt is satisfied with this arrangement," argued Wheeler, "you fellows certainly should be." They were not satisfied, however, and attempted the following day to substitute a resolution instructing for Roosevelt instead of Wheeler. But the Senator, a battle-hardened veteran of Montana politics, had thoughtfully brought a number of friendly followers into the galleries, and the chairman of the convention, Arthur Lamey, was Wheeler's choice for governor. The result was that despite repeated pleadings by the Roosevelt men for a roll call the Wheeler resolution was shouted in by a voice vote, with most of the voices coming from the galleries. Indeed, the Wheeler forces controlled the entire convention by voice vote, allowing not one single roll call on anything.[186]

Weak though he may have been behind the scenes, Wheeler and his sponsor, John L. Lewis, continued to hammer away at Roosevelt's foreign policy in public. Before the N.A.A.C.P. convention in June, Lewis not only attacked the Administration's movements toward intervention and termed the Democratic party the "war party," but he even violently attacked the New Deal as the cause of seven long years of depression. Had Hoover remained in office, he asserted, the depression would soon have been over. Of all the nations involved in the economic collapse "the United States alone went backward after the election of Franklin D. Roosevelt, and under his policies it has stayed depressed ever since."[187] Attending the Republican platform hearings at the end of the month, he was cheered to the rafters when he described the President's plans for conscripting men into the army as "a fantastic suggestion from a mind in full retreat."[188] The same day Wheeler denounced the newly appointed Republican Secretaries of War and Navy, Henry L. Stimson and Frank Knox, as warmakers and repeated his threat to "disavow any candidate who may lead this country down the road to war."[189] Two days later he strongly urged a liberal peace movement outside the two major parties, but he informed reporters that his name would go before the Democratic Convention regardless of what anyone else did, joining Garner and Farley in that category.[190] On July 11, however, he was somewhat mollified by the President's special message to Congress asking for an additional four billion dollars for defense but asserting, "We will not use our arms in a war of aggression; we will not send our men to take part in European wars."[191] Wheeler announced that he was gratified and was withdrawing from the race,[192] an intention which was rather short-lived. By convention time no one was sure what he intended to do.

Although it was clear, as Wheeler had observed, that Roosevelt could have the nomination if he wanted it, the New Dealers were still very much concerned that he might not be willing to accept it. Following the smashing California primary victory, Robert Jackson had written exultantly, "Some months ago I thought that no one could stop Roosevelt except Roosevelt. Now I don't think that even Roosevelt can stop Roosevelt for he will have to submit to the conscription."[193] Others were not so certain that he was not still bent on having Hull for his successor, so that the New Dealers were campaigning not only to win the nomination for Roosevelt but also to get him to accept it as well. At the convention of Sidney Hillman's Amalgamated Clothing Workers in Madison Square Garden in May, New Dealers Ickes, Robert Wagner, Herbert Lehman, Mayor La Guardia, and others praised the New Deal and over and over again demanded the President accept a third term. Roosevelt himself, probably because of concern over Lewis' attacks, called Hillman once to ask eagerly how things were going.[194] They were going very well, indeed, to the extent that the Clothing Workers became the first C.I.O. union to endorse the third term since Lewis predicted an "ignominious defeat" for the President.[195] Once the ice was broken, a good many others followed suit.

Senator Claude Pepper's contribution to the drive, he reported, was to join with a group (Kelly, Hague, Hopkins?) to convince the other candidates that they should withdraw. "Jim Farley ought to head the list," wrote Pepper darkly, "and I hope he will."[196] Paul McNutt dropped out publicly on May 30 with the statement that the renomination of Roosevelt was a necessity because of the war emergency, but a few days later a private circular was sent out from his campaign headquarters to the various local McNutt leaders to declare that the statement changed nothing and the campaign was to continue.[197]

Others sought directly to encourage the President to seek a third term by letters to him. Wrote Maury Maverick passionately, "THERE IS NOT A QUESTION WHETHER YOU RUN FOR A THIRD TERM OR NOT ANY MORE. It is the duty of every man to fight like hell for *militant democracy* and to have a *strong foreign policy*."[198] Justice Frank Murphy, with "faith . . . of the militant kind," wrote placidly, "Because it is just, your re-election is as certain as your renomination,"[199] and political scien-

tist Louis B. Wehle encouraged him to run because "of your standing with labor, liberals and radicals," which would enable him "to
be a bulwark against unnecessary and unfair encroachments by
capital in the emergency. . . ."[200] According to the compilations
of Administrative Assistant James Rowe, a total of 6,100 letters
were received at the White House on the subject of the third term
between May and the first of July. Of these, 6,015 favored it, and
only 85 were opposed. Between July 1 and July 12 an additional
5,450 were received, running 89 to 1 in favor of the third term.[201]

In addition, a steady stream of major and minor politicians
poured into the White House to plead with the President to accept
another term. Said Congressman John McCormack, leader of the
Farley-pledged Massachusetts delegation, after an interview with
Roosevelt, "We urged him just as strongly as we could to be a
candidate or consent to be drafted. I think it's absolutely indispensable that the President run."[202]

The question of when Roosevelt decided to accept the draft
or what caused him to change his mind about supporting Hull cannot be answered with any certainty. Reports had been leaking out
of the White House for almost six months that he definitely intended to retire unless the nation were faced with a national crisis
resulting from German victories. There was nothing inconsistent,
then, in his acceptance of the nomination after the fall of France,
and certainly there was no evidence that he was absolutely determined to run before that occurred. In the fall of 1939 he had tried
to arrange to have Sam Rosenman move up to Duchess County so
that they could work together at Hyde Park on his papers after
his retirement, and as late as February Harry Hopkins was talking
of buying a home in that neighborhood.[203] Late in January Roosevelt signed a contract to be a contributing editor for *Colliers* to
begin in January 1941,[204] and he told Tom Corcoran that he had
gone about as far as he could with domestic reform, and it would
be up to someone else to "mop up" after him.[205] Sometime in the
spring, according to Frances Perkins, he told Dan Tobin, President
of the Teamsters Union, that he definitely was finished as President.

> I have to get over this sinus, I have to have a rest. I
> want to go home to Hyde Park. I want to take care
> of my trees. I have a big planting there, Dan. I want

> to make the farm pay. I want to finish my little house
> on the hill. I want to write history. No, I just can't
> do it, Dan.[206]

In late April, Frank Walker sent him two charts showing electoral votes for all the previous elections back to 1880. Replied Roosevelt slyly, "Do you think that this year we should put this into the Hyde Park Library—or hand it on to some fellow who is still interested in electoral votes?"[207] In early May, Roosevelt still seemed to doubt that he would run again. On the fourth he spoke from the White House balcony to a group from the Women's Division of the National Democratic Committee. Molly Dewson noticed that he looked strained and tired, and she told Eleanor "with considerable emotion" that he had done enough for his country and should be allowed to retire. Before she left, Mrs. Roosevelt told her she had talked to the President about it, and he had replied, "Tell Molly that as things look I do not think it will be necessary for me to run."[208] Indeed, on June 20 he gave Cordell Hull the impression that he still did not intend to run,[209] and the New Dealers, who, as Hull remarked, were offering more opposition to his candidacy than the Republicans,[210] were still afraid they might be asked to support the Secretary of State.[211] The April Gallup Poll had shown him running ahead of both Roosevelt and the leading Republican contender at the time, Arthur Vandenberg,[212] and the poll for May showed Hull the leading Democrat except for Roosevelt.[213]

It seems probable that sometime between June 20 and July 3 Roosevelt definitely determined to accept the nomination. On July 3 he suggested rather halfheartedly to Hull that he might write a letter to someone like George Norris and end with the statement that he merely wished to go back to Hyde Park. Hull pointed out that such a letter would not delay his nomination a split second, and he had the rather strong impression that Roosevelt had decided to accept the nomination by that time.[214] By July 11, when Ickes was preparing to leave Washington for the convention, Roosevelt indicated the type of campaign he expected to wage, and Ickes was fairly sure that his mind was completely made up.[215]

The only thing that now stood in the way of his third nomination was the presumed opposition of Jim Farley and the motley group of conservatives who still held out against the Roosevelt tidal wave. There was no question that the President would have a vast majority of the delegates at the convention; the only question was, Would the majority be vast enough? Roosevelt insisted on going through all the motions of a genuine draft and even seemed to believe at times that the convention had some freedom of choice with which he did not wish to interfere. When the New Dealers asked for a plan and a floor leader for the convention, he merely grinned and said he was trusting in God, though Robert Jackson did pry from him the opinion that Jimmy Byrnes would be the most desirable floor leader.[216] Indeed, at a meeting of the third-term professionals—Ed Flynn, Ed Kelly, Frank Walker, Jimmy Byrnes, and Harry Hopkins—less than a week before the convention was to open, he was still expressing some misgivings about breaking the third-term precedent, although the politicians had little difficulty in showing him that there was no other Democrat left who could possibly win.[217] He did, however, insist on writing a short letter to William Bankhead, the keynote speaker of the convention, asking that Bankhead inform the delegates that he did not wish to remain in office after January.[218]

The convention was scheduled to open Monday, July 15. On Saturday, the thirteenth, Roosevelt and Rosenman went for a cruise on the Potomac, working on drafts of the platform and acceptance speech. The President said that he did not want to give the appearance of making a fight for the nomination or pressuring the delegates to vote one way or the other.[219] By that time, however, it was no longer necessary to fight for votes. Only a miracle of mismanagement by his friends could prevent his third nomination.

Virtually all of those close to Roosevelt—with the exception of Jesse Jones, who had become quite hostile by the time he put his opinions in writing,[220] and, of course, Garner and Farley—have expressed the opinion that the fall of France was the determining factor in Roosevelt's decision.[221] As dispassionate a historian as James McGregor Burns believes, however, that Roosevelt would have run again even if there had been no intensified international crisis,[222] and it seems quite probable, though by no means provable, that had the major issue at the convention still been liberalism vs.

conservatism Roosevelt would have been quite unwilling to throw the liberal forces to the wolves. The President apparently sincerely believed in his own mind until the latter part of June that he would retire at the end of his second term, but whether it would have been psychologically possible for him to forget the violent opposition and bitter defeats at the hands of the conservatives the previous three years and silently bow to the final defeat, a conservative Democratic nominee, may well be doubted.

CHAPTER VI

JEFFERSON'S LAST STAND

The long struggle between liberals and conservatives which had broken into the open in the spring of 1937 for control of the Democratic party was at last approaching the moment of truth. The conservatives and party regulars had won control of nearly everything but the presidency, but it was clear by convention time that unless President Roosevelt declined to run again, that office was out of reach. For most of the party faithful it was not an unsatisfactory situation. Clearly, the President did not have sufficient power to impose a New Dealer on the convention as his successor; if he withdrew, it would have to be in favor of an acceptable moderate like Cordell Hull. On the other hand, the majority of the delegates probably really wanted Roosevelt to run for a third term. He stood the best chance of retaining control of the presidency for the Democratic party, his name at the head of the ticket would strengthen the local party tickets immeasurably, and he himself showed every indication of being willing to heal the breach in the ranks in the interest of support for his foreign policy. The most agonizing soul searching had to be done by those who had called him a would-be dictator in the Court fight of 1937 and the Purge of 1938, a spendthrift and a wastrel when his budget messages were debated in Congress each year, and a destroyer of one of America's most cherished traditions when he refused to say he would not be a candidate for a third term. They now had the uncomfortable choice of eating their words, fighting to the last ditch, or remaining coldly aloof. Each had to decide which meant most to him: his political life—or at least his political influence—or his hatred for Roosevelt. With few exceptions, "principles" were for those who had nothing to lose.

Chicago: the Purge Revisited

As the hundreds upon hundreds of party faithful converged on Mayor Ed Kelly's hot, gusty city of Chicago, it was evident that President Roosevelt held the whip hand. What was not evident, even to his closest associates, was how or when or, indeed, if he would use it. "It is all very well for him to try to create the impression generally that he had nothing to do with the third-term movement and was indifferent to it," fumed Ickes, who was almost as much in the dark about the President's plans as anyone, "but I know that this has not been his state of mind."[1] To the Secretary of Interior's intense disgust, he found on reaching Chicago that someone else apparently did know what was on the President's mind. A Roosevelt headquarters had firmly been established in the Blackstone Hotel, presided over by Harry Hopkins with a direct telephone hookup from the lavatory to the White House. It was clear at once that if anyone knew anything about what was supposed to go on, it would be Harry Hopkins, and it was to Hopkins rather than third-term leader Ickes or National Chairman Farley that the politicians swarmed for directions. "I can't find out what's going on," complained one delegate from Georgia. "The word has been passed around that the Secretary of Commerce—what's his name? Oh yes, Hopkins—that Harry Hopkins is going to tell us what to do."[2]

The effect was galling to everyone. Hopkins, sure at least that the Roosevelt forces had the votes to overcome all opposition one way or another was not very tactful by all accounts.[3] Democrats who had been less than one hundred per cent behind the New Deal found the atmosphere at the Blackstone chilly indeed, and no pledges or promises of any kind were given to any of the delegates.[4] Farley and those close to him were, of course, more than mildly irritated by the situation. On one occasion, the National Chairman was talking to a group of delegates when someone came up to him and whispered something in his ear. "If Harry Hopkins wants to see me," he exploded, "he can see me in the office of the Democratic National Committee, where everybody else sees me."[5]

Nor were the New Dealers particularly happy about the situation. They gave the impression, one observer noted, of being "fearful, panicky, and weak."[6] Ickes, bitterly jealous of Hopkins and embarrassed because, after having led the third-term movement for two years, he was completely in the dark about what was going on, stayed in his hotel room to avoid being forced to admit it.[7] Ironically, Hopkins himself was equally ignorant of Roosevelt's intentions and desires. Although the telephone was hooked up, no vital information was coming through it. It was a symbol of authority and as such useful, but it really had no authority behind it.[8]

In such an atmosphere of uncertainty, inexperience, and ignorance, rumors spread like lightning, and anything seemed possible. Especially frightening to the New Dealers were reports that Farley's strength was growing, that he was spreading all kinds of lies about being promised the presidency by Roosevelt, and that he had retained a sizable bloc of tickets with which to pack the galleries with Roosevelt haters to mislead the radio audience about his real strength.[9] As a result, the third-term politicians on the scene convinced Roosevelt that the reading of his message denying any desire for a third term should not be done by William Bankhead, the convention keynoter, the first night, but by Permanent Chairman Alben Barkley, who was more friendly to the third term, on the second night.[10]

After the opening sessions on Monday, the strategy change seemed wise indeed. Mayor Kelly in his opening address of welcome, which sounded more like a nominating speech, appeared to be trying to start an early stampede for Roosevelt, but his final peroration, "We will stand—and put forward—and CONFIRM AGAIN—that God-sent guardian of our liberties—THE KIND OF MAN THAT MANKIND NEEDS: OUR BELOVED PRESIDENT, FRANKLIN D. ROOSEVELT,"[11] was met by an embarrassingly polite spattering of dutiful applause. It appeared, remarked one pro-New Deal newspaper, that the convention was moving toward a draft with all the enthusiasm of a chain gang.[12] Farley, who had spent the day fending off political bosses trying to make him change his position,[13] received a greater ovation at the evening session when he told the delegates poetically that the differences of opinion within the party "have no more significance than the ripples on the sea, or even the great storm waves that rise and pass, leaving the ocean still a great international highway."[14] Most important of all, it was agreed by friends and foes alike that Bankhead's keynote address, at which Roosevelt's message was originally to have been read, was dull and listless. The New Dealers interpreted it rather paranoiacly as a demonstration of hostility to the Administration; Farley thought it showed fatigue and ill health.[15]

The New Dealers were by now in something of a panic. It was quite evident to everyone that the convention was in a rather restless and resentful mood, though at whom or what was not so clear. Farley had the impression that the majority were opposed to the third term,[16] though it is likely that he was being told what he wanted to hear. Ed Flynn noted that the majority of the delegates had no great enthusiasm for the third term but knew they needed Roosevelt to win in November.[17] Certainly they resented the dictation of Harry Hopkins, and as one reporter noted, they resented being used as scenery like the Hawaiian leis and the brass bands.[18] An undercurrent of renewed interest in other candidates seemed to be sweeping through the convention as the apparent lack of excitement about Roosevelt became evident.[19]

Harold Ickes once more attempted to leap into the breach and lead the Roosevelt forces to a speedy victory. At a gathering of Ickes, Jackson, Hopkins, and Byrnes in Ickes' rooms at the Stevens Hotel, it was determined to take control of the convention and renominate the President without further delay. The easiest way to reach their goal, they decided, was to have the Rules Committee provide that the nomination should be the order of business before the reading of the platform, which normally came first and would not be ready for another day and a half. Alvin Wirtz and Oscar Chapman of the Interior Department were delegated to bring the members of the committee into line. By nine the next morning all appeared to be going very well. Wirtz and Chapman reported an enthusiastic approval by the committee members they had been able to contact, and it seemed likely they might be able to stampede the convention for Roosevelt that night. The roof fell in on their plans, however, when Hopkins reported that he had talked to the President that morning, and he did not want the convention stampeded. He did not care that it was drab and he was quite satisfied with the way things were going. There was nothing to do but forget their plans and proceed with their regular schedule.[20]

Ickes, however, was still sure some dramatic coup would be necessary to salvage the convention from the wily conservatives, and he was nearly thrown into a panic when Herbert Agar and Ulric Bell, the editor and Washington correspondent for the Louisville *Courier Journal*, reported that the Farley forces thought they might be able to win, and there was talk of a Farley-Wheeler ticket. At their urging he fired off a long and dramatic telegram to the President pleading that "you must see to it that that nomination is forthcoming in circumstances that will assure a successful campaign against appeasers . . . the control of this convention is in the hands of men who are determined to destroy you at any cost." The President should, he thought, make a personal appearance, demand a short platform of his own dictation, and "insist upon a candidate for Vice President who sees eye to eye with you on both domestic and foreign questions, a man who will be generally considered to have sufficient stature to be the head of the nation."[21] A second and understandably shorter telegram was also sent by Agar, Bell, Maury Maverick, newspapermen John Franklin Carter and Harry Bingham, and Verda W. Barnes, Vice President of the Young Democratic Clubs of America, also requesting the President to come to the convention.[22]

At the same time Frances Perkins, who was also alarmed at the bad feelings and the antithird-term mood she encountered, was moved—by Robert Allen, who had predicted in his column that the President would fly out to the convention—to call the President and ask him to come to Chicago. He refused point blank but did suggest that Eleanor might come if Miss Perkins called her. "You know," he said, "Eleanor always makes people feel right. She has a fine way with her."[23] After some wheedling and an invitation from Jim Farley, Eleanor agreed to come, though she did not arrive until her husband was already nominated.

Tuesday night, the second of the convention, was in some respects the low point of the third-term drive. Senator Alben Barkley, as Permanent Chairman, delivered his address, a scathing denunciation of Republican nominee Wendell Willkie, and inadvertently touched off a twenty-five minute demonstration for Roosevelt when he was only a third of the way through his speech.[24] It was genuine and enthusiastic, but it was premature.[25] When his diatribe was finished, Barkley read the long-awaited message to the convention from Roosevelt, making it clear that "all of the delegates to this convention are free to vote for any candidate."[26] This, of course, included Roosevelt, and it was expected to touch off a giant demonstration which might well stampede the convention. Had Mayor Kelly left it to the delegates to start the demonstration, however, there would have been none; they sat in stunned silence trying to determine what the message signified. Kelly had left nothing to chance, however, and a few seconds later the famous "voice from the sewer," Thomas D. McGarry, the Chicago superintendent of sewers, began bellowing "We want Roosevelt" from a microphone hidden in the basement of the hall. Immediately the aisles filled with demonstrators whom Mayor Kelly had also thoughtfully provided. The shabby proceedings went on for nearly forty-five minutes, with McGarry periodically chanting "Chicago wants Roosevelt; the party wants Roosevelt; New York wants Roosevelt," and so on down the line, and with Alben Barkley occasionally chiming in to remind the silent galleries that they were guests and should behave themselves.

For those who still could not get the drift of the President's message, Hopkins spelled it out to the press.

"Do you expect President Roosevelt to be renominated on the first ballot?" asked one reporter.

"Yes, sir," snapped Hopkins happily.

"Then the President's statement makes no change in your plans here?"

"Not any, brother."[27]

At this point it appeared that the only major hurdle the New Dealers faced to Roosevelt's renomination by a reasonably united party was the platform and particularly the troublesome foreign-relations plank. A group led by Senators Wheeler, David I. Walsh of Massachusetts, Pat McCarran of Nevada, Bennett Clark of Missouri, Edwin Johnson of Colorado, Worth Clark of Idaho, and former Under Secretary of War Harry Woodring, were threatening to bolt the convention unless a thoroughly isolationistic plank was accepted.[28] Their proposal included the statement, "We, therefore, dedicate ourselves to the proposition that we shall never use our armed forces in a war of aggression, nor shall we send those armed forces to engage in wars in Europe and Asia."[29] Cordell Hull, on the other hand, who felt that Roosevelt's internationalist stand was the only real excuse for a third term, was warning that such a plank would be a clear invitation to further aggression by Japan.[30] Indeed, the plank originally suggested by Adolph Berle for the State Department contained the statement, "We affirm that the surest way to preserve the safety of the United States is and has been to render all material aid and assistance consistent with international law to nations combating those forces of destruction and violence which threaten our national safety. . . ." There was no mention at all of not sending troops anywhere, though later State Department drafts included pledges against "sending our boys" to foreign wars.[31] Eventually Byrnes was able to work out a compromise satisfactory to everyone but Hull by adding to the pledge against foreign wars the words, "except in case of attack."[32]

That left only the problem of winning sufficient votes on the first ballot to insure a convincing Roosevelt draft. To this end, pressure of the most ruthless kind was applied to the opposition, particularly those New York and Massachusetts delegates still loyal to Farley. Even Ambassador Joseph Kennedy received a cable in Great Britain suggesting that his son, Joseph, Jr., a member of the Massachusetts delegation, change his mind about voting for Farley. In this instance, however, the pressure failed.[33] In addition, William Bankhead was induced to withdraw from the race by the promise of a fair chance for the vice presidency,[34] and it was Senator Lister Hill of Alabama who placed Roosevelt's name before the convention.[35] Senator Wheeler, on the fence until the very last minute, was also forced to withdraw. Before the convention ever began, his intentions appeared fairly clear. While he was standing in the lobby of the Stevens Hotel, someone tried to pin one of Mayor Kelly's "Just Roosevelt" buttons on his coat. "Like hell you will," he snapped, tearing it off. "My name is going before the convention too."[36] He had a four-room headquarters in the Stevens, with pretty girls passing out Wheeler buttons, and Bennett Clark had been asked to place his name before the convention.[37] New Deal pressure was sufficient, however, to shake his own none-too-enthusiastic Montana delegation,[38] and the Kelly "demonstrators" reportedly smashed up the signs prepared for his demonstration.[39] Senator Clark never got a chance to give his speech. Cordell Hull, too, had a message to the convention prepared in case someone tried to put his name forward in competition with Roosevelt, but it was not found necessary to read it.[40] In addition to all the backstage preparations, the galleries for the nominating session Wednesday night were jammed with Kelly followers primed to cheer and hiss at the proper times,[41] and other Kelly-hired "demonstrators" were on hand to make any show of enthusiasm for anyone other than Roosevelt very difficult.[42]

That left only the three recalcitrant antithird-term conservatives—Farley, Garner, and Tydings—standing between a necessary first vote and a far more impressive renomination by acclamation, and the feeling against them in some circles was, for a time, rather intense.[43] Nevertheless, despite boos and catcalls from the galleries, their names went before the convention. Carter Glass, muttering inaudibly at a microphone that was too high for him most of the time, touched off a rather pathetic five-minute demonstration for Farley (the Kelly musicians were totally silent), and then added that he had just received two anonymous messages objecting to Farley because of his Catholicism. "When I reflect that one of the three achievements of Thomas Jefferson which he most valued was the Virginia statute in favor of religious freedom, it made me more determined to present his name than I otherwise would be," said the eighty-year-old Virginian.[44] "When I think of Carter's failure in 1928 to lift one little finger against the raising of the religious issue in Virginia," sneered Roosevelt waspishly, "it lowers my respect for the fundamental integrity of the old man."[45]

Wright Morrow of Texas placed Garner's name before the convention in a rather lengthy speech that contained no attack on anyone,[46] but Edward J. Colgan, Jr., of Maryland, who gave the nominating speech for Millard Tydings, opened old wounds by the score. Not only did he reject the notion that Roosevelt was indispensable but he also lauded Tydings for fighting to preserve the Court in the "historical struggle" in defense of Constitutional government and for defeating "a great and popular President" in the Maryland primaries of 1938.[47]

The first and only ballot proved at once that all fears and alarms over rising conservative strength had been groundless. Of the 1100 total votes, Roosevelt received 946½, or 86 per cent of the total; Farley received 72½, Garner 61, Tydings 9½, and Hull 5½. When Farley followed Sam Rayburn to the platform to move the rules be suspended and Roosevelt nominated by acclamation, however, there was no question about his personal popularity. The cheers and wild applause were for Farley, not Roosevelt.[48] Farley was bitter toward the third termers, but he was a party man to the end, and as one young observer noted, "Farley received tremendous ovation in announcing his support of the nominee. Situation appears more harmonious than appeared possible earlier."[49]

That the situation did not remain harmonious was largely the result of Roosevelt's refusal to take anyone into his confidence about his intentions once he was nominated. It was known that Cordell Hull was his first choice for the vice presidency, and Robert Jackson flatly told reporters the day before the convention opened that Hull would be the vice-presidential candidate.[50] But Hull refused point blank to be "kicked upstairs" ("I said 'No, by God!' and 'By God, No!'"),[51] and Jimmy Byrnes, the man who would have been Roosevelt's second choice, had been eliminated earlier because he had abandoned the Catholic religion and was vulnerable to bigots from both sides.[52] Probably there would have been relatively few serious objections had Roosevelt made it clear at once that he wanted Wallace for his running mate. To be sure, Wallace had little or no strength at the convention and could not

even win the support of his own Iowa delegation, which was inclined to favor Clyde Herring,[53] but no one seriously questioned
the President's right to name the man who would be running with
him. What angered many was that the word had been passed by
the New Dealers, who lacked any instructions and were apparently
eager to insure total third-term support, that the field was open,
and enthusiastic campaigning had been going on ever since.[54]

Within a matter of hours after the word was given that it
would be an open fight, a dozen candidates were vying for the
honor, ignorant that Roosevelt had already privately dismissed
almost all but one of them. Speaker Bankhead, who had been personally assured by Hopkins that the field was open, had already
been written off by Roosevelt as too old and in poor health,[55] and,
indeed, he did die the following September. Burton K. Wheeler,
who had previously refused to consider the vice presidency, now
changed his mind and set about letting the New Dealers know it.[56]
Louis Johnson, Assistant Secretary of War, whose plan for the
regimentation of industry in case of war had roused intense liberal
distrust,[57] was going about informing everyone that the President
had given him "the green light."[58] Governor Lloyd Stark of Missouri, whom Roosevelt dismissed as a conservative with no sense
of humor, had thrown his hat in the ring[59] as had Scott Lucas of
Illinois, Culbert Olson of California, Sam Rayburn and Jesse Jones
of Texas, and Paul McNutt of Indiana.

Many of the candidates had strong followings behind them,
and all were orthodox Democrats with a long record of party
loyalty. It was with considerable anguish of spirit, then, that they
and the other party professionals learned of Roosevelt's decision
to back Wallace.[60] The result was a sullen grumbling among the
delegates that boded ill for the President's choice. Some eighty-five
Olson-pledged delegates from thirty-two states went so far as to
send Roosevelt what amounted to a rather insulting round-robin
telegram protesting the choice of Wallace, who, they predicted,
would be "crucified and cannot carry Western States and Southern
States." As to the effect of the choice on the convention, "The
morale of the delegates," they asserted, "is typified by a sense of
keen disappointment in the democratic process. The common ex-
pression is to the effect that you have made a grave mistake and

that such dictatorial tactics should at least have been more subtly planned."[61]

Roosevelt attributed the opposition to the "old-line conservatives" and "the Hater's Club" making their final stand against a "true liberal,"[62] and Claude Pepper referred to them as "a little group of willful men,"[63] but it is quite evident that unless one considers the vast majority of the delegates in that category, both were wrong. It was certainly not the view of New Dealer Harold Ickes, who, seeing the sharp opposition to Wallace, took the bull by the horns and wired the President to suggest the Chancellor of the University of Chicago, Robert Hutchins or, in the very likely event that that choice did not appeal to him, Ickes himself as his running mate.[64] "Dear old Harold," laughed Roosevelt. "He'd get fewer votes even than Wallace in that convention."[65]

In addition to being the dictated candidate to an unhappy convention, Wallace's unpopularity was intensified by the fact that he was a former Republican with little political support from anyone and because he had a growing reputation of being a dreamer and perhaps even something of a crackpot with a taste for astrology and other occult practices.[66] Roosevelt, however, wanted a New Dealer to succeed him if anything happened to him,[67] and he was grimly determined that the party should take the man of his choice and that the galling defeats of the previous three years should be avenged. "Well, I suppose all the conservatives in America are going to bring pressure on the convention to beat Henry," he growled. "The fellow they want is either Jesse or Bankhead. I'm going to tell them that I won't run with either of those men or with any other reactionary. . . . I won't deliver that acceptance speech until we see whom they nominate."[68] He made it even more abundantly clear when Hopkins called to tell him about the anti-Wallace feeling at the convention. "Well, damn it to hell," he snapped, "they will go for Wallace or I won't run and you can jolly well tell them so."[69]

By the time of the vice-presidential nominating session, most of the other candidates who had been "given the green light" had ceased campaigning for votes and made it clear they were for Wallace or at least not interested in running themselves. Their reactions ran the gamut from Lloyd Stark, who fired off a wire to Wallace five minutes after he heard of the President's choice, expressing his delight and "sincerest congratulations on your certain nomination and election,"[70] to Jesse Jones, who was receiving the strong backing of Jim Farley and Elliott Roosevelt, though not his own Texas state delegation, right up to nomination time, when Eleanor Roosevelt arrived and got both Elliott and Farley to cease campaigning.[71]

Despite Mrs. Roosevelt's efforts to calm the convention with a soothing talk, it was soon clear that the delegates were openly hostile to Wallace and eager to cheer and vote for anyone who would stay in the race against him. A bitter floor fight ensued. Speaker William Bankhead, who had refused to withdraw in favor of Wallace, was placed in nomination first and received an enthusiastic fifteen-minute demonstration. Maryland's conservative National Committeeman, Howard Bruce, nominated Jesse Jones; Philip Kornbein nominated anti-New Deal Senator Alva Adams of Colorado; and John Wells of Oklahoma received the loudest applause of all when he placed the name of Paul McNutt before the convention. McNutt, who could probably have won the nomination in spite of Roosevelt, went to the speaker's platform to withdraw his name, but it was a full twenty minutes before the wildly cheering and stomping crowd ran out of breath long enough for him to put three sentences together to withdraw his name from contention.[72] Before the roll call was completed, Senator Prentiss Brown of Michigan, Scott Lucas of Illinois, and newspaperman Bascom Timmons were all added to the roll of candidates, though Jesse Jones, Brown, and Lucas also withdrew their names.[73] By the time the balloting started, it was clear that Wallace would not win without an embarrassingly close fight.

In the meantime Jimmy Byrnes learned that Elliott Roosevelt was circulating in the convention hall and telling the delegates that anyone of three candidates would be acceptable to his father. Rushing to a phone, Byrnes called the White House and was informed that Elliott had not seen his father in more than a month and, further, that the President would not accept the nomination if Wallace were not nominated.[74] Pleading and cajoling, he rushed from delegation to delegation with the President's threat.[75] At the same time Jim Farley caused a near panic among the third-term forces when a worried Senator Joseph Guffey rushed up to him with the news that Roosevelt would not run again unless Wallace were nominated. "Good," cracked Chairman Farley. "Let's not nominate him."[76] The report was soon spreading that the conservatives were waging a last-ditch "stop Wallace" drive. Indeed, Farley did gain some measure of revenge for the "theft" of his New York votes in the presidential balloting. Nearly half of the delegates from that state assumed that Wallace would be nominated by acclaim or were too disgusted to care and went home. Governor Lehman, who had refused Farley the votes he felt he had coming to him, expected to cast the state's ninety-six votes for Wallace anyway until Farley warned him he would demand a roll call. The governor was forced to allow those present to vote for whom they wished,[77] and Wallace received forty-seven of fifty-eight votes instead of all ninety-six.[78]

The Secretary of Agriculture won on the first ballot, but the margin was uncomfortably narrow. He received only 628 votes to 459 for his combined rivals, which was not much more than the bare majority needed to win.[79] During the course of the voting Roosevelt became so worried and angered that he wrote out a speech declining the nomination and placing the blame for his action squarely on the "forces of conservatism and reaction" within the party.[80] While it is impossible to determine how much of the opposition to Wallace was ideological and how much the result of disappointment and the sheer desire for a good brawl, it is certain that most conservatives found Wallace's nomination obnoxious to say the least. Typical of their point of view was the comment of Governor Sam Jones of Louisiana, who remarked, "I'm one thousand per cent against Wallace,"[81] or that of Governor Leon Phillips of Oklahoma, who admitted that Wallace was his second choice, his first choice being "anyone—red, white, black or yellow—that can get the nomination."[82]

So unhappy was the convention over the necessity of nominating Wallace that Byrnes and Hopkins talked him out of addressing the delegates for fear of the storm of protest that was likely to greet him.[83] Eventually the hall quieted down to hear President Roosevelt's calm voice—somewhat like a father talking to unruly children, someone remarked—accepting the draft because, having called so many others to emergency duty, he could not, he said, now refuse the call to serve again.[84]

Several things immediately seemed clear as the delegates disgustedly wended their way out of the hot convention hall that night. To many observers the most important single development appeared at the time to be the seizure of control of the party machinery by the New Dealers.[85] The conservatives were left without a place on the ticket or a place in the platform, and it seemed, as one reporter noted, that the days of Democrats like Garner, Farley, Tydings, Van Nuys, and Harrison were as much a part of the past as were those of Al Smith, John Raskob, John W. Davis and James Reed. The party now belonged to people like Sherman Minton, Claude Pepper, Harry Hopkins, Frances Perkins, and Harold Ickes.[86] In effect, Roosevelt's drive to liberalize and modernize the Democratic party which had apparently foundered for good in the Purges of 1938 had at last borne fruit. The purge of 1940 had been successful. Historian Edgar Robinson has gone so far as to state that the traditional national Democratic party disappeared to be succeeded by the Roosevelt party.[87] Later developments in the campaign, however, make that analysis appear to be a trifle extreme.

Certainly Roosevelt's ability to jam Wallace down the throats of the unhappy delegates seemed to indicate an almost dictatorial control over the party, and it was some measure of his confidence in his own power and his determination to overcome his adversaries of the previous four years or wreck the party in the process that he held out for Wallace against the pleas of almost all his advisers. Though Hopkins and Paul Appleby begged him to call the six other leading contenders for the vice presidency and smooth their ruffled feathers, he refused to talk to more than one. Hopkins and Wallace, neither of whom was noted for tact or suavity, were told to see the others.[88] Perhaps the extent of Roosevelt's victory was best expressed by Washington humorist George Allen when an irate Louisiana delegate grabbed him by the lapels as he was leaving the convention and told him indignantly, "No one wanted Wallace—absolutely no one. Name me just one man that did." Said Allen calmly, "Brother, that I can do—and that one man was Roosevelt."[89]

Although most of the party regulars were able to swallow their chagrin—like Senator Pat Harrison, who told reporters solemnly, "To me, Wallace is fine"[90]—it was obviously one thing to nominate an all New Deal ticket and something else again to engender enough party enthusiasm to get it elected. As Roosevelt noted, the battle over Wallace was likely to cost the party a good many votes in the fall.[91] Control of the party machinery Roosevelt now had, but he was a wily enough politician to realize that it would not be worth much in the hands of New Deal amateurs.

The Campaign: Return to Normalcy

It was soon evident that the sulphurous emotions released at the convention were not going to die down at once. Senator Clyde Herring, who had had some designs on the vice presidency himself, wrote that while he still had some hopes of winning Iowa from the Republicans in November, "the unfavorable reaction to the control of the Convention by a little group who never voted the Democratic ticket, and the ticket itself below the President, is not going to help us in our state very much."[92] Frank McHale, who was already beginning the McNutt campaign for 1944, found that a number of the delegates were remaining "very frank and bitter," and were indicating they would not support the ticket, although others "have cooled off and have reconsidered their first reaction to the convention."[93] Antithird-term letters, which poured into the White House once the President was renominated, reiterated over and over the fear of dictatorship and, perhaps more often, a hearty dislike for Hopkins, Corcoran, Jackson, Ickes, and New Dealers in general.[94]

A certain number of defections from the party was to be expected, especially among conservatives with nothing to lose like Al Smith, who wanted the Democratic party defeated so it could rid itself of the minority bloc of New Dealers and return to the principles of Thomas Jefferson;[95] Senator Ed Burke, who had been defeated in his bid for renomination; John O'Connor, the only member of Congress who was successfully purged in 1938; former Senator James Reed of Missouri; and Stephen Chadwick, the National Commander of the American Legion.[96] What was surprising and somewhat alarming was the number of political amateurs and intellectual leaders who had formerly been in the Roosevelt camp but were now defecting—men like former Director of the Budget Lewis Douglas; former Under Secretary of the Treasury John Hanes; Alan Valentine, President of the University of Rochester; Hamilton Holt, President of Rollins College; Ernest Hopkins, President of Dartmouth; and Charles Seymour, President of Yale.[97] To be sure, many of them had always been conservative—Roosevelt remarked of Hanes and Douglas that their slant of mind ran more to dollars than to humanity[98]—but their numbers were, nevertheless, impressive. Most of the leaders of the Garner movement outside of Texas could also be found in the Willkie camp. The defectors made themselves useful to Willkie in two ways. A Democrats-for-Willkie organization was set up under the leadership of Hanes, Douglas, Valentine, and Mrs. Roberta Campbell Lawson, who was president of the General Federation of Woman's Clubs, to campaign among the rank-and-file Democrats.[99] The motto on their letterhead was, appropriately enough, "We Want Our Party Back." In the Senate, Ed Burke called together his Judiciary Subcommittee to hold hearings on his proposed amendment to the Constitution to limit the presidential term of office to one six-year term. The hearings were, of course, a sounding board for anti-third term witnesses like Bainbridge Colby, Secretary of State for a short time under Wilson; John W. Davis, former Democratic presidential nominee; Young B. Smith and Ignatius Wilkinson, deans of the Columbia and Fordham law schools; and scores of others.[100] The hearings lasted throughout most of the campaign.

By far the most serious defection, however, was John L. Lewis, especially since it occurred barely a week before the election. Since Lewis headed organizations totalling ten million members—if their families were added in, nearly a fourth of the total population[101]— it appeared that a devastating blow had been struck the third-term cause, particularly since Lewis stated that if Roosevelt were reelected, he would consider it a vote of no-confidence in his judgment by the members of the C.I.O. and would resign as president.[102] When Sidney Hillman called at the White House the day after Lewis' speech, he found the President and Harry Hopkins more depressed and frightened than he had ever seen them.[103]

It was obvious almost at once, however, that whatever motives Lewis had for opposing Roosevelt, they were not shared by the vast majority of the leaders and members of the C.I.O. or even, for that matter, by the majority of members of the U.M.W. All of the large unions within the C.I.O. except the U.M.W. almost immediately repudiated Willkie, and all six of the C.I.O. vice presidents continued to work for Roosevelt.[104] Letters reassuring the President of their support poured in from politicians and labor leaders great and small throughout the nation. Typical of the latter was one from the secretary of a local of mine workers in West Virginia. Said the miners, "In regard to a broadcast we heard John L. Lewis make on the 25th of October concerning the election of Windel Wilkey [sic]. He may want Wilkey for President but we dont [sic] want him for anything."[105] Others were more bitter, even accusing Lewis of selling out to big business. Only the extreme left wing of the C.I.O., represented by leaders like Harry Bridges of the West Coast Longshoremen and Warehousemen, Joseph Curran of the National Maritime Union, Mike Quill of the Transport Workers, and Leo LaMotte of the Automobile Workers, followed the Communist party line, which found both Roosevelt and Willkie unacceptable, and remained silent.[106] Clearly the differences between Lewis and Roosevelt were more personal than ideological, and the vast majority of union leaders did not find the Democratic party so conservative that the Republicans looked liberal by comparison.

Probably more devastating in the long run than any of the noisy defections was the quiet sit-down strike of antithird-term party regulars and especially Jim Farley. Liberals of the *New Republic* sort might rejoice that Farley's hand had been removed from the party's tiller,[107] but Roosevelt knew he needed Farley and needed him badly. At the July 26 Cabinet meeting the President pleaded with him to remain on as National Committee Chairman because "otherwise there would be serious repercussions within the party and I know you would be the last one to want that." If he did not care to do any of the work, would he at least leave his name on the party's letterheads as chairman?[108] Farley, however, was still coldly furious at the "theft" of his New York delegates at the convention and, for that matter, for several years of neglect and abuse by the New Dealers.[109] He refused all entreaties then and later to retain the post, although he did pledge his full support to the Roosevelt-Wallace ticket.[110]

His full support, however, turned out to be considerably less than Roosevelt might have desired. It was widely remarked that at the New York state convention Farley, who had retained his state chairmanship, praised Lehman as a great governor but did not once mention Roosevelt.[111] Despite the fact that over a dozen letters a day were being received at Democratic headquarters pleading for a national radio address by Farley in order to save the Catholic vote,[112] Farley would not be moved. He did appear with Roosevelt at the President's Madison Square Garden speech and at the Brooklyn Academy of Music three days later,[113] but he said nothing. Finally, on the very eve of the election he wired New York party workers urging that "every possible vote obtainable is brought to the polls on election day in support of President Roosevelt and the entire Democratic ticket."[114] His total contribution to the campaign was limited entirely to New York and of virtually no use at all to people like Mrs. Earl F. Ketcham, National Committee Woman from Nebraska, who wrote:

> I have just talked to Jim Quigley, our National Committeeman, . . . and we feel that there is nothing can be done for our state to carry it for the President that would help as much as having Jim Farley come into Omaha and give a talk at the big City Auditorium. . . . Next to the President, he is undoubtedly the best loved man in our party and Nebraskans would follow his advice. . . . The situation in Nebraska is worse than I have ever known it but we have many loyal workers and you may be sure I am going to work night and day trying to save us from the disgrace of being classed with Maine and Vermont.[115]

Reports that Democratic leaders were irked with Farley's behavior were quite true, and some of them stayed irked for a good many years thereafter.[116]

Nor were the other antithird-term Democrats any more help-ful, though none of those actually holding office bolted the party. There were reports almost immediately after the convention that most of those Senators who had opposed the Court bill in 1937 and the Purge in 1938 would go on a sit-down strike during the campaign,[117] and most of them did. Senator Van Nuys was the most outspoken. Said he, "I am still opposed to a third term for anybody and I doubt its acceptability by the American people."[118] "Cotton Ed" Smith, like Vice President Garner, refused to take any part in the campaign or vote at all. "I don't approve of him and I couldn't vote for him," said Smith of the President. "It is impossible for me to consider voting anything but the Democratic ticket and there is no Democrat to vote for."[119] The situation in Maryland was reportedly dangerous to the Democratic cause be-cause of defections of some of the leaders and the attitude of men like National Committeeman Howard W. Bruce and Senator Mil-lard Tydings. Tydings said nothing publicly against (or for) Roosevelt, but he made his opinion clear by openly advocating Burke's Constitutional Amendment.[120] Reports from local leaders to the President indicated apathy and foot-dragging by the state and local machines. Said one disgustedly, "Our so-called leaders have shown remarkable agility to avoid an open endorsement of your candidacy."[121]

In Virginia Senators Glass and Byrd agreed not to campaign for Roosevelt, even to the extent of not mentioning his name in any of their speeches.[122] Glass did eventually relent to the extent of making a public statement that anyone who took part in the party's convention was honorably obliged to abide by its decision, and he was, therefore, voting the Democratic ticket.[123]

The Texas state organization, under the direction of the newly elected National Committeeman Myron Blaylock, a Garner backer, limited its campaign to optimistic statements about the outcome.[124] Senator Tom Connally, however, who had been at odds with the Administration from time to time and openly opposed the third term as a matter of principle, campaigned for Roosevelt in several states to "make sure of winning the forthcoming election and pre-vent the isolationist Republicans from taking over."[125] Senator Wheeler, who himself was running—very successfully—for re-election, and Senator Alva Adams of Colorado, both of whom had been on record as opposing the third term, stated grudgingly they would vote for Roosevelt as a matter of party loyalty.[126]

Whether the opposition to Roosevelt's re-election by the anti-third-term dissidents went any further than mere foot dragging cannot be proved. Alan Valentine, Executive Director of the Democrats-for-Willkie organization, suspected the loyalty of some enough to request Emil Hurja, a former Garner backer, to ask Senators Alva Adams, Bennett Clark, Worth Clark, and Millard Tydings to suggest the best possible state advisory chairman for the Willkie Democrats in their states,[127] and Labor's representative at the Democratic campaign headquarters, Dan Tobin,, felt that the "sincerity and unity necessary to win did not prevail amongst many of the former leaders of the Democratic party."[128]

Faced with so much disaffection within the regular party organization, Roosevelt realized that party leaders would have to be mollified, and the New Dealers were accordingly called sharply to heel. The first indication that they were not heirs apparent to the party machinery was the appointment of Bronx boss Ed Flynn to succeed Farley as Democratic National Chairman. Growled an unhappy Harold Ickes:

> For whatever reason the appointment was made, in my judgment it was an unfortunate one. Flynn is a typical big-city political boss in alliance with Tammany Hall. . . . a man who has become rich out of politics and who has enriched his friends, while building up what is acknowledged to be a very powerful machine in the Bronx.[129]

The dislike was mutual, and Flynn wasted no time in letting the New Dealers know he was no Jim Farley and would not be ignored or passed over for any reason.

His first action was to inform the President that he did not want the New Deal amateurs associated with his professional National Committee in any way during the campaign. The two groups were, he said, like oil and water, and he would be in no way responsible for the activities of the New Dealers. He suggested they establish their own headquarters and campaign in their own way. After some discussion Roosevelt agreed.[130] Flynn also made it clear that he expected political appointments to be cleared through him and to go largely to members of the regular party organizations. "The trouble was," recalled Flynn, "that the New Dealers who surrounded him were constantly belittling the Democratic organizations and were continually suggesting names of people who were opposed to the organizations." When the President appointed a New Dealer to be Federal District Attorney in New York without consulting him, Flynn promptly got on the phone and told Roosevelt he was resigning. He was talked into staying on the job, but on his own terms.[131]

His problems with the New Dealers in the Cabinet were of a different sort. They could not be dismissed as political amateurs, and with the President refusing to do any active campaigning until quite late, they were forced to carry much of the brunt of the campaign. Flynn considered them "prima donnas" because of their demand for national radio time, which was an extremely expensive item.[132] One sizzling encounter occurred when Ickes was scheduled by the National Committee to speak in Oregon and several other places in the West. Willis Mahoney and the Oregon Democrats apparently wanted nothing to do with him and so informed Paul Aiken, chairman of the party's speaker's bureau. Ickes, who was already on his way West when he heard about it, was furious, but his anger then was quite mild compared to his reaction to a Steve Early suggestion (via Charles Michelson) that he make his western trip an inspection tour of reclamation, power, and natural resources projects, after which he might get some radio time—without any audience, without mentioning Willkie, and without any vituperation—to discuss power. Replied Ickes, "Cancellation of my trip at this stage is humiliating enough but to go sneaking about the West and Northwest (inspecting reclamation, power and other projects and then whispering inanities from radio studios, provided that I could get the time) is something that should not be asked of me and something that I cannot do." But the crux of the matter was, "I believe that the President is being imposed upon by men who don't want anyone outside the regular organization to have any credit for his victory, if he wins."[133] Eventually Roosevelt himself smoothed over the differences. Under the circumstances it is not surprising that Flynn referred to Ickes as a prima donna, and Ickes described Flynn as an "inept" National Chairman.[134]

Another victim of the exigencies of party unity during election year was the volatile Tom Corcoran, whose ruthlessness and aggressiveness, particularly in the field of political appointments, had made him a major liability to the Administration.[135] Roosevelt suggested that he go to New York and work with the Citizens' Committee for Roosevelt, which was the organization of New Dealers that Flynn had suggested to Roosevelt. According to Ickes, in that capacity he "lifted the campaign by its own bootstraps and made a contribution to the final victory in 1940 for which others have claimed and received credit that was not theirs."[136] He was, nevertheless, through as a presidential confidante.

Perhaps even more striking evidence that the liberal victory of July was more apparent than real was the replacement of Harry Hopkins with Jesse Jones as Secretary of Commerce in August. Roosevelt had told Jones before that his conservatism was good for the Administration and that he wanted him in the Cabinet;[137] by August he deemed the time had come to get rid of Hopkins and bring Jones into the spotlight. Undoubtedly it was one of the shrewdest gestures of the campaign. Congress was not only happy to confirm Jones, but unanimously passed a joint resolution allowing him to not only hold the Cabinet post but retain his position as head of all the lending agencies as well. Said Republican Senator Robert Taft, "I do not think that with the exception of the President of the United States any man in the United States ever enjoyed such power. I have no objection to giving Mr. Jones the additional power to act as Secretary of Commerce, but I think it is an extraordinary precedent justified only by the character of the man, and which I hope may not be repeated."[138] Jones made only one speech during the campaign, but it was not for his speaking ability that he had been appointed.

Part of the reason for the eclipse of the New Dealers after the convention was the nature of the campaign. Businessmen were being invited in great numbers to take part in the government's preparedness efforts, whereas many liberals, especially in the West, were isolationistic. Although there was a strong effort made to picture Willkie as "a tool of Wall Street,"[139] and various economic groups were reminded of the benefits they had received from the Democrats and were in danger of losing at the hands of the Republicans, the major stress was placed on national unity, peace, and freedom.[140] Significantly, one of the most popular and effective Democratic campaigners after the President himself, if one may judge from his many invitations to speak throughout the nation, was Senator Robert Wagner of New York.[141] An internationalist, he was a sufficiently orthodox Democrat to receive a long and cordial invitation from Mayor Kelly to address the annual Governor's Day gathering at the Illinois State Fair,[142] and enough of a New Dealer to go into Wisconsin and back Robert La Follette against James Finnegan, the conservative Democratic nominee for the Senate.[143] It was he, and not Secretary of Labor Frances Perkins, who answered John L. Lewis' blast against the Administration.[144]

Thus, by the time election day rolled around, it was apparent that although some conservatives had "taken a walk," and others were just sitting, the bulk of the campaigning had been done by and under the direction of the same sort of men who were directing campaigns when Roosevelt appeared on the scene in 1932. Besides Ed Flynn, the leaders were John Bankhead for the South, Sam Rayburn for the Southwest, Scott Lucas for the Midwest, and Leslie Miller for the Far West.[145] All had been around the party for a long time, and their methods of campaigning were the tried and true ones developed many long years before.[146] Max Lerner, in reviewing Farley's book *Behind the Ballots* one year before, observed that the day of the "pure politicians" like Farley was over because the New Deal had introduced the new "politics of the deed." Farley had been an innovator, but because he had not kept up with the times, he and his kind were about to become as extinct as the dodo. "Today there are new men for new methods—a Hopkins, an Ickes, a Wallace, a Lilienthal, above all a Corcoran."[147] If the campaign of 1940 proved anything, however, it was that the day of the "pure politician" was far from over, and the day of a Hopkins and "above all a Corcoran" had not yet dawned.

Any effort to determine the effects the liberal-conservative struggle within the Democratic party had on the 1940 election returns is doomed to failure from the start. There are simply too many important determinants such as the third-term issue and, above all, the foreign-policy issue to allow any clear cut analysis of voter motivation in other terms. Nevertheless, there are a few hints of the importance of the issue or lack thereof available.

Conservatives, New Dealers, and the Voters

First, it is clear that despite Roosevelt's trend toward the right before and during the campaign, his victory was largely attributable to the accomplishments of the New Deal. With the exception of the farmers, the grand coalition of 1936 had remained largely intact; the vote was, if anything, even more sharply divided along class lines than it had been in 1936.[148] The victory was won in the twelve largest cities, and according to analyst Samuel Lubell the dividing point between precincts that voted for Roosevelt and those that voted for Willkie in every case was income as expressed in housing rentals. Those who lived in areas where the rentals were lower than $45 a month voted heavily for Roosevelt; a majority of those who paid more than $60 a month voted for Willkie. The cutoff point was somewhere in between.[149] This analysis is complicated considerably, of course, when one takes into consideration the pro-Ally attitudes of ethnic groups like the Poles, the Slavs, and the Jews and the isolationist attitudes of the Germans and Italians. Moreover, where a political machine was particularly powerful, as in Jersey City, for example, it seems evident that the vote would have been delivered regardless of whether the Democratic candidate was liberal or conservative.[150] It would seem, however, that the economic lines were sharply enough drawn to suggest that the Democratic politicians were correct in assuming that no conservative Democratic candidate could have won the election.[151]

No certain conclusions can be drawn either about the effect of defectors from the party or opposition to Roosevelt's policies. It has been fairly well determined that John L. Lewis' endorsement of Willkie had next to no effect at all on the election. To be sure, Roosevelt's margin of victory in those areas heavily populated by members of the C.I.O. declined from 1936 by 6.2 per cent, but nationally it declined by 7.5 per cent. Had Lewis been able to swing as much as 20 per cent to 25 per cent of the C.I.O. vote to Willkie where it was most heavily concentrated, Roosevelt would have been defeated. As it was, Lewis' influence accounted for a change of less than 2 per cent of the national vote.[152]

It is probable that Jim Farley's lack of enthusiasm for the third term was slightly more serious. At least one leading New Dealer, Senator Sherman Minton, felt that he had been defeated partly because "we were double crossed in Indianapolis by our crowd and the Catholics in particular."[153] They were angered, he had been told, by the party's treatment of Farley.[154] By and large, however, Irish Catholic defections were not serious even where they might have meant the difference of a good many electoral votes—in Boston for instance. There the New Deal had meant federal jobs and prestige such as they had never known before, and neither the unhappiness of Farley nor the Administration's foreign policy was able to shake the loyalty of a very large number of them.[155] To be sure, on a nationwide scale Samuel Lubell found that the defection of voters of Irish ancestry from the Democratic party in 1940 was exceeded only by those of German and Italian ancestry,[156] but it seems more than probable that their feelings for Farley ranks well down on the list of reasons for this phenomenon.

There is, likewise, no way of showing any strong trend toward or away from the philosophy of the New Deal in the 1940 elections such as seemed so apparent to observers in 1938, other than by the continuing loyalty of the lower classes in the cities toward Roosevelt. As staunch a New Dealer as Minton was defeated in Indiana, but Edward Burke in Nebraska and William King in Utah were defeated in Democratic primaries specifically on the issue of their hostility to the New Deal.[157] Further, both liberal Burton K. Wheeler, who had frequently expressed disapproval of the third term and was bitterly critical of the Administration's foreign policy, and conservative Harry Byrd, who opposed the third term but approved of the foreign policy, ran well ahead of Roosevelt in their respective states,[158] although the President on the average ran better than Democratic candidates for Congress throughout the nation.[159]

One can only conclude that dissension in the Democratic ranks was a very mild and relatively unimportant motivation for voting in 1940, even though the dissenters included people as important as Jim Farley and John L. Lewis. Far more important were economic considerations based on class lines and the Administration's foreign policy, largely based on ethnic lines. From the point of view of retaining its power and control of federal offices, there is little doubt that the Democratic party owed a debt of gratitude to President Roosevelt and the New Dealers who had so long and faithfully worked for his third term.

CHAPTER VII

CONCLUSIONS

In retrospect, the nomination of Roosevelt in 1940 was hardly the lopsided victory for the New Dealers that it appeared at the time; there were elements of both defeat and compromise intermingled with the apparent success. To be sure, those conservatives and party regulars who had aspired to seize control of the party machinery as well as the office of the presidency had been thwarted. Those whose careers in national politics depended on being successful in this venture, such as Jim Farley and John Nance Garner, found the 1940 Democratic Convention the end of the trail. Some of lesser rank, such as Edward Burke, left the party entirely, but most were willing to "wait till next time."

As far as the liberals were concerned, however, the third-term drive, which had begun in the summer of 1938, was a confession of weakness, if not failure. President Roosevelt and the New Dealers had had visions of making the Democratic party over until it became a haven for liberals regardless of their political antecedents, of redrawing political lines so that voters would have a genuine, clear-cut choice at every election between a liberal and conservative ticket. To this end was the attempt to get rid of party conservatives in the Purge of 1938, the support of progressive third-party groups in a number of states at the expense of conservative Democratic party organizations, and even the entrusting of patronage power in the hands of Tom Corcoran rather than Jim Farley. As early as 1938, however, it was clear to some that the effort would end in failure. The conservatives and travel-worn "pure politicians" were as deeply entrenched as ever, and most of the insiders even then realized that no New Dealer, even—or perhaps especially—with President Roosevelt's backing could win the nomination in 1940. Perhaps Harry Hopkins, had he not become ill, might have been a threat, but in view of the tremendous storm of party protest against Henry Wallace at the convention even that seems highly improbable. One clear indication of New Deal weakness was the fact that Roosevelt had indicated more than once to intimates that his first choice as successor would be William O. Douglas, and yet even he did not dare suggest Douglas for Vice President in 1940. Because of his tremendous hold on the voters of the great coalition assembled in 1936, and because of his power to make and break local party bosses with the power of patronage, and because of his long, drawn-out silence which effectively hampered any campaigning by his rivals, and because of the war crisis, President Roosevelt was the overwhelming choice of the members of his party to be the 1940 Democratic nominee. Not included in the list of reasons is an overwhelming commitment to the aims and ideals of the New Deal on the part of the great majority of the delegates. Roosevelt was undoubtedly the only New Deal liberal who could have been nominated in July of 1940, but his New Deal liberalism was not the reason he was the party's choice.

As has already been pointed out before, Professor Edgar Robinson has suggested that when the 1940 Democratic Convention was led, dragging and kicking, to nominate Henry Wallace for Vice President, it marked the completion of the Roosevelt revolution; the New Dealers had succeeded in making over the Democratic party into a Roosevelt party, with only the forms and title of a by-gone day remaining. It was also the impression of contemporary commentators that the New Dealers had at last come into their own as political heavyweights. Two scenes at the convention dramatize rather graphically the impossibility of such a development. One is the picture of the immaculately groomed, perfectly tailored Baltimore aristocrat, Sumner Welles, being pushed and shoved down the aisle in the midst of a Roosevelt demonstration, with a tight little smile frozen on his face to indicate that he was wildly enthusiastic and having the time of his life. The other is the picture of the arrogant, acerbic, politician-baiting Rex Tugwell trying to drum up delegates for Henry Wallace before Roosevelt gave any indication that Wallace was his choice. To be sure, neither Welles nor Tugwell was part of the current inner circle, but they demonstrate the difficulties experienced by political amateurs in understanding and dealing with political leaders on the grass roots level. Similar but less picturesque examples might be given of Hopkins' treatment of friendly, hat-in-hand delegates or of Ickes' bid for the vice presidency for either himself or Robert Hutchins.

The fact was that after the National Democratic Convention of 1940 and the nomination of the Roosevelt-Wallace ticket the political alignment within the party remained unchanged. Some of the leaders had fallen by the wayside, but inasmuch as the forces they represented remained unchanged (one of the major forces being the determination to remain in office), others with different names and different faces but the same ideas immediately took their places. The New Dealers still retained control of the presidency and had gained control of the vice presidency—indeed, failure to win the vice presidency would have been an indication of incredible weakness and total repudiation—but the hollowness of even that victory for liberalism is rather well symbolized by the departure of Corcoran and the entry into the Cabinet of Jesse Jones. Congressional conservatives suffered no noticeable diminution of their power and no apparent change of principles, although the war emergency had pushed the entire New Deal issue into the background. Perhaps even more important, control of the machinery of the Democratic party remained firmly in the hands of party professionals. New Dealers found that Ed Flynn was merely another Jim Farley, only with sharper fangs, and the proceedings at the convention had only made him, if anything, more antagonistic toward them. As far as political appointments went, they had been better off with Farley. The party policies would continue to originate from the White House, but that represented no change from the previous eight years. There were, moreover, times during those previous eight years when the President's policies were both more liberal and far less subject to question by members of his own party than they were in 1940, as the struggle over the foreign-relations plank in the platform indicates.

For the other Democratic candidates the nomination of Roosevelt represented an experience in frustration. Of all those mentioned as presidential prospects undoubtedly Cordell Hull came the closest to seeing his rather mild ambitions realized. It seems quite likely that had Roosevelt withdrawn in favor of Hull at the convention as he had originally indicated to Hull that he would, the Secretary of State, with the aid of Farley and the Roosevelt endorsement, would have been nominated on the first ballot. Farley, who had no genuine presidential ambitions for himself, was said to control more than four hundred second-choice votes, and Hull was generally very satisfactory to party regulars everywhere. Further, the only other real threats left were Burton K. Wheeler and Paul McNutt. Wheeler would have had to contend with Roosevelt's well-known antipathy for him and support of Hull. Further, although the isolationists in the party were demonstrative and highly vocal at the convention, they were clearly a minority.

Paul McNutt's popularity is less easy to evaluate. Throughout the three years he was actively seeking the nomination, he demonstrated convincingly that he was the purest of pure politicians not excluding Farley, who at least made a stand for the principle of rotation of offices. McNutt's policies, if one may call them that, varied from a "middle-of-the-road wait-and-see" attitude in 1938, when the country appeared to be on the crest of a conservative wave, to cradle-to-grave welfare statism in the spring of 1940, when Roosevelt's approval was all important. Undoubtedly, under his suave exterior he was as cold and hard as the political writers of that day described him, but William Allen White's characterization of him as a Fascist was surely ludicrous. In many respects McNutt resembled Roosevelt himself more nearly than any of the other candidates. Like the Governor of New York in 1932, he was a pleasant young man who wanted very much to be President, and his policies were largely shaped by what his advisers of the moment thought the majority of citizens would vote for. Like Roosevelt, he was extremely handsome, an excellent speaker, and a tireless campaigner. He was, no doubt, ruthless—like Roosevelt—but he had the additional problem of having allowed this to become quite noticeable during his term as governor, something the aristocrat of Hyde Park never did. Perhaps the chief difference between them was the difference between New York politics and Indiana politics. No one knows how many delegates had given him second-choice pledges, probably a goodly number in the South and Far West, but it seems quite possible that had Hull been unable to capture a majority of the votes on the first ballot, the convention might have swung to McNutt. There was certainly no question of his popularity with the delegates. Farley and the New Dealers would have been most unhappy, but Roosevelt could hardly have complained, since he himself had appointed him to the responsible post of Security Administrator.

The voting in the 1940 election seems to indicate that no Democrat except Roosevelt could have defeated Willkie. The third-term nomination was no clear-cut victory for either side in the four-year war between liberals and conservatives, but a happy compromise with some benefits to both sides. The question of whether the same compromise could have been made without the pressure of World War II is what Roosevelt used to call an "iffey" one. It seems quite probable, however, that faced with the loss of office and program after probable defeat at the polls, the New Dealers and party regulars would have smoothed their differences in a time of the profoundest peace and drafted Roosevelt for a third term. Certainly Harold Ickes and others of the inner circle were trumpeting the call for a third term over a year before war broke out, and such non-New Dealish types as Mayor Ed Kelly and Mayor Frank Hague were also on record as favoring a third term before the war. In the last analysis the logic of numbers would probably have issued the call for a third term and a temporary truce in the liberal-conservative power struggle. Organized labor had more votes than management, debtors had more votes than creditors, farmers formed a more vocal voting bloc than consumers, there were far more people in the low income-tax brackets than the higher ones, and liberals, Negroes, and the unemployed loved Roosevelt more and in greater numbers than the wealthy hated him. Whether Roosevelt would have answered the call is a question which cannot be answered, but it seems almost certain that the call would have come.

NOTES

Notes to Chapter I

1. Arthur Schlesinger, Jr., *The Coming of the New Deal* (Boston, 1958), p. 568.
2. Arthur Schlesinger, Jr., *The Politics of Upheaval* (Boston, 1960), p. 592.
3. Interview with James Farley, November 9, 1963; William Leuchtenburg, *Franklin D. Roosevelt and the New Deal, 1932-1940* (New York, Evanston, and London, 1963), p. 190.
4. Rexford G. Tugwell, *The Democratic Roosevelt* (New York, 1957), p. 412.
5. William Allen White, New York *Times*, August 15, 1937.
6. Institute of Public Opinion Poll cited in Wilfred Binkley, *American Political Parties: Their Natural History*, 3rd ed. rev. (New York, 1959), p. 380.
7. Hugh Johnson, "Third Term????" *Saturday Evening Post*, CCXI (December 17, 1938), 56.
8. Stanley High, "Whose Party Is it?" *Saturday Evening Post*, CCIX (February 6, 1939), 11; Wilfred Binkley, *op. cit.*, p. 374.
9. Wilfred Binkley, *op. cit.*, pp. 367-368.

10. William Leuchtenburg, *op. cit.*, pp. 3-4.

11. New York *Times*, September 28, 1938.

12. Samuel Lubell, *The Future of American Politics* (New York, 1952), p. 48.

13. William Leuchtenburg, *op. cit.*, p. 188.

14. Saul Alinsky, *John L. Lewis: An Unauthorized Biography* (New York, 1949), p. 177.

15. Institute of Public Opinion Poll, cited by Wilfred Binkley, *op. cit.*, p. 380.

16. *Ibid.*

17. Franklin D. Roosevelt, *Public Papers of Franklin D. Roosevelt*, Vol. IX, ed. Samuel Rosenman (New York, 1941), p. 27.

19. *Ibid.;* Raymond Moley, *27 Masters of Politics* (New York, 1949), p. 40.

20. Stanley High, *Roosevelt—and Then?* (New York, 1937), p. 211.

21. Frank Walker, unpublished memoirs, Walker Papers (University of Notre Dame Archives, Notre Dame, Indiana). For a description of Roosevelt's brain-picking operations, see Raymond Moley, *After Seven Years* (New York, 1939), p. 20.

22. Joseph Alsop and Robert Kintner, *Men Around the President* (New York, 1939), p. 5.

23. For two views of the "First and Second New Deal thesis" see Arthur Schlesinger, Jr., *The Politics of Upheaval* (Boston, 1960), pp. 389, 392, 690-692.

24. Rexford G. Tugwell, *op. cit.*, p. 415.

25. Joseph Alsop and Robert Kintner, *op. cit.*, p. 113.

26. Joseph Alsop and Robert Kintner, *op. cit.*, p. 132; Stanley High, *op. cit.*, p. 46.

27. Alva Johnston, "White House Tommy," *Saturday Evening Post*, CCX (July 31, 1937), 7.

28. *Ibid.*, p. 65.

29. *Ibid.*, p. 5

30. Stanley High, *op. cit.*, p. 45.

31. Alva Johnston, *loc. cit.*, p. 65.

32. Blair Bolles, "Cohen and Corcoran: Brain Twins," *American Mercury*, XLIII (January, 1938), 44.

33. Frank Walker, unpublished memoirs, Walker Papers.

34. Joseph Alsop and Robert Kintner, *op. cit.*, p. 114; James McGregor Burns, *The Lion and the Fox* (New York, 1956), p. 325.

35. Stanley High, *op. cit.*, pp. 242, 247; also Stanley High, "Fog Over Washington," *Saturday Evening Post*, CCX (April 9, 1938), 110.

36. Gerald Johnson, *Roosevelt: Dictator or Democrat* (New York, 1941), p. 258.

37. Stanley High, "Whose Party Is It?" *Saturday Evening Post*, CCIX (February 6, 1937), 38.

38. Stanley High, *op. cit.*, pp. 141-143.

39. U.S., *Congressional Record*, 75 Cong., 1 Sess. (May 21, 1937), p. 4901.

40. Robert Sherwood, *Roosevelt and Hopkins*, Bantam Edition, 2 vols. (New York, 1950), Vol. I, pp. 110-111.

41. *Ibid.*, p. 94.

42. Stanley High, *op. cit.*, p. 135.

43. Robert Sherwood, *op. cit.*, p. 113.

44. Delbert Clark, "Who Will It Be in 1940? The Guessing Starts," *New York Times Magazine*, November 21, 1937, p. 23; Stanley High, "Will It Be Wallace?" *Saturday Evening Post*, CCX (July 3, 1937), 6.

45. *Fortune*, XV (April, 1937), 111.

46. New York *Times*, January 7, 1940.

47. *Ibid.*, March 5, 1940.

48. Sherman Minton to Franklin Roosevelt, March 22, 1937; Roosevelt to Minton, April 4, 1937 (Franklin D. Roosevelt Library, Hyde Park, New York, President's Secretary's File, Box 52). Cited hereafter as FDRL-PSF.

49. James A. Farley, *Jim Farley's Story: The Roosevelt Years* (New York, 1948), p. 82.

50. Joseph Alsop and Turner Catledge, *The 168 Days* (Garden City, New York, 1938), p. 204.

51. New York *Times*, June 24, 1937.

52. *Time*, July 5, 1937, p. 12.

53. Press Conference No. 377, June 29, 1937, FDRL.

54. *Fortune*, XV (July, 1937), 96-97.

55. "Third Term: Bad Medicine," *The Nation*, CVL (July 3, 1937), 5.

56. Steve Early to Franklin Roosevelt, September 3, 1937, in *F.D.R.: His Personal Letters*, ed. Elliot Roosevelt (New York, 1947-1950), p. 710. Cited hereafter as *Personal Letters*.

57. New York *Times*, June 25, 1937.

58. Albert Shaw, "Third Term Reticence," *Literary Digest*, CXXIV (October 9, 1937), 12.

59. William Leuchtenburg, *op. cit.*, pp. 252-253.

60. "Washington Bulletin," *Business Week* (September 4, 1937), p. 5.

61. New York *Times*, August 23, 1937.

62. *Ibid.*, August 27, 1937.

63. Washington *Herald*, September 24, 1937.

64. Interview with James Farley, November 9, 1963.

65. New York *Times*, October 5, 1937.

66. *Fortune*, XV (October, 1937), 109.

67. Stanley High, *op. cit.*, p. 310.

68. Donald McCoy, *Angry Voices: Left-of-Center Politics in the*

New Deal Era (Lawrence, 1958), pp. 158, 161; George Creel, "Parade to the Post," *Colliers*, C (October 2, 1937), 25.

69. George Creel, *loc. cit.*, p. 26; Bruce Bliven, "Pennsylvania under Earle," *New Republic*, XCII (August 18, 1937), 38; Eugene Pharo, "Governor Earle of Pennsylvania," *American Mercury*, XLIII (February, 1938), 166.

70. New York *Times*, April 10, 1937.

71. "The Labor Governors," *Fortune*, XV (June, 1937), 140.

72. *Ibid.*, p. 144; Bruce Bliven, *loc. cit.*, p. 38.

73. George Creel, *loc. cit.*, p. 26.

74. New York *Times*, April 5, 1937.

75. Stanley High, *op. cit.*, pp. 316-317.

76. The Labor Governors," *Fortune*, XV (June, 1937), 80-81, 138.

77. *New York Times Magazine*, February 21, 1937, p. 5; George Creel, *loc. cit.*, p. 26.

78. J. Woodford Howard, "Frank Murphy and the Sit-Down Strikes of 1937," *Labor History*, I (Spring, 1960), 114-115.

79. Franklin Roosevelt to Frank Murphy, February 11, 1937, FDRL-President's Personal File 1662. Cited hereafter as FDRL-PPF.

80. George Creel, *loc. cit.*, p. 26.

81. "The Labor Governors," *Fortune*, XV (June, 1937), 140.

82. J. Woodford Howard, *loc. cit.*, p. 137.

83. Joseph Alsop and Turner Catledge, *The 168 Days* (New York, 1938), p. 128.

84. V. O. Key, *Southern Politics in State and Nation* (New York, 1949), pp. 19-35.

85. Robert T. Cochran, Jr., "Virginia's Opposition to the New Deal, 1933-1940" (unpublished master's dissertation, Georgetown University, 1950), pp. 8-9.

86. Cited in *Personal Letters*, p. 443.

87. U.S., *Congressional Record*, 75 Cong., 1 Sess. (January 27, 1937), p. 496.

88. Carter Glass to William McAdoo, April 29, 1940, William McAdoo Papers (Library of Congress, Washington, D.C.), Box 471. Cited hereafter as McAdoo Papers.

89. U.S., *Congressional Record*, 75 Cong., 1 Sess. (January 12, 1937), p. 180.

90. *Time*, August 29, 1938, p. 11.

91. Joseph Alsop and Turner Catledge, *op. cit.*, p. 122.

92. Edward Burke to Franklin Roosevelt, August 17, 1934, FDRL-Official File 300, Box 43. Cited hereafter as FDRL-OF.

93. *Time*, April 12, 1937, p. 17.

94. *Ibid.*, August 2, 1937, p. 13.

95. Raymond Clapper, "Roosevelt Tries the Primaries," *Current History*, IL (October, 1938), 19.

96. E.g., Delbert Clark, "Who Will It Be in 1940? The Guessing Starts," *New York Times Magazine*, November 21, 1937, p. 22; Mark Sullivan, New York *Tribune*, November 19, 1939.

97. Joseph Alsop and Turner Catledge, *op. cit.*, p. 129. A much milder version of the same incident was given by the same authors in their article "Tom Jeff—He Loves the President, But—" *Saturday Evening Post*, CCIX (January 9, 1937), 6.

98. U.S., *Congressional Record*, 75 Cong., 3 Sess. (May 28, 1938), p. 7681.

99. A. Blair Crownover, "Franklin Roosevelt and the Primary Campaigns of the 1938 Congressional Elections" (unpublished senior essay, Princeton University, 1955), appendix ii.

100. Arthur Schlesinger, Jr., *The Politics of Upheaval* (Boston, 1960), p. 417.

101. Edward J. Flynn, *You're the Boss* (New York, 1947), p. 153.

102. Stanley High, *op. cit.*, p. 238.

103. Summary of Gallup Polls in Washington *Post*, August 29, 1937.

104. Delbert Clark, *loc. cit.*, p. 23.

105. "Farley for President," *American Mercury*, XLII (November, 1937), 257.

106. Mary Dewson, unpublished memoirs, Mary Dewson Papers, FDRL, pp. 50-51.

107. Interview with James Farley, November 9, 1963.

108. Samuel Rosenman, *Working with Roosevelt* (New York, 1952), p. 201.

109. Grace Tully, *F.D.R. My Boss* (New York, 1949), p. 180.

110. Raymond Moley, *27 Masters of Politics* (New York, 1949), p. 109.

111. Frank Walker, unpublished memoirs, Walker Papers.

112. "New York's Election," *New Republic*, XCIII (November 10, 1937), 5.

113. Cordell Hull, *The Memoirs of Cordell Hull* (New York, 1948), Vol. I, p. 855.

114. Thomas Stokes, Washington *Daily News*, May 6, 1937.

115. Frank Walker, *loc. cit.*

116. "Washington Bulletin," *Business Week* (August 21, 1937), p. 5.

117. Franklin Roosevelt to Jesse Jones, December 14, 1937, Jesse Jones Papers (Library of Congress, Washington, D.C.), Box 29.

118. Frank Walker, *loc. cit.*

119. George Creel, *loc cit.*, p. 26.

120. *Time*, March 1, 1937, p. 10; Joseph H. Friend, "Watch Paul McNutt," *Nation*, CXLVII (July 23, 1938), 87.

121. Oscar Ewing to Wesley Winans Stout, Editor of *Saturday*

Evening Post, January 27, 1940, Paul McNutt Papers (Lilly Library, Indiana University).
  122. Joseph H. Friend, *loc. cit.,* p. 88; *Time,* March 1, 1937, p. 10.
  123. James Farley, *Behind the Ballots* (New York, 1938), pp. 111, 146.
  124. James Farley, *op. cit.,* pp. 71-72.

Notes to Chapter II

  1. John Morton Blum, *From the Morgenthau Diaries: Years of Crisis, 1928-1938* (Boston, 1959), p. 327.
  2. Frank Walker, unpublished memoirs, Walker Papers.
  3. Arthur Krock, New York *Times,* February 5, 1937.
  4. *Time,* September 12, 1938, p. 23.
  5. Bascom N. Timmons, *Jesse H. Jones: The Man and the Statesman* (New York, 1956), p. 257.
  6. Raymond Moley, *After Seven Years* (New York, 1939), p. 83.
  7. Rexford G. Tugwell, *The Democratic Roosevelt* (Garden City, New York, 1957), p. 378.
  8. James Farley, *Jim Farley's Story: The Roosevelt Years* (New York, 1948), p. 183.
  9. Edward J. Flynn, *You're the Boss* (New York, 1947), p. 150.
  10. William Smathers to Franklin Roosevelt, June 21, 1937, Franklin D. Roosevelt Library, President's Personal File 4470. Cited hereafter FDRL-PPF.
  11. New York *Times,* April 7, 1940.
  12. *Ibid.*
  13. New York *Times,* January 7, 1937.
  14. The fullest account of the Court fight is Joseph Alsop and Turner Catledge, *The 168 Days* (New York, 1938).
  15. E.g., Rexford G. Tugwell, *The Democratic Roosevelt* (New York, 1957), p. 405; Dennis Brogan, *The Era of Franklin D. Roosevelt* (New Haven, 1950), p. 229; Arthur Mullen, *Western Democrat* (New York, 1940), p. 330.
  16. Joseph Alsop and Turner Catledge, *op. cit.,* p. 178.
  17. T.R.B., "Washington Notes," *New Republic,* XCII (August 4, 1937), 361.
  18. Burton K. Wheeler with Paul F. Healy, *Yankee from the West* (New York, 1962), pp. 322-323.
  19. Joseph Alsop and Turner Catledge, *op. cit.,* p. 87.
  20. Samuel I. Rosenman to Franklin D. Roosevelt, undated, FDRL-PPF 64.
  21. Josephus Daniels to Franklin Roosevelt, March 8, 1937,

Josephus Daniels Papers (Library of Congress, Washington, D.C.), Box 18. Cited hereafter as Daniels Papers.

22. Joseph Alsop and Turner Catledge, *op. cit.*, p. 93.

23. Interview with James Farley, November 9, 1963.

24. Joseph Alsop and Turner Catledge, *op. cit.*, p. 192.

25. Josephus Daniels to Franklin Roosevelt, February 27, 1937, Daniels Papers, Box 16.

26. James Farley, *op. cit.*, p. 82.

27. Roosevelt to Paul V. McNutt, May 17, 1937, FDRL-PPF 2836.

28. Arthur Krock, New York *Times*, June 16, 1937.

29. *Ibid.*, July 4, 1937.

30. U.S., *Congressional Record*, 75 Cong., 1 Sess. (July 6, 1937), p. 6798.

31. *Ibid.*

32. John Bankhead to Franklin Roosevelt, July 23, 1937, FDRL-PPF 1362.

33. Turner Catledge, New York *Times*, June 27, 1937.

34. New York *Times*, July 16, 1937. Copy of the press release in FDRL-PPF 3160.

35. *Ibid.*, July 16, 1937.

36. The alignment between liberals and conservatives was not perfect by any means. Claude Pepper, an ardent New Dealer, for instance, supported Harrison because of his close personal friendship with Harrison. Similar personal motives accounted for some of the Barkley votes. Interview with Claude Pepper, August 26, 1963.

37. James Farley, *op. cit.*, pp. 92-93. Alben Barkley, *That Reminds Me* (Garden City, New York, 1954), p. 155. A different story of the pressure put on Truman is told by Harold Gosnell in *Champion Campaigner: Franklin D. Roosevelt* (New York, 1952), pp. 169-170, but the weight of evidence is heavily on the side of the above interpretation.

38. *Time*, July 26, 1937, p. 12.

39. U.S. *Congressional Record*, 75 Cong., 1 Sess. (August 12, 1937), p. 8732.

40. New York *Times*, August 17, 1937.

41. Press Conference No. 360, April 15, 1937, FDRL.

42. New York *Times*, March 21, 1937.

43. Press Conference No. 360, April 15, 1937, FDRL.

44. New York *Times*, January 22, 1937.

45. Press Conference No. 338, January 22, 1937; New York *Times*, January 23, 1937.

46. U.S., *Congressional Record*, 75 Cong., 1 Sess. (April 2, 1937), p. 3066.

47. *Ibid.*, p. 3078.

48. *Ibid.*, p. 3136. The best source for how each Senator stood on the Court plan is the New York *Times*, July 11, 1937, and July 23, 1937.

49. *Ibid.* (April 5, 1937), p. 3136.

50. New York *Times*, April 8, 1937.

51. William Leuchtenburg, *Franklin D. Roosevelt and the New Deal, 1932-1940* (New York, Evanston, and London, 1963), p. 242.

52. Press Conference No. 377, June 29, 1937, FDRL.

53. New York *Times*, September 4, 1937.

54. *Ibid.*, August 21, 1937.

55. *Ibid.*, January 9, 1937.

56. Joseph Alsop and Turner Catledge, *op. cit.*, p. 128.

57. U.S., *Congressional Record*, 75 Cong., 1 Sess. (April 20, 1937), p. 3612.

58. *Ibid.* (May 20, 1937), pp. 4887-4890.

59. *Ibid.* (May 21, 1937), p. 4900.

60. New York *Times*, June 22, 1937.

61. Franklin D. Roosevelt, *The Public Papers of Franklin D. Roosevelt*, Vol. VI, ed. Samuel Rosenman (New York, 1941), pp. 190-194.

62. Harold Ickes, *The Inside Struggle, 1936-1939*, Vol. II: *The Secret Diary of Harold Ickes* (New York, 1953), p. 182.

63. John Morton Blum, *op. cit.*, p. 381.

64. *Ibid.*, p. 396.

65. New York *Times*, November 9, 1937.

66. *Time*, December 6, 1937, p. 15.

67. *Time*, March 20, 1939, p. 12.

68. According to William McAdoo, Garner had actually had nothing to do with the deadlock-breaking swing of the California delegates to Roosevelt inasmuch as he had no control over them and was only informed of it after it was decided by the California caucus. William McAdoo to Sam Rayburn, April 28, 1939, William McAdoo Papers (Library of Congress, Washington, D.C.), Box 469.

69. Joseph Alsop and Turner Catledge, *op. cit.*, p. 69.

70. Bascom Timmons, *Garner of Texas* (New York, 1948), p. 219.

71. Frank Walker, unpublished memoirs, Walker Papers.

72. Raymond Moley, *27 Masters of Politics* (New York, 1949), p. 74.

73. William Leuchtenburg, *op. cit.*, p. 4.

74. John N. Garner to Roosevelt, October 1, 1934, FDRL-PPF 1416.

75. Bascom Timmons, *Garner of Texas* (New York, 1948), p. 212.

76. Garner to Roosevelt, June 20, 1937, FDRL-PPF 1416.

77. *Supra*, pp. 50-51.

78. Bascom Timmons, *op. cit.*, p. 216.

79. *Ibid.*, pp. 215-216.

80. Joseph Alsop and Turner Catledge, *op. cit.*, p. 132.

81. *Ibid.*, p. 237.

82. James Farley, *op. cit.*, p. 84.

83. New York *Times*, June 19, 1937.

84. Garner to Roosevelt, June 19, 1937, FDRL-PSF, Box 52.

85. James Farley, *op. cit.*, pp. 84-86.

86. Roosevelt to Garner, July 7, 1937, FDRL-PSF, Box 52.

87. James Farley, *op. cit.*, p. 95.

88. *Ibid.*, p. 94.

89. Thomas L. Stokes, "Garner Turns on F.D.R.," *Nation*, CXLIV (June 26, 1937), 722; Henry M. Hyde, "White House No Man," *Saturday Evening Post*, CCX (June 25, 1938), 53; Earnest K. Lindley, Washington *Post*, December 16, 1938.

90. New York *Times*, September 5, 1937.

91. *Ibid.*, September 8, 1937.

92. *Ibid.*, December 19, 1937.

93. James Farley, *op. cit.*, p. 111.

94. Delbert Clark, "Who Will It Be in 1940? The Guessing Starts," *New York Times Magazine*, November 21, 1937, p. 23.

95. Joseph K. Howard, "The Decline and Fall of Burton K. Wheeler," *Harper's* (March, 1947), p. 227.

96. Joseph Alsop and Turner Catledge, *op. cit.*, p. 237.

97. Frank Walker, unpublished memoirs, Walker Papers; Charles Michelson, *The Ghost Talks* (New York, 1944), p. 140; Joseph K. Howard, *loc. cit.*, p. 229.

98. George Creel, "Parade to the Post," *Colliers* (October 2, 1937), p. 26.

99. Robert Sherwood, *Roosevelt and Hopkins*, Bantam Edition, 2 vols. (New York, 1950), I, p. 109.

100. Joseph K. Howard, *loc. cit.*, pp. 231-232.

101. U.S., *Congressional Record*, 75 Cong., 1 Sess. (July 8, 1937), p. 6895.

102. Richard Neuberger, "Wheeler of Montana," *Harper's* CLXXX (May, 1940), 614.

103. New York *Times*, October 17, 1937.

104. James Farley, *op. cit.*, p. 125.

105. Richard T. Ruetten, "Showdown in Montana, 1938: Burton Wheeler's Role in the Defeat of Jerry O'Connell," *Pacific Northwest Quarterly*, LIV (January, 1963), 19.

106. Tom Connally as told to Alfred Steinberg, *My Name Is Tom Connally* (New York, 1954), p. 189.

107. Russell Lord, *The Wallaces of Iowa* (Boston, 1947), p. 464.

108. Robert Sherwood, *op. cit.*, p. 109.

109. Allan Nevins, *Herbert H. Lehman and His Era* (New York, 1963), p. 192.

110. New York *Times*, June 18, 1937.

111. Frank McHale to Paul McNutt, July 12, 1937, Paul McNutt Papers (Lilly Library, Indiana University).

112. New York *Times*, August 26, 1937.

113. Interview with James Farley, November 9, 1963.

114. Rexford G. Tugwell, *op. cit.*, p. 404.

Notes to Chapter III

1. E.g., Raymond Moley, *27 Masters of Politics* (New York, 1949), p. 41.

2. James Farley, *Jim Farley's Story: The Roosevelt Years* (New York, 1948), p. 142.

3. Edward J. Flynn, *You're the Boss* (New York, 1947), p. 152.

4. James Farley, *op. cit.*, p. 111.

5. Eugene Gerhart, *America's Advocate: Robert Jackson* (Indianapolis, 1958), p. 132.

6. New York *Times*, January 9, 1938.

7. James Farley, *op. cit.*, p. 117; interview with James Farley, November 9, 1963.

8. Euguene Gerhart, *op. cit.*, p. 138.

9. New York *Times*, January 22, 1938.

10. U.S., *Congressional Record*, 75 Cong., 3 Sess. (March 4, 1938), p. 2833.

11. *Ibid.*, p. 2836.

12. Robert Sherwood, *Roosevelt and Hopkins*, Bantam Edition, 2 vols. (New York, 1950), I, pp. 115-116.

13. Raymond Moley, *op. cit.*, p. 41.

14. U.S., *Congressional Record*, 75 Cong., 3 Sess. (May 25, 1938), pp. 7460-7461; New York *Times*, May 29, 1938.

15. Robert Sherwood, *op. cit.*, p. 121.

16. Arthur Krock, New York *Times*, October 18, 1938.

17. New York *Times*, April 1, 1938.

18. U.S., *Congressional Record*, 75 Cong., 3 Sess. (April 5, 1938), pp. 4761-4762.

19. Paul Leach, "Iffies on the Wabash," *Saturday Evening Post*, CCX (December 11, 1938), 11.

20. New York *Times*, February 20, 1938.

21. *Ibid.*, February 11-20, 1938.

22. *Ibid.*, February 20, 1938.

23. *Ibid.*, IV, 6, February 27, 1938.

24. *Ibid.*, February 23, 1938.

25. *Ibid.*, March 17, 1938.

26. *Ibid.*, speeches given March 23 and 25, but first cited July 13, 1938.

27. New York *Times*, April 29, 1938.

28. George Norris to Franklin Roosevelt, July 28, 1937 (Franklin D. Roosevelt Library, President's Secretary's File), Box 52. Cited hereafter as FDRL-PSF.

29. Elmer Davis, "The Wisconsin Brothers: A Study in Partial Eclipse," *Harpers*, CLXXVII (February, 1939), 274.

30. Russell B. Nye, *Midwestern Progressive Politics* (Lansing, 1951), p. 373.

31. John Morton Blum, *From the Morgenthau Diaries: Years of Crisis, 1928-1938* (Boston, 1959), p. 381.

32. Robert Sherwood, *op. cit.*, I, p. 115.

33. Roosevelt to William Phillips, May 18, 1938 in Franklin D. Roosevelt, *F.D.R.: His Personal Letters*, ed. Elliot Roosevelt (New York, 1947-1950), p. 785. Cited hereafter as *F.D.R.: Personal Letters*.

34. New York *Times*, April 3, 1938.

35. The best general summary is in Charles W. Van Devander, *The Big Bosses* (New York, 1944), pp. 156-157.

36. *Time*, May 2, 1938, p. 12.

37. *Ibid.*, May 9, 1938, p. 14.

38. Harold Ickes, "My Twelve Years with F.D.R.," *Saturday Evening Post*, CCXX (July 10, 1948), 33.

39. New York *Times*, May 17, 1938.

40. *Ibid.*, May 19, 1938.

41. *Ibid.*, May 19, 1938.

42. James Farley, *op. cit.*, p. 133.

43. New York *Times*, July 26, 1938.

44. *Time*, August 8, 1938, p. 11.

45. *Newsweek*, August 8, 1938, p. 8.

46. Samuel Rosenman, *Working with Roosevelt* (New York, 1952), p. 176.

47. *Time*, September 12, 1938, p. 22.

48. *Ibid.*, p. 23.

49. Franklin D. Roosevelt, *Public Papers of Franklin D. Roosevelt*, ed. Samuel Rosenman, VII (New York, 1941), pp. 1-14. Cited hereafter as *Public Papers*.

50. The best detailed account of this decision is Joseph Alsop and Robert Kintner, *Men Around the President* (New York, 1939), pp. 133-156.

51. "Planters' Punch," *New Republic*, XCIV (March 16, 1938), 162.

52. *Daniel Roper Memorandum to Franklin Roosevelt*, April 6, 1938, in FDRL-PSF, Box 18.

53. U.S., *Congressional Record*, 75 Cong., 3 Sess. (April 8, 1938), p. 5123.

54. O. R. Altman, "Second and Third Sessions of the Seventy-Fifth Congress, 1937-8," *American Political Science Review*, XXXII (December 1938), 1120.

55. U.S., *Congressional Record*, 75 Cong., 3 Sess. (May 28, 1938), p. 7681.

56. Basil Rauch, *The History of the New Deal*, 1933-1938 (New York, 1944), p. 311.

57. Albert Alexander, "The President and the Investigator," *Antioch Review*, XV (Spring, 1955), 107; August R. Ogden, *The Dies Committee* (Washington, 1943), p. 45.

58. New York *Times*, November 24, 1938.

59. *Ibid.*, November 25, 1938.

60. Senator William Smathers to Josephus Daniels, January 12, 1938, Daniels Papers (Library of Congress, Washington, D.C.), Box 735. Cited hereafter as Daniels Papers.

61. J. B. Shannon, "Presidential Politics in the South: 1938," *Journal of Politics*, I (May, 1939), 1950.

62. Blair A. Crownover, "Franklin Roosevelt and the Primary Campaigns of the 1938 Congressional Elections" (unpublished senior essay, Princeton University, 1955), pp. 48-49; *Time*, May 2, 1938, p. 10.

63. Press Conference No. 432, February 8, 1938. FDRL.

64. Claude Pepper to Franklin Roosevelt, May 4, 1938, FDRL-President's Personal File, 4773. Cited hereafter as FDRL-PPF.

65. Fred P. Cone to Franklin Roosevelt, May 4, 1938, FDRL-Official File 300, Box 21. Cited hereafter as FDRL-OF.

66. New York *Times*, May 7, 1938; U.S., *Congressional Record*, 75 Cong., 3 Sess. (May 24, 1938), p. 7449.

67. New York *Times*, April 11, 1938.

68. *Time*, May 30, 1938, p. 13.

69. Reverend Maurice S. Sheehy to Franklin Roosevelt, May 25, 1938, FDRL-OF 300, Box 29.

70. New York *Times*, May 26, 1938.

71. U.S., *Congressional Record*, 75 Cong., 3 Sess. (May 25, 1938), p. 7460.

72. *Ibid.*, p. 7478.

73. *Time*, June 13, 1938, p. 16.

74. *Ibid.*

75. New York *Times*, June 7, 1938.

76. Turner Catledge, *ibid.*, May 27, 1938.

77. *Time*, September 12, 1938, p. 23.

78. Jay Franklin, "We, the People," Washington *Star*, May 30, 1938.

79. Russell Lord, *The Wallaces of Iowa* (Boston, 1947), p. 464; New York *Times*, May 27, 1938.

80. Interview with Benjamin V. Cohen, November 22, 1963.

81. Harold Ickes, "My Twelve Years with F.D.R.," *Saturday Evening Post*, CCXX (June 23, 1938), 78.

82. *Ibid.*

83. New York *Times*, June 7, 1938.

84. *Public Papers*, VII, p. 401.

85. Josephus Daniels to Franklin Roosevelt, September 21, 1938, Daniels Papers, Box 18.

86. Blair Crownover, *loc. cit.*, Appendix II, pp. v, vi; Edward J. Flynn, *op. cit.*, pp. 149-150.

87. Lester Weisse to James A. Farley, December 9, 1938, in the Charles Broughton Papers (Wisconsin State Historical Society Library, Madison, Wisconsin).

88. New York *Times*, July 6, 1938.

89. *Ibid.*, July 13, 1938.

90. Paul McNutt to Frank McHale, July 19, 1938, Paul McNutt Papers (Lilly Library, Indiana University). Cited hereafter as McNutt Papers.

91. *Ibid.*

92. McNutt to Frank McHale, August 15, 1938, McNutt Papers.

93. William Kitchen to Paul McNutt, August 31, 1938, McNutt Papers.

94. Press Conference No. 482, September 2, 1938, FDRL.

95. *Public Papers*, VII, pp. 559, 562.

96. *Ibid.*, pp. 562, 566, 570-1, 577.

97. *Time*, October 17, 1938, p. 18.

98. Donald McCoy, *Angry Voices: Left-of-Center Politics in the New Deal Era* (Lawrence, 1958), pp. 181-182.

99. G. Gould Lincoln, Washington *Star*, November 12, 1938.

100. Democratic National Committee Papers, FDRL-OF 300, Box 104-107.

101. Thomas Stokes, *Chip Off My Shoulder* (Princeton, 1940), pp. 534-536.

102. Democratic National Committee Papers, FDRL-OF 300, Box 104-107.

103. Calvin Conklin to James Farley, November 12, 1938, FDRL-OF 300, Box 105.

104. Interview with James Farley, November 9, 1963.

105. Harry Hopkins to Harold Baker, February 4, 1939, Harry Hopkins Papers (Franklin D. Roosevelt Library, Hyde Park).

106. New York *Times*, November 29, 1938.

107. *Ibid.*, December 24. 1938.

108. Arthur Krock, *ibid.*, November 13, 1938.

109. *Ibid.*, September 11, 1938.
110. Arthur Krock, *ibid.*, November 9, 1938.
111. *Ibid.*, September 11, 1938.
112. *Ibid.*, November 24, 1938.
113. *Ibid.*
114. Paul McNutt to Admiral H. E. Yarnell, December 24, 1938, McNutt Papers.
115. *Ibid.*
116. T.R.B., "McNuttus, Venit, Vidit, Vicit," *New Republic*, XCIX (July 26, 1939), 333.
117. Paul McNutt Memorandum to Franklin Roosevelt, November 5, 1938, McNutt Papers.
118. Richard T. Reutten, "Showdown in Montana, 1938: Burton K. Wheeler's Role in the Defeat of Jerry O'Connell," *Pacific Northwest Quarterly*, LIV (January, 1963), 26.
119. Frank Murphy to James Farley, December 7, 1938, FDRL-OF 300, Box 105; Frank Murphy, "Tragic Interruption," *Nation*, CXLVII (December 3, 1938), 589-590.
120. Franklin Roosevelt to Joseph Daniels, November 14, 1938, Daniels Papers, Box 18.
121. *Time*, October 24, 1938, p. 10.
122. James Byrnes, *All in One Lifetime* (New York, 1958), p. 103.
123. Democratic National Committee Papers, FDRL-OF 300, Boxes 104, 105.
124. Josephus Daniels to Franklin Roosevelt, November 9, 1938, Daniels Papers, Box 18.
125. Paul Douglas to Abraham Epstein, November 10, 1938, Mary W. Dewson Papers (Franklin D. Roosevelt Library, Hyde Park).
126. Robert Sherwood, *op. cit.*, I, pp. 115-116.
127. Joseph Alsop and Robert Kintner, New York *Times*, June 1, 1938.
128. New York *Times*, July 11, 1938.
129. *Ibid.*, August 27, 1938.
130. James Farley, *op. cit.*, p. 183; Edward J. Flynn, *op. cit.*, p. 153; Samuel Rosenman, *op. cit.*, p. 177.
131. New York *Times*, November 6, 1938.
132. Democratic National Committee Papers, FDRL-OF 300, Boxes 104-107.
133. New York *Times*, June 1, 1938.
134. Thomas Stokes, Washington *Star*, July 13, 1938.
135. John Morton Blum, *op. cit.*, p. 418; New York *Times*, April 12, 1938.
136. Press Conference No. 450, April 12, 1938, FDRL.

137. New York *Times*, July 5, 1938.

138. *Ibid.*, August 7, 1938.

139. *Ibid.*

140. *Ibid.*

141. *Ibid.*, September 16, 1938.

142. *Ibid.*, December 7, 1938.

143. John O'Connell and Doris Fleeson, "Capital Stuff," Washington *Times*, December 12, 1938.

144. Daniel Roper to Marvin McIntyre, November 26, 1938, FDRL-PSF, Box 18.

145. Roosevelt to Garner, November 28, 1938, *F.D.R.: Personal Letters*, p. 831.

146. Joseph Alsop and Robert Kintner, "The Capital Parade," Washington *Star*, December 29, 1938.

147. Paul Hutchinson, "Cordell Hull for President?" *New Republic*, XCV (June 1, 1938), 92-94.

148. James Farley, *op. cit.*, p. 135.

149. Carl E. Bailey to Jesse Jones, May 23, 1938, Jesse Jones Papers (Library of Congress, Washington, D.C.), Box 186.

150. Bascom Timmons, *Garner of Texas* (New York, 1948), p. 252.

151. New York *Times*, December 2, 1938.

152. Fred Essary, Baltimore *Sun*, October 16, 1938.

153. Jack Alexander, "Missouri Dark Mule," *Saturday Evening Post*, CCXI (October 8, 1938), 6.

154. Joseph T. Davis to Franklin Roosevelt, August 20, 1938, FDRL-OF 300, Box 41.

155. Tom Corcoran to Steve Early, October 5, 1938, FDRL-PPF 1560.

156. New York *Times*, October 9, 1938.

157. *Ibid.*, December 2, 1938.

158. *Ibid.*, January 29, 1938.

159. *Ibid.*, July 13, 1938.

160. Joseph Alsop and Robert Kintner, "Capital Parade," Washington *Star*, July 8, 1938.

161. Robert Sherwood, *op. cit.*, I, p. 208.

162. *Ibid.*; Ickes, *loc. cit.* (July 10, 1948), p. 33.

163. Paul Anderson, "The Third Term," *Nation*, CXLVII (July 23, 1938), 82.

164. New York *Times*, July 25, 1938.

165. *Ibid.*, July 29, 1938.

166. *Ibid.*

167. *Ibid.*, September 16, 1938.

168. *Ibid.*, December 5, 1938.

169. *Ibid.*, October 20, 1938.

170. *Ibid.*, November 11, 1938.

171. *Ibid.*

172. Wright Patman to Franklin Roosevelt, November 25, 1938, FDRL-OF 288.

173. New York *Times*, December 13, 1938.

174. Raymond Clapper, "Return to the Two Party System," *Current History*, XLIX (December, 1938), 14-15.

175. New York *Times*, December 14, 1938.

176. David McClugage to Jime Farley, December 19, 1938. The author did not make a mathematical tabulation of the letters for and against a third term in the Democratic National Committee Papers, FDRL-OF 300, Boxes 104-107. The statement of their relative numbers is based only on a rough estimate.

177. G. Gould Lincoln, Washington *Star*, November 13, 1938. There is an extremely interesting estimate of 1940 convention strength for a third term in the Democratic National Committee Papers for 1938, OF 300, Box 107, chiefly based on the attitudes of the political leaders of the respective states. The convention votes of those states which presumably would favor a third term total 232; those opposed, 290; and those uncertain, 540. The prognosis was apparently made by a New Dealer. Neither the staff at the Roosevelt Library nor Jim Farley had any idea of the author's identity.

178. John Gilbert Winant, *Letter from Grosvenor Square* (Boston, 1947), p. 19.

Notes to Chapter IV

1. Franklin D. Roosevelt, Public Papers, VIII (New York, 1941), p. 68.

2. Josephus Daniels to George Creel, January 20, 1939, Daniels Papers, Box 736.

3. Oswald Garrison Villard, "Issues and Men," *Nation*, CXLVIII (January 21, 1939), 94.

4. Robert T. Cochran, Jr., "Virginia's Opposition to the New Deal, 1933-1940" (unpublished master's dissertation, Georgetown University, 1950), pp. 90-94.

5. *Newsweek*, February 6, 1939, p. 16.

6. Thomas Amlie to Franklin D. Roosevelt, April 7, 1939, in U.S., *Congressional Record*, 76 Cong., 1 Sess. (Appendix, pp. 1530-1).

7. Robert T. Cochran, Jr., *loc. cit.*, p. 115.

8. New York *Times*, February 15, 1939.

9. Floyd Riddick, "The First Session of the Seventy-Sixth Congress," *American Political Science Review*, XXXIII (December 1939), 1022-1043.

10. *Newsweek*, August 28, 1939, p. 15.

11. U.S., *Congressional Record*, 76 Cong., 1 Sess. (August 5, 1939), p. 11166.

12. *Ibid.*, pp. 11165-6.

13. "Democratic Party Is No Longer Mr. Roosevelt's, And Not Yet Anybody Else's," *Fortune*, XX (October 1939), 71.

14. Raymond Clapper, Washington *News*, January 3, 1939.

15. Frank Kent, Baltimore *Sun*, January 5, 1939.

16. Ernest K. Lindley, Washington *Post*, January 4, 1939.

17. New York *Times*, January 4, 1939.

18. Turner Catledge, *ibid.*, January 8, 1939, IV, 3.

19. New York *Times*, January 17, 1939.

20. *Newsweek*, January 23, 1939, p. 13.

21. *Ibid.*, February 6, 1939; Joseph Alsop and Robert Kintner, Washington *Star*, January 24, 1939.

22. Harlan Miller, Washington *Post*, January 31, 1939.

23. *Ibid.*, January 26, 1939.

24. Floyd Riddick, *loc. cit.*, p. 1027.

25. *Time*, April 3, 1939, pp. 12-13.

26. Joseph Alsop and Robert Kintner, New York *Times*, July 25, 1939.

27. New York *Times*, July 22, 1939.

28. Joseph Guffey to Franklin Roosevelt, July 29, 1939, FDRL-PSF, Box 52.

29. New York *Times*, March 26, 1939.

30. *Ibid.*, May 21, June 14, 1939.

31. Bascom Timmons, *Garner of Texas* (New York, 1948), p. 253.

32. Raymond Clapper, Washington *News*, March 31, 1939.

33. T.R.B., "Washington Notes," *New Republic*, XCIX (June 21, 1939), 187.

34. Washington *Post*, May 26, 1939.

35. *Time*, June 5, 1939, p. 20.

36. Marquis James, "Poker-Playing, Whiskey-Drinking, Evil Old Man!" *Saturday Evening Post*, CCXII (September 9, 1939), 25.

37. *Ibid.*, p. 25; Jed Johnson to Franklin Roosevelt, June 13, 1939, FDRL-OF, Box 6.

38. Philadelphia *Record*, June 18, 1939. Clipping from Jones Papers.

39. Interview with Benjamin V. Cohen, November 22, 1963. Mr. Cohen emphasized that there was nothing particularly organized about the gatherings in his offices. For no apparent reason, he claimed, men hotly in favor of the third term dropped in to chat quite frequently until the place began to get the reputation of being the center of the third-term movement.

40. "Congress Begins Looking at Presidential Prospects," *Congressional Digest*, XVIII (May 1939), 129.

41. Drew Pearson and Robert Allen, "Washington Merry-Go-Round," Washington *Times Herald*, February 17, 1939.

42. *Ibid.*, April 18, 1939.

43. Cited in the Washington *Post*, June 6, 1939.

44. New York *Times*, July 26, 1939.

45. New York *Times*, July 28, 1939.

46. Marquis James, *loc. cit.*, p. 25.

47. Kenneth Crawford, "Real John Garner," *Nation*, CIL (August 5, 1939), 140.

48. New York *Times*, August 13, 1939.

49. Dwight C. Dorough, *Mr. Sam* (New York, 1962), p. 253.

50. Joseph Alsop and Robert Kintner, New York *Times*, May 28, 1939; Raymond Moley, "Mercy and the Big Chance," *Newsweek*, May 15, 1939, p. 56.

51. *Newsweek*, May 15, 1939, p. 15.

52. Burton K. Wheeler with Paul F. Healy, *Yankee from the West* (Garden City, New York, 1962), p. 354.

53. Joseph Alsop and Robert Kintner, New York *Times*, May 28, 1939.

54. E.g., "Third Term Strategy," *New Republic*, XCVII (January 11, 1939), 273; T.R.B., "Washington Notes," *New Republic*, XCVIII (May 3, 1939), 377.

55. Oswald Garrison Villard, "No Third Term," *Nation*, CXLVIII (June 17, 1939), 702.

56. U.S., *Congressional Record*, 76 Cong., 1 Sess. (Appendix, pp. 2723-5).

57. New York *Times*, June 17, 1939.

58. *Ibid.*, June 21, 1939.

59. *Ibid.*, June 22, 1939.

60. Copy of the speech in FDRL-PSF, Box 52.

61. New York *Times*, July 14, 1939.

62. Tom Corcoran to Missy LeHand, July 22, 1939, FRDL-OF 1560.

63. New York *Times*, June 20, 1939.

64. *Ibid.*, July 9, 1939.

65. *Supra*, p. 133.

66. Robert Divine, *The Illusion of Neutrality* (Chicago, 1962), p. 284.

67. *Time*, July 31, 1939, p. 8.

68. *Ibid.*

69. New York *Times*, April 1, 1939.

70. James Farley, *Jim Farley's Story: The Roosevelt Years* (New York, 1948), p. 153.

71. Interview with James Farley, November 9, 1963.

72. New York *Times*, February 10, 1939.

73. *Ibid.*, July 24, 1939.

74. James Farley, *op. cit.*, pp. 173-178.

75. *Ibid.*, pp. 186-188.

76. *Newsweek*, May 1, 1939.

77. E.g., "I am not in any sense in politics and have no personal political plans or purposes for the future." Cordell Hull to Clinton Noble (a Democrat from Utica, N.Y.), October 12, 1939, Hull Papers (Library of Congress, Washington, D.C.).

78. *Time*, December 18, 1939, p. 12.

79. New York *Times*, July 23, 1939.

80. Robert Sherwood, *Roosevelt and Hopkins*, Bantam Edition, 2 vols. (New York: 1948), Vol. I, p. 137.

81. U.S., *Congressional Record*, 76 Cong., 1 Sess. (January 5, 1939), pp. 92-93.

82. *Newsweek*, January 30, 1939, p. 14.

83. New York *Times*, January 24, 1939.

84. U.S., *Congressional Record*, 76 Cong., 1 Sess. (January 19, 20, 23, 1939), pp. 475-502, 544-574, 598-628.

85. *Ibid.*, pp. 554-555.

86. New York *Times*, January 24, 1939.

87. Robert Sherwood, *op. cit.*, I, p. 136.

88. Situation summarized in a letter from Henry Morgenthau to Roosevelt, March 1939, in Franklin D. Roosevelt, *F.D.R.: His Personal Letters*, ed. Elliot Roosevelt (New York, 1947-1950), pp. 869-870. Cited hereafter as *Personal Letters*.

89. New York *Times*, February 25, 1939.

90. *Ibid.; Newsweek*, March 6, 1939, p. 17; *Time*, March 6, 1939, p. 12.

91. *Time*, March 6, 1939, p. 12.

92. *F.D.R.: Personal Letters*, p. 870.

93. Arthur Krock, New York *Times*, March 10, 1939.

94. Marriner Eccles, *Beckoning Frontiers*, ed. Sidney Hyman (New York, 1951), p. 318.

95. Robert Jackson to Harry Hopkins, March 24, 1939, Harry Hopkins Papers (Franklin D. Roosevelt Library, Hyde Park), Confidential Political File.

96. New York *Times*, April 5, 1939.

97. *Ibid.*, April 5, 1939.

98. Robert Sherwood, *op. cit.*, I, p. 137.

99. *Ibid.*, p. 143.

100. *Ibid.*, p. 143.

101. *Ibid.*, p. 148.

102. *Newsweek*, January 2, 1939, p. 14.

103. New York *Times*, May 14, 1939, IV, p. 10.

104. Information in a memorandum by Edward Eicher to Roosevelt, July 26, 1939, FDRL-President's Personal File 4898. Cited hereafter as FDRL-PPF.

105. Edward Eicher to Roosevelt, July 19, 1939, FDRL-PPF 4989.

106. *Ibid.*, July 26, 1939.

107. New York Times, June 8, 1939.

108. *Time*, July 31, 1939, p. 12.

109. James Farley, *op. cit.*, p. 184.

110. Houston *Post*, February 25, 1939, from Jones Papers.

111. Los Angeles *Daily News*, August 9, 1939.

112. *Time*, July 31, 1939, p. 9.

113. Jesse Jones to Harry Hopkins, September 4, 1939, Jones Papers, Box 14.

114. Minneapolis *Tribune*, June 3, 1939.

115. Boston *Observer*, October 27, 1939.

116. New York *Times*, August 24, 1939; Washington *Star*, August 5, 1939.

117. E.g., Frank McHale to Josephus Daniels, May 16, 1939, Daniels Papers, Box 738.

118. New York *Times*, June 11, 1939.

119. *Ibid.*, June 14, 1939.

120. *Ibid.*, June 19, 1939.

121. *Ibid.*, July 11, 1939.

122. *Ibid.*, July 12, 1939.

123. Alva Johnston, "I Intend to Be President," *Saturday Evening Post*, CCXII (March 16, 1940), 70.

124. James Farley, *op. cit.*, p. 170; Raymond Moley, "McNutt Moves In," *Newsweek*, XIV (July 24, 1939), 48.

125. *Newsweek*, July 17, 1939, pp. 14-15.

126. T.R.B., "Washington Notes," *New Republic*, XCIX (June 21, 1939), 187.

127. *Ibid.*, July 26, 1939, p. 333.

128. Douglas MacArthur to Paul McNutt, July 12, 1939, Paul McNutt Papers (Lilly Library, Indiana University).

129. New York *Times*, October 1, 1939.

130. George Norris to Claude Pepper, August 28, 1939, FDRL-PSF, Box 52.

131. Frank Walker Papers.

132. *Ibid.*

133. New York *Times*, October 1, 1939.

134. *Ibid.*, May 16, 1939.

135. Memorandum from E. M. Watson to Edward Kannee, FDRL-OF 300, Box 52.

136. Drew Pearson and Robert Allen, "Washington Merry-Go-Round," Washington *Times Herald*, March 27, 1939.

137. *Time*, August 21, 1939, p. 14.

138. *F.D.R.: Public Papers*, Vol. VIII, p. 437.

139. New York *Times*, August 5, 13, 1939.

140. Harold Ickes, *The Lowering Clouds, 1939-1941*, Vol. III, *The Secret Diary of Harold Ickes* (New York, 1954), p. 103.

141. *Time*, July 24, 1939.

142. New York *Times*, October 28, 1939.

143. Turner Catledge, New York *Times*, October 1, 1939, IV, 7.

144. New York *Times*, October 26, 1939.

145. *Ibid.*, October 27, 1939.

146. *Ibid.*, October 26, 1939.

147. *Ibid.*, November 16, 1939.

148. Drew Pearson and Robert Allen, "Washington Merry-Go-Round," Madison *Capital Times*, December 1, 1939; Washington *Times Herald*, November 21, 1939; Madison *Capital Times*, December 31, 1939.

149. E. M. Watson to David K. Niles, November 9, 1939, FDRL-OF 300, Box 41.

150. Turner Catledge, New York *Times*, March 19, 1939, IV, 6.

151. George Creel, *Rebel at Large: Recollections of Fifty Crowded Years* (New York, 1947), p. 311.

152. Franklin Roosevelt to Eleanor Roosevelt, August 12, 1939, *Personal Letters*, p. 801.

153. James McGregor Burns, *Roosevelt: The Lion and the Fox* (New York, 1956), p. 411.

154. James Farley, *op. cit.*, p. 184.

155. Burton K. Wheeler, *op. cit.*, p. 357.

156. Richard Neuberger, "Lewis and the Third Term," *Nation*, CXLIX (November 25, 1939), 571.

157. Norman Littell to Roosevelt, June 30, 1939, FDRL-PPF 6093.

158. Roosevelt to Littell, July 1, 1939, *ibid.*

159. Saul Alinsky, *John L. Lewis: An Unauthorized Biography* (New York, 1949), pp. 138-139.

160. New York *Times*, October 31, 1939.

161. Ickes, *op. cit.*, p. 53.

162. New York *Times*, November 1, 1939.

163. Madison *Capital Times*, December 21, 1939. One indication of how thoroughly Lewis had done his work is that twenty-four years later Ben Cohen, who was supposed to be one of those working on the plan, could not recall that it ever existed. Interview November 22, 1963.

164. *Newsweek*, October 30, 1939.

165. New York *Times*, November 28, 1939.

166. Harold Ickes, *op. cit.*, pp. 66, 74-75.

167. Interview with Benjamin V. Cohen, November 22, 1963.

168. *Ibid.*

169. Harold Ickes, *op. cit.*, pp. 66-67.

170. *Ibid.*, p. 81.

171. *Ibid.*, p. 83; James Farley, *op. cit.*, p. 214.

172. New York *Times*, December 15, 1939.

173. *Ibid.*, December 16, 1939.

174. T.R.B., "Washington Notes," *New Republic*, XCIX (June 28, 1939), 214.

175. New York *Times*, June 28, 1939.

176. *Ibid.*, July 2, 1939.

177. Oswald Garrison Villard, "Issues and Men," *Nation*, CXLIX (July 15, 1939), 72.

178. *Supra*, p. 19.

179. Burton K. Wheeler, *op. cit.*, p. 363.

180. New York *Times*, December 12, 1939.

181. *Supra*, p. 153.

182. Madison *Capital Times*, December 9, 1939.

183. James Farley, *op. cit.*, p. 224.

184. *Newsweek*, April 3, 1939; Arthur Krock, New York *Times*, April 7, 1939.

185. Arthur Krock, *ibid.*, April 7, 1939.

186. New York *Herald Tribune*, October 22, 1939; Arthur Krock, *ibid.*, October 26, 1939.

187. *Time*, December 18, 1939, p. 11.

188. Frank Walker, unpublished memoirs, Walker Papers.

189. James Farley, *op. cit.*, p. 184.

190. Ulric Bell, "Little Jack Garner," *American Mercury*, XLVII (May 1939), 7.

191. T.R.B., "Washington Notes," *New Republic*, XCVIII (April 12, 1939), 278.

192. Fred Pasley, Washington *Times Herald*, April 12, 1939.

193. New York *Herald Tribune*, June 4, 1939; Jay Franklin, "We the People," Washington *Star*, June 12, 1939.

194. New York *Times*, July 27, 1939.

195. *Supra*, p. 148.

196. Anonymous undated memorandum in FDRL-PSF, Box 52.

197. Washington *News*, February 10, 1939.

198. *Current History*, L (December 1939), 7.

199. New York *Times*, December 17, 1939.

200. *Ibid.*, December 9, 1939.

201. Harold Ickes to Raymond Robbins, December 6, 1939, Raymond Robbins Papers (Wisconsin State Historical Society Library, Madison, Wisconsin).

Notes to Chapter V

1. Franklin D. Roosevelt, *Public Papers*, Vol. IX, pp. 1-10.
2. Ernest K. Lindley, Washington *Post*, January 5, 1940.
3. New York *Times*, January 1, 1940.
4. Sherwood Eddy to Raymond Robbins, January 4, 1940, Raymond Robbins Papers (Wisconsin Historical Society Library, Madison, Wisconsin).
5. Washington *Star*, February 26, 1940.
6. New York *Times*, January 7, 1940.
7. *Fortune*, XXI (January 1940), 56.
8. Washington *Post*, January 3, February 25, 1940.
9. E.g., Drew Pearson and Robert Allen, "Washington Merry-Go-Round," New York *Times Herald*, January 2, 1940; *Time*, January 1, 1940, p. 8; *Newsweek*, January 15, 1940.
10. Cordell Hull, *The Memoirs of Cordell Hull* (New York, 1948), I, p. 856.
11. Interview with James Farley, November 9, 1963.
12. Cordell Hull, *op. cit.*, p. 749.
13. *Ibid.*, p. 857.
14. Madison *Capital Times*, January 2, 1940.
15. Harold Ickes, *The Lowering Clouds, 1939-1941*, Vol. III, *The Secret Diary of Harold Ickes* (New York, 1954), p. 108. Cited hereafter as Ickes, *The Lowering Clouds*.
16. *Ibid.*
17. Harold Ickes, "My Twelve Years with F.D.R.," *Saturday Evening Post*, CCXX (July 10, 1948), 108. Cited hereafter as Ickes, "My Twelve Years."
18. J. E. Pollard, *The Presidents and the Press* (New York, 1947), p. 826.
19. James Farley, *Jim Farley's Story: The Roosevelt Years* (New York, 1948), p. 224; Harold Ickes, *The Lowering Clouds*, p. 122.
20. Franklin Roosevelt to Henry Horner, March 27, 1940, Franklin D. Roosevelt, *F.D.R.: His Personal Letters*, ed. Elliot Roosevelt (New York, 1947-1950), pp. 1011-1012. Cited hereafter as *Personal Letters*.
21. Rexford G. Tugwell, *The Democratic Roosevelt* (Garden City, New York, 1957), p. 532.
22. *United States News*, February 2, 1940, p. 7; *ibid.*, February 16, p. 9.
23. Robert Jackson to William McAdoo, February 14, 1940, William McAdoo Papers (Library of Congress, Washington, D.C.), Box 471. Cited hereafter as McAdoo Papers.
24. Interview with Benjamin V. Cohen, November 22, 1963.

25. Interview with Claude Pepper, August 26, 1963.

26. Josephus Daniels to F. W. Buxton, March 13, 1940, Josephus Daniels Papers (Library of Congress, Washington, D.C.), Box 740. Cited hereafter as Daniels Papers.

27. Harold Ickes, *Lowering Clouds*, p. 160.

28. New York *Times*, January 13, 1940.

29. Marguerite LeHand memorandum to Franklin Roosevelt, January 8, 1940, FDRL-President's Secretary's File, Box 18. Cited hereafter as FDRL-PSF.

30. New York *Times*, January 27, 140.

31. *Time*, February 5, 1940, p. 18.

32. New York *Times*, January 28, 1940.

33. *Ibid.*, January 25, 1940.

34. *Ibid.*, February 1, 1940.

35. *Ibid.*, February 1, 1940.

36. New York *Herald Tribune*, January 28, 1940.

37. Harold Ickes, *Lowering Clouds*, p. 121.

38. *Newsweek*, February 19, 1940, p. 11.

39. Harry Sauthoff to Merlin Hull, February 19, 1940, Merlin Hull Papers (Wisconsin State Historical Society Library, Madison, Wisconsin).

40. New York *Times*, April 2, 1940.

41. New York *Times*, February 21, 1940.

42. *Ibid.*

43. *Ibid.*, February 23, 25, 1940.

44. Frank McHale to Paul McNutt, January 23, 1940, Paul McNutt Papers (Lilly Library, Indiana University). Cited hereafter as McNutt Papers.

45. Drew Pearson and Robert Allen, "Washington Merry-Go-Round," Madison *Capital Times*, February 20, 1940.

46. Robert Allen, "Wheeler and the Liberals," *Current History*, LI (March 1940), 25.

47. T.R.B., "Washington Notes," *New Republic*, CII (January 1, 1940), 21.

48. George Creel, *Rebel at Large: Recollections of Fifty Crowded Years* (New York, 1947), p. 312.

49. Drew Pearson and Robert Allen, "Washington Merry-Go-Round," Madison *Capital Times*, January 12, 29, March 6, 1940.

50. New York *Times*, January 24, 1940.

51. William Allen White, "Candidates in the Spring," *Yale Review*, XXIX (March 1940), 439.

52. Jonathan Mitchell, "McNutt, Beauty in Distress," *New Republic*, CII (April 29, 1940), 565; Milton Mayer, "Men Who Would Be President: Pretty Boy McNutt," *Nation*, CL (March 30, 1940), 415-416.

53. Oscar Ewing to Wesley Winans Stout, January 27, 1940, McNutt Papers.

54. Alva Johnston, "I Intend to Be President," *Saturday Evening Post*, CCXII (March 16, 1940).

55. D. J. Richards to Paul McNutt, January 27, 1940, McNutt Papers.

56. *Time*, March 25, 1940, p. 22.

57. J. Patrick Beacom to Frank McHale, January 14, 1940; Frank McHale to Ed Stanley, January 21, 1940, McNutt Papers.

58. *Time*, March 25, 1940, p. 22.

59. Oscar Ewing to Paul McNutt, May 6, 1940, McNutt Papers.

60. Washington *News*, March 21, 1940.

61. T.R.B., "Washington Notes," *New Republic*, CII (April 1, 1940), 440.

62. Maurice Judd to Paul McNutt, April 2, 1940, McNutt Papers.

63. J. Patrick Beacom to Frank McHale, January 14, 1940, McNutt Papers.

64. Manuscript of the book is in FDRL-President's Personal File 2836. Cited hereafter as FDRL-PPF. The book was never published.

65. Oscar Ewing to Fowler Harper, April 29, 1940, McNutt Papers.

66. Harper to Ewing, April 25, 1940, McNutt Papers.

67. Harold Ickes, "My Twelve Years" (November 25, 1940), 86.

68. Dean Albertson, *Roosevelt's Farmer: Claude R. Wickard* (New York, 1961), p. 126.

69. Pencilled notation on the cover of the manuscript. Early's note to McNutt over Roosevelt's signature, April 10, 1940, in the McNutt Papers.

70. Harold Ickes, "My Twelve Years" (November 25, 1948), 86.

71. Washington *Post*, January 3, 1940.

72. Bascom Timmons, *Garner of Texas* (New York, 1948), p. 271.

73. *Ibid.*, p. 257.

74. Harold Ickes, *Lowering Clouds*, p. 140.

75. Thomas Stokes, Washington *News*, April 2, 1940.

76. Allan Michie, "Men Who Would Be President: John Nance Garner," *Nation*, CL (March 2, 1940), 301.

77. Arthur Krock, New York *Times*, March 1, 1940.

78. New York *Journal and American*, May 18, 1940, in Jesse Jones Papers (Library of Congress, Washington, D.C.), Box 186. Cited hereafter as Jones Papers.

79. Jesse Jones to William Randolph Hearst, May 22, 1940, Jones Papers, Box 186.

80. William Rankin to Jesse Jones, undated, Jesse Jones Papers.

81. Interview with James Farley, November 9, 1963; New York *Times*, January 25, 1940.

82. Copy of the speech in FDRL-Official File 300. Cited hereafter as OF.

83. James Farley, *op. cit.*, pp. 223-224.

84. Interview with James Farley, November 9, 1963.

85. James Farley, *op. cit.*, p. 225; Providence *Journal*, February 21, 1940.

86. New York *Times*, February 13, 1940.

87. *Ibid.*, February 29, 1940.

88. John McCormack to Steve Early, February 19, 1940, FDRL-OF 1871, Box 1.

89. Washington *Post*, March 4, 1940.

90. Press Conference No. 628, March 5, 1940, FDRL.

91. Press Conference No. 630, March 19, 1940, FDRL.

92. Washington *Post*, March 21, 1940.

93. Washington *Star*, March 18, 1940; Interview with James Farley.

94. Charles Michelson, *The Ghost Talks* (New York, 1944), p. 157.

95. Franklin Roosevelt to Herbert Lehman, March 26, 1940, FDRL-PPF 93.

96. New York Times, March 13, 1940.

97. Turner Catledge, *ibid.*, March 17, 1940.

98. New York *Times*, May 24, May 25, June 5, 1940.

99. *Ibid.*, April 2, 1940.

100. Madison *Capital Times*, February 13, 1940.

101. Interview with James Farley, November 9, 1963.

102. Gustave Keller to James Farley, January 3, 1940; Farley to Keller, January 17, 1940, Charles Broughton Papers (Wisconsin State Historical Society Library, Madison, Wisconsin). Cited hereafter as Broughton Papers.

103. Frank McHale to Paul McNutt, August 24, 1939, McNutt Papers; Charles Broughton to James Farley, December 12, 1939, Broughton Papers.

104. Washington *Star*, March 27, 1940. As head of the Wisconsin delegation in 1932, Callahan had refused admission tickets to the Roosevelt members of his delegation, which may have been the origin of the bad blood between them. Arthur Mullen, *Western Democrat* (New York, 1940), p. 269.

105. Aldric Revell, Madison *Capital Times*, February 29, 1940.

106. Rudolph Penn to Harry Bolens, May 18, 1939, Harry Bolens Papers (Wisconsin State Historical Society Library, Madison, Wisconsin).

107. Madison *Capital Times*, April 2, 1940.

108. Leo T. Crowley to Franklin Roosevelt, April 3, 1940, FDRL-PSF, Box 44.

109. Madison *Capital Times*, February 11, 1940.

110. *Ibid.*, April 2, 1940.

111. New York *Herald Tribune*, March 12, 1940.

112. New York *Times*, March 28, 1940.

113. *Ibid.*, April 4, 1940.

114. Baltimore *Sun*, April 5, 1940.

115. T.R.B., "Washington Notes," *New Republic*, CII (April 15, 1940), 504.

116. Arthur Krock, New York *Times*, April 7, 1940.

117. Tom Connally as told to Alfred Steinberg, *My Name Is Tom Connally* (New York, 1954), p. 234.

118. Washington *Star*, February 9, 1940.

119. New York *Times*, April 11, 1940.

120. *Ibid.*

121. Edward Burke to William McAdoo, May 10, 1940, William McAdoo Papers (Library of Congress, Washington, D.C.), Box 471. Cited hereafter as McAdoo Papers.

122. New York *Times*, April 23, 1940.

123. Albert S. Brown to Steve Early, April 18, 1940, FDRL-OF 12.

124. Robert Burke, *Olson's New Deal for California* (Berkeley and Los Angeles, 1953), p. 142.

125. On a memorandum from James Rowe reporting that Olson, through Voorhis, had asked that Roosevelt give some assurance that he would not endorse any other group, Roosevelt pencilled "o.k." in the margin. FDRL-PSF, Box 28.

126. Harold Ickes, *Lowering Clouds*, p. 140.

127. *Ibid.*, p. 150; Ickes to Raymond Robbins, March 20, 1940, Raymond Robbins Papers (Wisconsin State Historical Society Library, Madison, Wisconsin); William McAdoo to Charles Brown, March 15, 1940, McAdoo Papers.

128. Robert Burke, *op. cit.*, p. 141; Ickes to McAdoo, March 24, March 25, 1940, McAdoo Papers.

129. New York *Times*, May 10, 1940.

130. Ickes to McAdoo, May 8, 1940, McAdoo Papers.

131. Harold Ickes, *Lowering Clouds*, p. 155.

132. Washington *News*, April 6, 1940.

133. Dallas *Morning News*, April 11, 1940, in Jones Papers.

134. Tom Miller to A. J. Wirtz, April 11, 1940, Harry Hopkins Papers, FDRL, Confidential Political File.

135. *Ibid.*

136. A. J. Wirtz to Ray Brooks, April 12, 1940, Harry Hopkins Papers, FDRL, Confidential Political File.

137. A. J. Wirtz to Harry Hopkins, April 12, 1940, in *ibid.*

138. Washington *Post*, April 19, 1940.

139. Austin *American*, April 25, 1940, in Hopkins Papers.

140. Harold Ickes, *Lowering Clouds*, pp. 167-169.

141. Jay Franklin, "We the People," Washington *Star*, May 2, 1940.

142. Willis Mahoney to Harry Hopkins, March 13, 1939, Harry Hopkins Papers, FDRL, Confidential Political File.

143. Mahoney to Hopkins, June 27, 1939, in *ibid.*

144. Portland *Oregonian*, May 15, 1940.

145. Mahoney to Hopkins, June 25, 1940, Hopkins Papers, FDRL, Confidential Political File.

146. New York *Times*, February 20, 1940.

147. Washington *Star*, March 16, 1940.

148. "Draft Roosevelt—How?" *The United States News*, VIII (January 5, 1940), pp. 15-16.

149. Washington *Post*, May 1, 1940.

150. FDRL-PSF, Box 18. Hugh Ross in his article, "Roosevelt's Third Term Nomination," *Mid America*, XLIV (April 1962), 91, has suggested that this was transparently designed to head off the third term. Wallace, on the other hand, pointed out to Roosevelt that the names of the fifty-three signers of the petition included Democrats of every shade, mentioning several strong New Dealers. What they were interested in chiefly, he suggested, was party harmony. Henry Wallace to Roosevelt, May 6, 1940, FDRL-PSF, Box 18.

151. New York *Times*, May 9, 1940.

152. James Farley, *op. cit.*, p. 240.

153. *Ibid.*

154. Washington *Post*, May 12, 1940.

155. Robert T. Cochran, Jr., "Virginia's Opposition to the New Deal, 1933-1940," (unpublished master's dissertation, Georgetown University, 1950), p. 140.

156. Washington *Post*, May 8, 1940.

157. *Newsweek*, April 29, 1940, p. 33; Washington *Post*, May 1, 1940.

158. Washington *Post*, April 19, 1940.

159. James Farley, *op. cit.*, p. 250.

160. Washington *Post*, May 1, 1940.

161. Cordell Hull to W. T. Kennerly, May 29, 1940, Cordell Hull Papers (Library of Congress, Washington, D.C.). Cited hereafter as Cordell Hull Papers.

162. J. W. Gardenhiser to Hull, June 22, 1940, Cordell Hull Papers.

163. *Time*, September 11, 1939, p. 17.

164. New York *Times*, April 26, 1940.

165. J. P. Newell to Frank McHale, April 22, 1940, McNutt Papers.

166. New York *Times*, May 16, 1940.

167. Senator Josh Lee to Harry Hopkins, May 26, 1939, Hopkins Papers, FDRL, Confidential Political File.

168. Josh Lee to Franklin Roosevelt, November 27, 1939, FDRL-OF 300, Box 56.

169. Josh Lee to Harry Hopkins, May 14, 1940, Hopkins Papers, FDRL, Confidential Political File; Lee to Roosevelt, June 11, 1940, FDRL-OF 300, Box 56.

170. James Farley, *op. cit.*, p. 250.

171. Washington *Post*, April 29, 1940.

172. Louis L. Snyder, *The War: A Concise History* (New York, 1960), pp. 73-109.

173. *Time*, May 27, 1940, p. 18.

174. New York *Times*, June 5, 1940.

175. *Time*, April 22, 1940.

176. Harold Ickes, "My Twelve Years" (July 17, 1948), 97.

177. *Time*, May 27, 1940, p. 21.

178. New York *Times*, May 27, 1940.

179. T.R.B., "Washington Notes," *New Republic*, CIII (July 8, 1940), 53.

180. Madison *Capital Times*, April 30, 1940.

181. New York *Times*, May 31, 1940.

182. *Ibid.*, June 13, 1940.

183. Interview with Benjamin V. Cohen, November 22, 1963.

184. Burton K. Wheeler with Paul F. Healy, *Yankee from the West* (Garden City, New York, 1962), pp. 361-362.

185. Interview with Benjamin V. Cohen.

186. J. C. Hallack to Steve Early, May 24, 1940, FDRL-OF 2526, Box 21. Replied the delighted Early at this evidence of Wheeler weakness, "I think I can say, without stretching the truth, that your letter of May 24 is the most interesting document that has come to me in the long years since March 4, '33."

187. *P.M.*, June 19, 1940.

188. *Time*, July 1, 1940.

189. *P.M.*, July 1, 1940.

190. New York *Times*, July 3, 1940.

191. *Ibid.*, July 11, 1940.

192. *Ibid.*, July 11, 1940.

193. Robert Jackson to William McAdoo, May 15, 1940, McAdoo Papers.

194. Matthew Josephson, *Sidney Hillman: Statesman of Labor* (Garden City, New York, 1952), pp. 477-478.

195. New York *Times*, May 21, 1940.

196. Claude Pepper to William McAdoo, May 15, McAdoo Papers.

197. Press Release, May 30, 1940; Circular to McNutt workers, June 4, 1940, in McNutt Papers.

198. Maury Maverick to Roosevelt, May 9, 1940, FDRL-PPF 3446.

199. Frank Murphy to Roosevelt, June 10, 1940, Harry Hopkins Papers, General Correspondence.

200. Louis B. Wehle to Roosevelt, May 24, 1940, FDRL-PPF 693.

201. FDRL-OF 2526, Box 21.

202. Baltimore *Sun*, July 9, 1940.

203. Samuel I. Rosenman, *Working with Roosevelt* (New York, 1952), p. 193.

204. Paul Appleby, "Roosevelt's Third Term Decision," *American Political Science Review*, XLVI (September 1952), 756.

205. Harold Ickes, *Lowering Clouds*, p. 107.

206. Frances Perkins, *The Roosevelt I Knew* (New York, 1946), p. 126.

207. Roosevelt to Frank Walker, April 26, 1940, Frank Walker Papers (University of Notre Dame Archives, Notre Dame, Indiana).

208. Mary Dewson, unpublished memoirs, p. 229, Mary Dawson Papers, FDRL.

209. Cordell Hull, *The Memoirs of Cordell Hull*, I (New York, 1948), p. 858.

210. *Ibid.*, p. 857.

211. Harold Ickes, *Lowering Clouds*, p. 216-219.

212. Washington *Post*, April 14, 1940.

213. *Ibid.*, May 15, 1940.

214. Cordell Hull, *op. cit.*, pp. 858-859.

215. Harold Ickes, *Lowering Clouds*, p. 238.

216. *Ibid.*, p. 235.

217. James Byrnes, *All in One Lifetime* (New York, 1958), pp. 117-118.

218. Samuel I. Rosenman, *Working with Roosevelt* (New York, 1952), p. 206.

219. *Ibid.*, p. 208.

220. Jesse H. Jones with Edward Angly, *Fifty Billion Dollars: My Thirteen Years with R.F.C.* (New York, 1951), p. 260.

221. Harold Ickes, *Lowering Clouds*, p. 107; Cordell Hull, *op. cit.*, p. 855; Alben Barkley, *That Reminds Me* (Garden City, New York, 1954), p. 185; Frances Perkins, *op. cit.*, p. 126; Mary Dewson, unpublished memoirs, p. 229, Mary Dewson Papers, FDRL; Benjamin Cohen, interview, November 22, 1963.

222. James McGregor Burns, *Roosevelt: The Lion and the Fox* (New York, 1956), pp. 532-533.

Notes to Chapter VI

1. Harold Ickes, *The Lowering Clouds, 1939-1941*, Vol. III, *The Secret Diary of Harold Ickes* (New York, 1954), p. 240. Cited hereafter as Ickes, *The Lowering Clouds*.
2. *Newsweek*, July 22, 1940, p. 15.
3. E.g., Eleanor Roosevelt, *This I Remember* (New York, 1949), pp. 214-215.
4. *Time*, July 29, 1940, p. 11.
5. *Newsweek*, July 22, 1940, p. 15.
6. Jonathan Mitchell, "Chicago—Family Stuff," *New Republic*, CIII (July 29, 1940), 137.
7. Ickes, *The Lowering Clouds*, p. 246.
8. Paul Appleby, "Roosevelt's Third Term Decision," *American Political Science Review*, XLVI (September, 1952), 755.
9. Samuel I. Rosenman, *Working with Roosevelt* (New York, 1952), pp. 209, 211; Harold Ickes, *The Lowering Clouds*, p. 243.
10. Samuel I. Rosenman, *op. cit.*, p. 209.
11. *Official Report of the Proceedings of the Democratic National Convention, 1940*, p. 5. Cited hereafter as *Official Proceedings*.
12. *P.M.*, July 18, 1940.
13. James Farley, *Jim Farley's Story: The Roosevelt Years* (New York, 1948), pp. 272-273.
14. *Official Proceedings*, p. 16.
15. Samuel I. Rosenman, *op. cit.*, p. 211; James Farley, *op. cit.*, p. 276.
16. James Farley, *op. cit.*, p. 261.
17. Edward J. Flynn, *You're the Boss* (New York, 1947), pp. 156-157.
18. *Newsweek*, July 22, 1940, p. 16.
19. New York *Herald Tribune*, June 16, 1940.
20. Harold Ickes, *The Lowering Clouds*, pp. 243-245.
21. *Ibid.*, pp. 249-250; Ickes to Roosevelt, July 16, 1940, Franklin D. Roosevelt Library, President's Secretary's File, Box 19. Cited hereafter as FDRL-PSF.
22. The wire is in FDRL-Official File 1871, Box 1. Cited hereafter as FDRL-OF.
23. Frances Perkins, *The Roosevelt I Knew* (New York, 1946), pp. 128-132.
24. *Official Proceedings*, pp. 60-61.
25. James Farley, *op. cit.*, p. 280.
26. *Official Proceedings*, p. 69.
27. New York *Herald Tribune*, July 17, 1940.

28. James Byrnes, *Speaking Frankly* (New York, 1947), p. 10; *P.M.*, July 15, 1940.

29. *P.M.*, July 15, 1940.

30. Cordell Hull, *The Memoirs of Cordell Hull* (New York, 1948), I, p. 862.

31. Robert Wagner Papers (Georgetown University, Washington, D.C.).

32. James Byrnes, *op. cit.*, p. 10; Cordell Hull, *op. cit.*, p. 862; *Official Proceedings*, p. 154.

33. James Farley, *op. cit.*, pp. 264-265; New York *Herald Tribune*, July 16, 1940; Washington *News*, July 16, 1940.

34. James Farley, *op. cit.*, pp. 329-330.

35. *Official Proceedings*, p. 166.

36. Chicago *Times*, July 14, 1940.

37. Marquis Childs, *I Write From Washington* (New York, 1942), p. 197; James Farley, *op. cit.*, p. 297.

38. James Farley, *op. cit.*, p. 297.

39. Burton K. Wheeler with Paul F. Healy, *Yankee from the West* (Garden City, New York, 1962), p. 366.

40. Cordell Hull Papers (Library of Congress, Washington, D.C.).

41. *P.M.*, July 18, 1940.

42. Burton K. Wheeler, *op. cit.*, p. 366; Bascom Timmons, *Garner of Texas* (New York, 1948), p. 275.

43. Bascom Timmons, *op. cit.*, p. 275.

44. *Official Proceedings*, p. 168.

45. Roosevelt to R. Walton Moore, August 3, 1940, FDRL-President's Personal File 2605. Cited hereafter as FDRL-PPF.

46. *Official Proceedings*, pp. 179-184.

47. *Ibid.*, pp. 172-174.

48. *Ibid.*, p. 195.

49. Albert Gore to Cordell Hull, July 18, 1940, Cordell Hull Papers.

50. Chicago *Times*, July 14, 1940.

51. James Farley, *op. cit.*, p. 331. Other accounts are Harold Ickes, *The Lowering Clouds*, p. 286, and Cordell Hull, *op. cit.*, pp. 860-861.

52. James Byrnes, *All in One Lifetime* (New York, 1958), pp. 118-120; Samuel I. Rosenman, *op. cit.*, p. 202; Interview with Claude Pepper, August 26, 1963.

53. Dean Albertson, *Roosevelt's Farmer: Claude R. Wickard in the New Deal* (New York, 1961), pp. 142-144.

54. New York *Herald Tribune*, July 16, 1940.

55. James Farley, *op. cit.*, p. 254.

56. Wheeler has stated bluntly that there were at least two administration offers for the vice presidency during the convention—one

by a lawyer, Mose Cohen, after a conversation with Hopkins and Frank Walker, and the other from William H. Hutchinson of International News Service, who told him that it came from Frank Murphy—and Wheeler turned them both down. (Burton K. Wheeler, *op. cit.*, pp. 366-368.) This is contradicted by Frank Walker, who thought that Mose Cohen was an emissary from Wheeler and "He'd have made up with Roosevelt in a minute if he could have secured the vice presidential nomination." (Frank Walker, unpublished memoirs, University of Notre Dame Archives, Notre Dame, Indiana.) William Hutchinson's report from the convention mentioned only that "insiders," with Roosevelt's knowledge, were approaching both Murphy and Wheeler to see if they were interested. (Washington *Times-Herald*, July 16, 1940.) Benjamin Cohen, certainly an "insider," has expressed strong doubts about the accuracy of that report. (Interview November 22, 1963.) Most important of all, James O'Connor, Congressman from Montana, called Harold Ickes after the foreign-relations plank had been agreed on to say that Wheeler was willing to accept the nomination, but did not want his name presented unless there was a chance the President would accept him. Ickes opined that the President would not. (Harold Ickes, *The Lowering Clouds*, p. 254.)

57. Jonathan Mitchell, "M-Day Man: Louis A. Johnson," *New Republic*, XCVIII (February 22, 1939), 63.

58. James Farley, *op. cit.*, p. 294.

59. Harold Ickes, *The Lowering Clouds*, p. 287.

60. Everyone who has written an account of what happened at the convention has a different version of where and how Roosevelt informed the party leaders of his choice, but all agree that the immediate reaction was dismay.

61. Wire is in FDRL-OF 1871, Box 1.

62. Roosevelt to George Norris, July 21, 1940, Franklin D. Roosevelt, *F.D.R.: His Personal Letters*, ed. Elliot Roosevelt (New York, 1947-1950), pp. 1046-1047.

63. Claude Pepper to Roosevelt, July 23, 1940, FDRL-PPF 4773.

64. Harold Ickes, *The Lowering Clouds*, pp. 256-257.

65. Samuel I. Rosenman, *op. cit.*, p. 213.

66. Alben Barkley, *That Reminds Me* (Garden City, New York, 1954), p. 186; George Creel, *Rebel at Large: Recollections of Fifty Crowded Years* (New York, 1947), p. 313.

67. Interview with Claude Pepper, August 26, 1963.

68. Samuel I. Rosenman, *op. cit.*, p. 213.

69. Grace Tully, *F.D.R. My Boss* (New York, 1949), p. 238.

70. Lloyd Stark to Henry Wallace, July 18, 1940, FDRL-PPF 4462.

71. Eleanor Roosevelt, *op. cit.*, p. 217; James Farley, *op. cit.*, pp. 300-301.

72. Paul Appleby, *loc. cit.*, p. 760, has stated that McNutt's sup-

port came almost entirely from galleries packed by his supporters and a few disappointed followers of other candidates. Interviews with Claude Pepper and James Farley and also the accounts of *Newsweek*, July 29, 1940, p. 9, and *Time*, July 29, 1940, p. 13, all indicate that the enthusiasm was genuine and McNutt could have taken the nomination had he so desired.

73. *Official Proceedings*, pp. 210-237.

74. Neil MacNeil, "How to Rig a Convention," *Saturday Evening Post*, CCXIII (October 26, 1940), 73, 75.

75. James Byrnes, *All in One Lifetime* (New York, 1958), pp. 124-125.

76. Interview with James Farley, November 9, 1963.

77. Allan Nevins, *Herbert H. Lehman and His Era* (New York, 1963), pp. 208-209.

78. *Official Proceedings*, p. 240.

79. *Ibid.*, pp. 240-241.

80. Samuel I. Rosenman, *op. cit.*, pp. 215-216.

81. *Time*, September 23, 1940, p. 13.

82. James Farley, *op. cit.*, p. 302.

83. Dean Albertson, *op. cit.*, pp. 146-147.

84. *Official Proceedings*, pp. 252-259.

85. "Who Willed the Third Term," *New Republic*, CIII (July 29, 1940), 135; *P.M.*, July 19, 1940.

86. Indianapolis *Star*, July 19, 1940.

87. Edgar E. Robinson, *The Roosevelt Leadership, 1933-1945* (Philadelphia and New York, 1955), p. 253.

88. Paul Appleby, *loc. cit.*, p. 259.

89. George Allen, *Presidents Who Have Known Me* (New York, 1950), pp. 130-131.

90. Washington *Times-Herald*, July 18, 1940.

91. Roosevelt to George Norris, July 21, 1940, *Personal Letters*, p. 1047.

92. Clyde Herring to William McAdoo, July 31, 1940, William McAdoo Papers (Library of Congress, Washington, D.C.). Cited hereafter as McAdoo Papers.

93. Frank McHale to Paul McNutt, August 6, 1940, Paul McNutt Papers (Lilly Library, Indiana University).

94. FDRL-OF 2526.

95. New York *Times*, July 31, 1940.

96. Donald Bruce Johnson, *The Republican Party and Wendell Willkie* (Urbana, 1960), p. 115.

97. *Time*, August 5, 1940, p. 14.

98. Press Conference No. 662, July 23, 1940, FDRL.

99. New York *Times*, July 23, 1940.

100. *Ibid.*, October 1, 3, 1940. Colby's speech to the committee

in the Bainbridge Colby Papers (Library of Congress, Washington, D.C.)

101. Irving Bernstein, "John L. Lewis and the Voting Behavior of the C.I.O.," *Public Opinion Quarterly*, V (June, 1941), 234.

102. New York *Times*, October 26, 1940.

103. Matthew Josephson, *Sidney Hillman: Statesman of Labor* (Garden City, New York, 1952), p. 488.

104. Irving Bernstein, *loc. cit.*, p. 237.

105. Sampy Keene to Roosevelt, October 28, 1940, FDRL-PPF 3183.

106. Saul Alinsky, *John L. Lewis: An Unauthorized Biography* (New York, 1949), p. 174; Irving Bernstein, *loc. cit.*, p. 236. Alinsky has suggested that Lewis endorsed Willkie instead of remaining silent to avoid giving aid and comfort to the Communists in the union.

107. "Who Willed the Third Term," *New Republic*, CIII (July 29, 1940), 135.

108. James Farley, *op. cit.*, pp. 307-309.

109. *Ibid.*, p. 312; interview with James Farley, November 9, 1963.

110. "Meeting of the Democratic National Committee, Friday, July 19, 1940," *Official Proceedings*, p. 364.

111 New York *Times*, October 1, 1940.

112. James T. Mathews to Frank Walker, October 24, 1940, Walker Papers, University of Notre Dame, Notre Dame, Indiana).

113. New York *Times*, October 29, November 3, 1940.

114. *Ibid.*, November 4, 1940.

115. Mrs. Earl Ketcham to Mary Dewson, September 27, 1940, Mary Dewson Papers, FDRL.

116. Frank Walker, unpublished memoirs, Walker Papers.

117. New York *Times*, July 23, 1940.

118. *Ibid.*

119. *Ibid.*, November 6, 1940.

120. *Ibid.*, November 3, 1940.

121. Louis Macht to Roosevelt, October 17, 1940, FDRL-OF 300, Box 36.

122. Robert T. Cochran, Jr., "Virginia's Opposition to the New Deal, 1933-1940" (unpublished master's dissertation, Georgetown University, June, 1950), p. 146.

123. New York *Times*, November 2, 1940.

124. *Ibid.*, October 6, 1940.

125. Tom Connally as told to Alfred Steinberg, *My Name Is Tom Connally* (New York, 1954), p. 235.

126. New York *Times*, July 24, 1940.

127. Alan Valentine to Emil Hurja, August 26, 1940, Emil Hurja Papers, FDRL.

128. Dan Tobin to Edward Flynn, November 11, 1940, FDRL-PPF, 1180.

129. Harold Ickes, *The Lowering Clouds*, pp. 278-279.

130. Edward J. Flynn, *op. cit.*, p. 161.

131. *Ibid.*, pp. 162-164.

132. *Ibid.*, pp. 166-167.

133. Ickes to Roosevelt, October 5, 1940; Steve Early to Charles Michelson, October 5, 1940; Ickes to Early, October 6, 1940; Early memorandum, October 10, 1940, FDRL-OF 6.

134. Harold Ickes, "My Twelve Years with Roosevelt," *Saturday Evening Post*, CCXX (July 10, 1948), 112. Cited hereafter as "My Twelve Years."

135. Samuel I. Rosenman, *op. cit.*, p. 227; Rexford G. Tugwell, *The Demcoratic Roosevelt* (Garden City, New York, 1957), p. 547. Tugwell suggests that Corcoran was the victim of the jealousy of Harry Hopkins, and he was actually less a liability than in 1937, when the President ignored all criticism of him. But 1937 was not an election year, and the President was considerably more sure of his power over the party then. Moreover, Hopkins had demonstrated in 1938, when he refused to have anything to do with Wallace's efforts to oust Ickes from the Cabinet, that he did not let his personal feelings stand in the way of what he thought was best for the Administration.

136. Harold Ickes, "My Twelve Years," p. 112.

137. Bascom Timmons, *Jesse Jones: The Man and the Statesman* (New York, 1956), p. 251.

138. *Ibid.*, pp. 280-281.

139. Theodore M. Black, *Democratic Party Publicity in the 1940 Campaign* (New York, 1941), p. 109.

140. Harold Gosnell, *Champion Campaigner: Franklin D. Roosevelt* (New York, 1952), p. 181.

141. E.g., lists presented by Paul Aiken to Wagner, September 28, September 30, 1940, Robert Wagner Papers (Georgetown University, Washington, D.C.).

142. Edward Kelley to Wagner, August 15, 1940, Wagner Papers.

143. Madison *Capital Times*, November 4, 1940.

144. Hugo Black to Robert Wagner, November 6, 1940, Wagner Papers.

145. Edward J. Flynn, *op. cit.*, p. 166.

146. Theodore Black, *op. cit.*, p. 66.

147. Max Lerner, "Jim Farley, Soldier and Artist," *New Republic*, XCVII (December 28, 1939), 237.

148. Harold Gosnell, *op. cit.*, p. 186.

149. Samuel Lubell, "Post Mortem: Who Elected Roosevelt?" *Saturday Evening Post*, CCXIII (January 25, 1940), 94.

150. Charles W. Van Devander, *The Big Bosses* (New York, 1944), p. 100.

151. James Farley is still of the opinion that Cordell Hull would have run far better than Roosevelt because he would have attracted the support of men like Al Smith and John W. Davis as well as the liberals. It seems likely, however, that the votes such men as these could deliver would have been more than offset by the lack of enthusiasm of organized labor, Negroes, and the unemployed. (Interview with James Farley, November 9, 1963.)

152. Irving Bernstein, *loc. cit.*, pp. 240-241.

153. Sherman Minton to William McAdoo, November 16, 1940, McAdoo Papers.

154. Sherman Minton to Josephus Daniels, November 20, 1940, Josephus Daniels Papers (Library of Congress, Washington, D.C.), Box 472.

155. Samuel Lubell, *loc. cit.*, p. 91.

156. Samuel Lubell, *Revolt of the Moderates* (New York, 1950), p. 80.

157. Mrs. Earl F. Ketcham to Mary Dewson, September 27, 1940, Mary Dewson Papers, FDRL; *Time*, September 16, 1940, p. 17.

158. Joseph Howard, "The Decline and Fall of Burton K. Wheeler," *Harper's*, CXCIV (March 1947), 227; Robert T. Cochran, Jr., *loc. cit.*, p. 147.

159. Malcolm Moos, *Politics, Presidents, and Coattails* (Baltimore, 1952), p. 11.

BIBLIOGRAPHY

PRIMARY SOURCES

MANUSCRIPTS

The most important collection of private papers for the Roosevelt years is, of course, at the Roosevelt Memorial Library, Hyde Park, New York. The Roosevelt Papers themselves are subdivided into the President's Personal File (PPF), the President's Secretary's File (PSF), and the Official File (OF). The Papers of the Democratic National Committee are listed in the Official File 300. Other private collections housed at the Roosevelt Library which proved useful were the Harry Hopkins Papers, the Mary Dewson Papers, especially her memoirs, and, to a lesser extent, the Emil Hurja Papers.

    Particularly valuable sources housed in the Manuscripts Division of the Library of Congress were the papers of Josephus Daniels, William Gibbs McAdoo, Jesse Jones, and Cordell Hull. The papers of Bainbridge Colby, Thomas Connally, George Creel, and Lewis Schwellenbach proved to be of very little significance.

The papers of Paul V. McNutt at the Lilly Library, Indiana University, and the Frank Walker Papers in the archives of the University of Notre Dame were especially important. Neither has been well explored by any previous historian. The papers of Senator Robert Wagner at Georgetown University, Washington, D. C., were of value only with regard to the fight over the platform of the 1940 Democratic Convention.

The Charles Broughton Papers at the State Historical Society Library, Madison, Wisconsin, were valuable for the 1940 Wisconsin primary, and the papers of Merlin Hull and Harry Bolens, housed in the same place, were enlightening on Wisconsin politics in general. The Raymond Robbins Papers, also at the State Historical Library, provided some interesting insights into the liberal mind of the late 1930's.

There are no John Nance Garner papers, inasmuch as the former Vice President had them burned shortly after his retirement. The closest thing to his version of the story is the biography of him by Bascom Timmons (listed under biography), to which Garner appended an endorsement of everything said therein. The recently opened papers of Frank Murphy at the University of Michigan were not consulted on the advice of Professor Sidney Fine of the University of Michigan, who has been through the papers and advised the author that there was nothing in them which has not already appeared in print with regard to the topic of this paper.

NEWSPAPERS AND PERIODICALS

The New York *Times* was used almost exclusively on a day by day basis from 1937 to 1940 for news stories; it was supplemented somewhat, especially from 1938 on, by the Washington *Post*. Three Washington papers—the *News, Star,* and *Times Herald*—as well as the *Baltimore Sun* and the New York *Herald Tribune*, were used largely for the columns of their Washington correspondents. From December, 1939, through 1940, the liberal Madison *Capital Times* and the New York *P.M.* were consulted.

The weekly or monthly news magazines and journals of opinion which were used from 1937 through 1940 were *The New Republic, Nation, Newsweek, Time,* and *Fortune.* From January, 1940, on, *United States News* was also of value.

MEMOIRS, DIARIES, AND AUTOBIOGRAPHIES

This period is especially rich in the published personal recollections of the principal figures on the political scene. Undoubtedly the most significant of these for this paper are

Blum, John Morton. *From the Morgenthau Diaries: Years of Crisis, 1928-1938*. Boston: Houghton-Mifflin Co., 1959.

Farley, James A. *Jim Farley's Story: The Roosevelt Years*. New York: Whittlesey House, McGraw-Hill Book Co., 1948.

———. *Behind the Ballots: The Personal History of a Politician*. New York: Harcourt, Brace and Co., 1938.

Flynn, Edward J. *You're the Boss*. New York: Viking Press, 1947.

Hull, Cordell. *The Memoirs of Cordell Hull*. 2 vols. New York: Macmillan Co., 1948, Vol. I.

Ickes, Harold L. *The Inside Struggle, 1936-1939*. Vol. II of *The Secret Diary of Harold Ickes*. New York: Simon and Shuster, 1953.

———. *The Lowering Clouds, 1939-1941*. Vol. III of *The Secret Diary of Harold Ickes*. New York: Simon and Shuster, 1954.

Rosenman, Samuel I. *Working with Roosevelt*. New York: Harper, 1952.

Wheeler, Burton K. with Paul F. Healy. *Yankee from the West*. Garden City, New York: Doubleday and Co., 1962.

Other books by members of the administration which proved valuable in varying degrees are

Eccles, Marriner. *Beckoning Frontiers*. Edited by Sidney Hyman. New York: Alfred A. Knopf Co., 1951.

Ickes, Harold L. *The Autobiography of a Curmudgeon*. New York: Reynal and Hitchcock, 1943.

Jones, Jesse H. with Edward Angly. *Fifty Billion Dollars: My Thirteen Years with R. F. C.* New York: Macmillan Co., 1951.

Perkins, Frances. *The Roosevelt I Knew*. New York: Viking Press, 1946.

Tully, Grace. *F. D. R. My Boss*. New York: Charles Scribner's Sons, 1949.

Books by members of Congress are

Barkley, Alben. *That Reminds Me*. Garden City, New York: Doubleday and Co., 1954.

Byrnes, James F. *All in One Lifetime.* New York: Harper, 1958.
———. *Speaking Frankly.* New York: Harper, 1947.
Connally, Tom as told to Alfred Steinberg. *My Name Is Tom Connally.* New York: Thomas Y. Crowell Co., 1954.
Norris, George. *Fighting Liberal: The Autobiography of George W. Norris.* New York: Macmillan Co., 1945.
Truman, Harry S. *Years of Decision.* Vol. I of *The Memoirs of Harry Truman.* Garden City, New York: Doubleday, Doran and Co., 1955-1956.
Voorhis, Horace Jeremiah. *Confessions of a Congressman.* Garden City, New York: Doubleday Co., 1947.

Finally, books by other relatively qualified observers are

Allen, George E. *Presidents Who Have Known Me.* New York: Simon and Schuster, 1950.
Brownlow, Louis. *A Passion for Anonymity.* 2 vols. Chicago: University of Chicago Press, 1958, Vol. II.
Childs, Marquis. *I Write from Washington.* New York: Harper and Brothers, 1942.
Clapper, Raymond. *Watching the World.* New York: Whittlesey House, McGraw-Hill Book Co., 1946.
Creel, George. *Rebel at Large: Recollections of Fifty Crowded Years.* New York: G. P. Putnam's Sons, 1947.
Michelson, Charles. *The Ghost Talks.* New York: G. P. Putnam's Sons, 1944.
Moley, Raymond. *After Seven Years.* New York: Harper and Brothers, 1939.
Mullen, Arthur F. *Western Democrat.* New York: Wilfred Funk, Inc., 1940.
Richberg, Donald. *My Hero: The Indiscreet Memoirs of an Uneventful but Unheroic Life.* New York: G. P. Putnam's Sons, 1954.
Roosevelt, Eleanor. *This I Remember.* New York: Harper and Brothers, 1949.
Roosevelt, James, and Shalett, Sidney. *Affectionately, F. D. R.: A Son's Story of a Lonely Man.* New York: Harcourt, Brace and Co., 1959.
Roosevelt, Nicholas. *A Front Row Seat.* Norman, Oklahoma: University of Oklahoma Press, 1953.
Smith, Merriman. *Thank You Mr. President.* New York: Harper and Brothers, 1946.

Stokes, Thomas L. *Chip Off My Shoulder.* Princeton: Princeton University Press, 1940.

Wehle, Louis B. *Hidden Threads of History: Wilson Through Roosevelt.* New York: Macmillan Co., 1953.

White, Walter. *A Man Called White.* New York: Viking Press, 1948.

Winant, John Gilbert. *Letter from Grosvenor Square.* Boston: Houghton-Mifflin Co., 1947.

PUBLISHED DOCUMENTS AND LETTERS

Cannon, Clarence. *Democratic Manual of the Democratic National Convention.* 4th Ed., 1940.

Official Report of the Proceedings of the Democratic National Convention, 1940.

Roosevelt, Franklin D. *F. D. R.: His Personal Letters.* Edited by Elliott Roosevelt. New York: Duell, Sloan and Pearce, 1947-1950.

————. *The Public Papers of Franklin D. Roosevelt.* 9 vols. Edited by Samuel I. Rosenman. New York: Random House, 1938 and 1941, Vols. VI, VII, VIII, and IX.

U. S. Congress. *Congressional Record,* 75 Cong., 1 Sess. through 76 Cong., 2 Sess. January, 1937, to February, 1940.

BOOKS OF CONTEMPORARY OPINION AND REPORTING

Alsop, Joseph, and Catledge, Turner. *The 168 Days.* Garden City, New York: Doubleday, Doran and Co., 1938.

Alsop, Joseph, and Kintner, Robert. *Men Around the President.* New York: Doubleday, Doran and Co., 1939.

Baldwin, Roger N., and Randall, Clarence B. *Civil Liberties and Industrial Conflict.* Cambridge, Massachusetts: Harvard University Press, 1938.

Chamberlain, John. *The American Stakes.* New York: Carrick and Evans, Inc., 1940.

High, Stanley. *Roosevelt—and Then?* New York: Harper and Brothers, 1937.

Johnson, Gerald. *Roosevelt: Dictator or Democrat.* New York: Harper and Brothers, 1941.

JOURNAL ARTICLES

Because the number of articles used would almost constitute a book in itself if listed here, I have chosen to omit those from journals already mentioned in the bibliography elsewhere, namely, *The New Republic*, *Nation*, *Time*, *Newsweek*, *Fortune*, and *United States News*. The articles taken from these sources may be found in the footnotes.

1937

Alsop, Joseph, and Turner, Catledge. "Tom Jeff—He Loves the President, But—" *Saturday Evening Post*, January 9, 1937, 5 ff.

Belair, Felix, Jr. "Two of the Selfless Six," *Nation's Business*, July, 1937, 25 ff.

Creel, George. "Parade to the Post," *Colliers*, October 2, 1937, 25-26 ff.

DeVoto, Bernard. "Desertion from the New Deal," *Harper's*, October, 1937, 557-560.

Essary, J. Fred. "Split in the Democratic Party," *Atlantic*, December, 1937, 751-758.

"Farley for President," *American Mercury*, November, 1937, 257-274.

"First Session Ends in Political Turmoil; Major Acts," *Congressional Digest*, August, 1937, 193-196.

High, Stanley. "Party Purge," *Saturday Evening Post*, August 21, 1937, 16 ff.

———. "Roosevelt: Democratic or Dictatorial," *Harper's*, October, 1937, 480-487.

———. "Whose Party Is It?" *Saturday Evening Post*, February 6, 1937, 10 ff.

———. "Will It Be Wallace?" *Saturday Evening Post*, July 3, 1937, 5 ff.

Johnston, Alva. "President Tamer," *Saturday Evening Post*, November 13, 1937, 8 ff.

———. "White House Tommy," *Saturday Evening Post*, July 31, 1937, 5 ff.

Leach, Paul. "Iffies on the Wabash," *Saturday Evening Post*, December 11, 1937, 10 ff.

Shaw, Albert. "Third Term Reticence," *Literary Digest*, October 9, 1937, 12.

"Washington Bulletin," *Business Week*, September 4, 1937, 5.

"Who's Who and Where in Congress," *Business Week*, October 30, 1937, 30.

1938

Alexander, Jack. "Missouri Dark Mule," *Saturday Evening Post*, October 8, 1938, 5 ff.

Altman, O. R. "Second and Third Sessions of the Seventy-Fifth Congress, 1937-8," *American Political Science Review*, XXXII (December, 1938), 1099-1123.

Banning, Margaret Culkin. "Conservative Front," *Saturday Evening Post*, January 8, 1938, 23 ff.

Bolles, Blair. "Cohen and Corcoran: Brain Twins," *American Mercury*, January, 1938, 38-45.

Clapper, Raymond. "Return to the Two-Party System," *Current History*, December, 1938, 13-15.

———. "Roosevelt Tries the Primaries," *Current History*, October, 1938, 16-19.

"Democrats Fight for 1940 Control," *Congressional Digest*, June, 1938, 161-163.

High, Stanley. "Fog Over Washington," *Saturday Evening Post*, April 9, 1938, 27 ff.

Hyde, Henry M. "White House No Man," *Saturday Evening Post*, June 25, 1938, 23 ff.

"If Politics Permits; Coalition of Democrats and Republicans," *Saturday Evening Post*, March 19, 1938, 22.

Johnson, Hugh S. "Third Term????" *Saturday Evening Post*, December 17, 1938, 12 ff.

Kent, Frank. "No Third Term for Roosevelt," *American Mercury*, January, 1938, 1-9.

Pharo, Eugene. "Governor Earle of Pennsylvania," *Amercian Mercury*, February, 1938, 164-174.

Sullivan, Mark. "Purge Has Left the Democratic Party Without Leadership," *Congressional Digest*, October, 1938, 255.

1939

Bell, Ulric. "Little Jack Garner," *American Mercury*, May, 1939, 1-8.

Clapper, Raymond. "Third Term for Roosevelt?" *Current History*, August, 1939, 13-16 ff.

"Congress Begins Looking at the Presidential Prospects," *Congressional Digest*, May, 1939, 129-131.

Davis, Elmer. "The Wisconsin Brothers: A Study in Partial Eclipse," *Harper's*, February, 1939, 268-277.

"Garner for President," *Current History*, July, 1939, 7.

James, Marquis. "Poker-Playing, Whiskey-Drinking, Evil Old Man!" *Saturday Evening Post*, September 9, 1939.

Kent, Frank R. "Great Corcoran Drive for the Third Term Idea," *Current History*, July, 1939, 40.

Lindley, Ernest K. "New Deal Faces 1940," *Virginia Quarterly Review*, XV, (July, 1939), 321-332.

Lyons, Eugene. "Beware the Third Termites," *American Mercury*, August, 1939, 385-391.

"McNutt for '40?" *Current History*, August, 1939, 7.

Owens, J. W. "Lewis vs. Garner: A Sign of Political Times," *Current History*, September, 1939, 36-37.

Riddick, Floyd. "The First Session of the Seventy Sixth Congress," *American Political Science Review*, XXXIII (December, 1939), 1022-1043.

Shannon, J. B. "Presidential Politics in the South: 1938," *Journal of Politics*, (May, 1939), 146-170; (August, 1939), 278-300.

Wilcox, Francis O. "The Neutrality Fight in Congress," *The American Political Science Review*, XXXIII (October, 1939), 811-825.

1940

Allen, Robert S. "Wheeler and the Liberals," *Current History*, March, 1940, 25-27.

"Congress Watches Politics and Battles the New Deal," *Congressional Digest*, May, 1940, 129-130.

Corey, Herbert. "Great God McNutt," *American Mercury*, January, 1940, 30-36.

Davis, Elmer. "Contradiction in Chicago," *Saturday Review of Literature*, August 3, 1940, 8-9.

Howard, Clinton N. "The Democratic Debacle: The Story of the Democratic Convention," *Progress*, XL (August, 1940).

"Jack, the Giant Killer, Heir Apparent?" *Business Week*, February 10, 1940, 24 ff.

Johnston, Alva. "I Intend to be President," *Saturday Evening Post*, March 16, 1940, 20-21 ff.

Lucey, C. "Did the President Sign Away 1940? What Will the Hatch Act Do to This Year's Election?" *Saturday Evening Post*, January 27, 1940, 27 ff.

MacNeil, Neil. "How to Rig a Convention," *Saturday Evening Post*, October 26, 1940, 29 ff.

Newberger, Richard L. "Wheeler of Montana," *Harper's*, May, 1940, 609-618.

"Presidential Politics Dominates the Legislative Situation," *Congressional Digest*, March, 1940, 65-66.

Pringle, Henry F. "McNutt is Willing," *Forum*, CIII (June, 1940), 311-316.

White, William Allen. "Candidates in the Spring," *Yale Review,* XXIX (March, 1940), 433-443.

1941

Alsop, Joseph and Kintner, Robert. "Never Leave Them Angry: Sam Rayburn Tackles His Biggest Job," *Saturday Evening Post,* January 18, 1941, 22 ff.

Bernstein, Irving. "John L. Lewis and the Voting Behavior of the C.I.O.," *Public Opinion Quarterly,* V (June, 1941), 233-249.

Lubell, Samuel. "Post-Mortem: Who Elected Roosevelt?" *Saturday Evening Post.* January 25, 1941, 11 ff.

SECONDARY SOURCES

BIOGRAPHIES

Albertson, Dean. *Roosevelt's Farmer: Claude R. Wickard in the New Deal.* New York: Columbia University Press, 1961.

Alinsky, Saul. *John L. Lewis: An Unauthorized Biography.* New York: G. P. Putnam's Sons, 1949.

Burns, James MacGregor. *Roosevelt: The Lion and the Fox,* New York: Harcourt-Brace Co., 1949.

Coit, Margaret L. *Mr. Baruch.* Boston: Houghton-Mifflin Co., 1957.

Dorough, C. Dwight. *Mr. Sam.* New York: Random House, 1962.

Frank, John P. *Mr. Justice Black: The Man and His Opinions.* New York: Alfred A. Knopf, 1949.

Gellermann, William. *Martin Dies.* New York: John Day, 1944.

Gerhart, Eugene. *America's Advocate: Robert H. Jackson.* Indianapolis: Bobbs-Merrill Co., 1958.

Gunther, John. *Roosevelt in Retrospect.* New York: Harper and Brothers, 1950.

James, Marquis. *Mr. Garner of Texas.* Indianapolis: Bobbs-Merrill Co., 1939.

Josephson, Matthew. *Sidney Hillman: Statesman of Labor.* Garden City, New York: Doubleday and Co., 1952.

Lord, Russell. *The Wallaces of Iowa.* Boston: Houghton Mifflin Co., 1947.

McKenna, Marian C. *Borah.* Ann Arbor: University of Michigan Press, 1961.

Moley, Raymond. *27 Masters of Politics.* New York: Funk and Wagnalls Co., 1949.

Morison, Elting. *Turmoil and Tradition: A Study of the Life and Times of Henry L. Stimson*. Boston: Houghton Mifflin Co., 1960.

Nevins, Allan. *Herbert H. Lehman and His Era*. New York: Charles Schribner's Sons, 1963.

Salter, J. T. (ed.). *Public Men In and Out of Office*. Chapel Hill, North Carolina: University of North Carolina Press, 1946.

Sherwood, Robert. *Roosevelt and Hopkins: An Intimate History*. 2 vols. New York: Harper (Bantam Book Edition), 1950. Vol. I.

Smith, Rixey, and Beasley, Norman. *Carter Glass, a Biography*. New York: Longmans, Green and Co., 1939.

Stimson, Henry L., and Bundy, McGeorge. *On Active Service in Peace and War*. New York: Harper and Brothers, 1947.

Timmons, Bascom. *Garner of Texas*. New York: Harper and Brothers, 1948.

———. *Jesse H. Jones: The Man and the Statesman*. New York: Henry Holt Co., 1956.

Tugwell, Rexford Guy. *The Democratic Roosevelt*. Garden City, New York: Doubleday Co., 1957.

Wechsler, James. *Labor Baron*. New York: W. Morrow and Co., 1944.

GENERAL BACKGROUND ON POLITICS IN THE 1930'S

Allen, Frederick Lewis. *Since Yesterday: The Nineteen-Thirties in America, 1929-1939*. New York: Harper, 1940.

Binkley, Wilfred N. *American Political Parties: Their Natural History*. 3rd Ed. Revised. New York: Alfred A. Knopf, 1959.

Burns, James MacGregor. *Congress on Trial: The Legislative Process and the Administrative State*. New York: Harper and Brothers, 1949.

Corwin, Edward S. *The Presidential Office and Powers, 1787-1948*. New York: New York University Press, 1948.

Crane, Milton. *The Roosevelt Era*. New York: Broni and Gaer, 1947.

Franklin, John Hope. *From Slavery to Freedom: A History of American Negroes*. New York: Alfred A. Knopf, 1956.

Goldman, Eric. *Rendezvous with Destiny*. New York: Vintage Books, 1956.

Harrison, Gordon. *Road to the Right: The Tradition and Hope of American Conservatives*. New York: William Morrow and Co., 1954.

Hofstadter, Richard. *The American Political Tradition and the Men Who Made It*. New York: Vintage Books, 1955.

Johnson, Walter. *1600 Pennsylvania Avenue: Presidents and the People, 1929-1959*. Boston: Little, Brown and Co., 1960.

Kempton, Murray. *Part of Our Time: Some Ruins and Monuments of the Thirties.* New York: Simon and Schuster, 1955.

Key, V. O., Jr. *Southern Politics in State and Nation.* New York: Alfred A. Knopf, 1949.

Lubell, Samuel. *The Future of American Politics.* New York: Harper and Brothers, 1952.

———. *Revolt of the Moderates.* New York: Harper and Brothers, 1956.

Mitchell, Broadus. *Depression Decade: From the New Era Through the New Deal, 1929-1941.* New York: Rhinehart Co., 1947.

Moos, Malcolm C. and Hess, Stephen. *Hats in the Ring.* New York: Random House, 1960.

———. *Politics, Presidents, and Coattails.* Baltimore: John Hopkins, 1952.

Nye, Russel B. *Midwestern Progressive Politics.* Lansing: Michigan State College Press, 1951.

Pollard, J. E. *The Presidents and the Press.* New York: Macmillan Co., 1947.

Roseboom, Eugene H. *A History of Presidential Elections.* New York: Macmillan Co., 1957.

Saloutos, Theodore and Hicks, John. *Agricultural Discontent in the Middle West, 1900-1939.* Madison: University of Wisconsin Press, 1951.

Shannon, Jasper Berry. *Toward a New Politics in the South.* Knoxville: University of Tennessee Press, 1949.

Snyder, Louis L. *The War: A Concise History.* New York: Julian Messner, Inc., 1960.

Stein, C. W. *The Third Term Tradition.* New York: Columbia University Press, 1943.

Taft, Philip. *The A.F. of L. from the Death of Gompers to the Merger.* New York: Harper and Brothers, 1959.

Tatum, Elbert Lee. *The Changed Political Thought of the Negro, 1915-1940.* New York: Exposition Press, 1951.

Van Devander, Charles W. *The Big Bosses.* New York: Howell, Soskin Co., 1944.

Wecter, Dixon. *The Age of the Great Depression, 1929-1941.* New York: Macmillan Co., 1948.

PROBLEMS AND POLITICS OF THE NEW DEAL

Brogan, Dennis. *The Era of Franklin D. Roosevelt.* Chronicles of America Series. New Haven: Yale University Press, 1950.

Burke, Robert. *Olson's New Deal for California*. Berkley and Los Angeles: University of California Press, 1953.

Cochran, Robert Thomas, Jr. "Virginia's Opposition to the New Deal 1933-1940," Unpublished Master's Dissertation, Department of History, Georgetown University, 1950.

Crownover, A. Blair. "Franklin Roosevelt and the Primary Campaigns of the 1938 Congressional Elections," Unpublished Senior Essay, Princeton University, 1955.

Derber, Milton, and Young, Edwin (eds.). *Labor and the New Deal*. Madison: University of Wisconsin Press, 1957.

Divine, Robert. *The Illusion of Neutrality*. Chicago: University of Chicago Press, 1962.

Einaudi, Mario. *The Roosevelt Revolution*. New York: Harcourt, Brace and Co., 1959.

Flynn, John T. *Country Squire in the White House*. New York: Doubleday, Doran and Co., 1940.

———. *The Roosevelt Myth*. New York: The Devin-Adair Co., 1948.

Gosnell, Harold. *Champion Campaigner: Franklin D. Roosevelt*. New York: Macmillan Co., 1952.

Greer, Thomas H. *What Roosevelt Thought: The Social and Political Ideas of Franklin D. Roosevelt*. East Lansing, Michigan State University Press, 1958.

Kifer, Allen Francis. "The Negro Under the New Deal, 1933-1940," Unpublished Doctoral Dissertation, Department of History, University of Wisconsin, 1961.

Johnson, Donald Bruce. *The Republican Party and Wendell Wilkie*. Urbana: University of Illinois Press, 1960.

Leuchtenburg, William E. *Franklin D. Roosevelt and the New Deal, 1932-1940*. The New American Nation Series. Edited by Henry Steele Commager and Richard B. Morris. New York, Evanston, and London: Harper and Row (Torchbooks Edition), 1963.

McCoy, Donald R. *Angry Voices: Left-of-Center Politics in the New Deal Era*. Lawrence: University of Kansas Press, 1958.

Ogden, August Raymond. *The Dies Committee*. Washington: Catholic University of America Press, 1943.

Perkins, Dexter. *The New Age of Franklin D. Roosevelt, 1932-1945*. Chicago: University of Chicago Press, 1957.

Rauch, Basil. *The History of the New Deal, 1933-1938*. New York: Creative Age Press, 1944.

Robinson, Edgar Eugene. *The Roosevelt Leadership: 1933-1945*. Philadelphia and New York: Lippincott, 1955.

————. *They Voted for Roosevelt: The Presidential Vote 1932-1944.* Stanford: Stanford University Press, 1947.

Schlesinger, Arthur M., Jr. *The Coming of the New Deal.* Vol. II of *The Age of Roosevelt.* Boston: Houghton Mifflin Co., 1958.

————. *The Politics of Upheaval.* Vol. III of *The Age of Roosevelt.* Boston: Houghton Mifflin Co., 1960.

JOURNALS AND PERIODICALS

Alexander, Albert. "The President and the Investigator; Roosevelt and Dies," *Antioch Review,* XV (Spring, 1955), 106-117.

Appleby, Paul. "Roosevelt's Third Term Decision," *American Political Science Review,* XLVI (September, 1952), 754-765.

Berdahl, Clarence A. "Political Parties and Elections," *American Political Science Review,* XXXVII (February, 1943), 68-81.

Blackwood, George D. "The Sit-Down Strike in the Thirties," *South Atlantic Quarterly,* LV (October, 1956), 438-448.

Cronon, E. David. "A Southern Progressive Looks at the New Deal," *Journal of Southern History,* XXIV (May, 1958), 151-176.

De Conde, Alexander. "The South and Isolationism," *Journal of Southern History,* XXIV (August, 1958), 332-346.

Heacock, Walter J. "William B. Bankhead and the New Deal," *Journal of Southern History,* XXI (August, 1955), 347-359.

Howard, Joseph K. "The Decline and Fall of Burton K. Wheeler," *Harper's,* March, 1947, 226-236.

Howard, J. Woodford. "Frank Murphy and the Sit-Down Strikes of 1937," *Labor History,* I (Spring, 1960), 103-140.

Ickes, Harold I. "My Twelve Years with F.D.R.," *Saturday Evening Post,* June 5 to July 24, 1948.

McCoy, Donald. "The National Progressives of America, 1938," *Mississippi Valley Historical Review,* XXXXIV (June, 1957), 75-93.

Rose, Kenneth. "The Recession of 1937-1938," *Journal of Political Economy,* LVI (June, 1948), 239-248.

Ross, Hugh. "Roosevelt's Third Term Nomination," *Mid-America,* XXXXIV (April, 1962), 80-95.

Rudolph, Frederick. "The American Liberty League, 1934-1940," *American Historical Review,* LVI (October, 1950), 19-33.

Reutten, Richard T. "Showdown in Montana, 1938: Burton Wheeler's Role in the Defeat of Jerry O'Connell," *Pacific Northwest Quarterly,* LIV (January, 1963), 19-29.

Adams, Alva, 96, 101, 116, 176, 184
Agar, Herbert, 169
Agricultural Adjustment Act, 5, 6, 44, 65, 66
Agriculture, Department of, 10, 12, 75
Aiken, Paul, 185
Alabama primary campaign of 1938, 67
Allen, George E., 113, 178
Allen, Robert, 32, 98, 135, 169
Alsop, Joseph, 82, 87
Amalgamated Clothing Workers of America, 129, 159
American, Austin, 148
American Association for Social Security, 80
American Business Clubs, 101
American Federation of Labor (A. F. of L.) 70, 133

American Institute of Public Opinion, 68, 89
American Labor Party, 59
American Mercury, 24
American Negro Congress, 134
American Youth Congress, 134
Amlie, Thomas, 93
Anderson, Marian, 98
Anderson, Paul, 87
Appleby, Paul, 178

Bailey, Carl, 84
Bailey, Josiah, 20, 31, 36, 93
Bankhead, John, 38, 122, 135, 187
Bankhead, William, 22, 42, 110, 151, 162, 168, 171, 174, 175, 176
Bannon, William M., 146
Barkley, Alben, 39, 72, 76, 79, 95, 96, 167, 170

Barnes, Verda W., 169
Baruch, Bernard, 104
Behind the Ballots, 187
Bell, Ulrich, 169
Benson, Elmer, 74, 81
Berle, Adolph, 171
Bilbo, Theodore, 152
Biltmore Hotel, 7
Bingham, Harry, 169
Birmingham, Ed., 106, 150
Black, Hugo, 26, 32, 40, 61
Blackstone Hotel, 166, 167
Blaylock, Myron, 183
Boettiger, John and Anna, 117
Boileau, Gerald, 43
Bolens, Harry, 75, 144
Borah, William, 36
Brain Trust, 7, 8
Bridges, Harry, 181
Bridges, Styles, 104
Brooks, Roy, 148
Broughton, Charles, 144, 145
Broun, Heywood, 125
Brower, Albert S., 147
Brown, Prentice, 176
Bruce, Howard, 176, 183
Bulkley, Robert, 21
Bureau of Internal Revenue, 137
Burke, Edward, 15, 16, 20, 40, 43, 45, 50, 82, 101, 115, 146, 179, 180, 189, 191
Burns, James McGregor, 117, 162
Business Advisory Council, 105
Byrd-Glass machine, 92, 93, 151
Byrd, Harry, 19, 21, 36, 115, 183, 189
Byrnes, James, 22, 33, 41, 42, 43, 48, 93, 96, 122, 123, 153, 162, 168, 171, 173, 176, 177

Cahill, John, 103
California primary campaign of 1940, 146, 147, 148, 159
Callahan, John, 144
Callahan, William, 144
Capital Times, Madison, 51
Caraway, Hattie, 72
Carter, John Franklin, 169
Catledge, Turner, 63
Chadwick, Stephen, 179
Chapman, Oscar, 98, 169
Civilian Conservation Corp, 111, 128

Civil Liberties, Bureau of, 17
Clapper, Raymond, 21, 89, 95, 97
Clark, Bennett Champ, 36, 85, 86, 115, 116, 122, 151, 171, 172, 184
Clark, Delbert, 24
Clark, Worth, 115, 171, 184
Claypool Hotel, 111
Cleveland, Grover, 19, 40
Cobb, Zach Lamar, 147
Coffee, Harry, 80
Cohen, Benjamin, 9, 33, 65, 71, 98, 106, 117, 156
Colby, Bainbridge, 180
Colgan, Edward, Jr., 173
Colliers, 160
Colorado Fuel and Iron Corporation Steel Workers Club, 86, 87
Columbia University, 7, 52, 180
Commerce, Department of, 84
Cone, Fred, 68
Congress of Industrial Organizations (C. I. O.), 5, 41, 48, 62, 66, 99, 147, 149, 159, 180, 181, 189
Connally, Tom, 22, 36, 104, 139
Connor, Michael, 152
Coolidge, Calvin, 52, 124
Cooper, Prentice, 104
Copeland, Royal, 20, 63
Corcoran, Thomas, 9, 32, 33, 51, 53, 65, 69, 71, 85, 87, 98, 103, 106, 117, 131, 154, 160, 179, 186, 187, 192, 193
Costigan, Howard, 5, 117
Council of National Defense, 155
Courier-Journal, Louisville, 94, 169
Cox, Eugene, 93
Coyle, David, 138
Creel, George, 27
Crowley, Leo T., 145
Cummings, Homer, 23, 34, 51, 92
Curley, James, 3
Curran, Joseph, 181
Current History, 135
Currie, Lauchlin, 10

Daniels, Josephus, 36, 37, 72, 80, 92, 132
Daughters of the American Revolution (D. A. R.), 98
Dartmouth College, 180
Davis, James J., 64
Davis, John W., 72, 80, 178, 180

Davis, Joseph T., 85
Democratic National Committee, 20, 23, 51, 56, 97, 167, 184
Democratic National Convention (1932), 28
Democratic National Convention (1940), 2, 14, 72, 114, 123, 133, 142, 154, 158, 161, 162, 166-179
Democratic Victory Dinner, 13
Democrats for Willkie, 180, 184
Denny, Ludwell, 137
Detroit Athletic Club, 18
Dewey, Thomas, 101
Dewson, Molly, 24, 161
Dies Committee, 66, 74, 83, 95
Dies, Martin, 66, 67
Dieterich, William, 23, 39
Dillon, Read and Company, 155
Dimock, Marshall, 118
Donahey, Vic, 150
Doughton, Robert, 4
Douglas, Lewis, 180
Douglas, Paul, 80
Douglas, William O., 10, 32, 121, 122, 192
Downey, Sheridan, 147, 148
Driscoll, Clara, 97, 145
Dubinsky, David, 133
Duffy, F. Ryan, 22, 74

Earle, George, 14, 16, 17, 53, 62, 63, 64, 73, 74, 75, 78, 86
Early, Steve, 86, 116, 185
Eccles, Marriner, 10, 65, 106
Economy Act of 1933, 48
Eddy, Sherwood, 129
Eicher, Edward, 109
Ely, Joseph, 97
Epstein, Abraham, 80
Ernst, Morris, 36
Evans, Silliman, 47
Evjue, William, 52
Ewing, Oscar, 138
Ezekiel, Mordecai, 10

Farley, James, 2, 4, 7, 13, 15, 16, 20, 23, 24, 25, 26, 28, 33, 36, 37, 48, 54, 56, 57, 60, 63, 71, 73, 75, 80, 81, 82, 83, 84, 85, 87, 89, 97, 102, 103, 104, 105, 109, 111, 112, 117, 120, 121, 129, 130,

Farley, James—Cont.
137, 140, 141, 142, 143, 144, 146, 153, 159, 161, 162, 166, 167, 168, 169, 170, 171, 172, 173, 176, 177, 181, 182, 184, 187, 189, 190, 191, 193, 194, 195
Federal Deposit Insurance Corporation, 145
Federal Public Health Service, 111
Federal Reserve System, Board of Governors of, 10
Finnegan, James, 187
Flanagan, John, 92
Florida primary campaign of 1938, 68
Florida primary campaign of 1940, 153
Flynn, Edward, 5, 33, 56, 72, 142, 162, 168, 184, 185, 187, 193
Flynn, John, 36
Foley, Edward, 157
Ford, Henry, 97
Fordham Law School, 180
Forrestal, James, 155
Fort Peck Dam, 52
Fortune, 14, 129
Franco, Francisco, 14
Frankfurter, Felix, 10, 32, 36
Franklin, Jay, 32, 71
Frazier, Lynn, 36

Gallagher, Thomas, 81
Gallup, Dr. George, 89
Gallup Poll, 17, 31, 62, 73, 79, 83, 85, 86, 95, 96, 108, 112, 114, 123, 129, 139, 154, 161
Gardenhiser, J. W., 152
Gardner, Max, 114
Garner, John Nance, 10, 22, 28, 31, 37, 38, 42, 46, 47, 48, 49, 50, 51, 57, 62, 73, 82, 83, 84, 85, 94, 95-101, 103, 112, 114, 122-125, 129, 138, 139, 143-149, 158, 162, 172, 173, 178, 183, 191
General Federation of Women's Clubs, 180
General Motors strike, 18, 40, 41
George, Walter, 21, 22, 33, 36, 80, 105, 115, 122, 139, 152
Germany, Eugene, 97, 145
Gerry, Peter, 36
Gilles, James, 114
Gillette, Guy, 69, 70, 71, 72, 75, 76, 77, 80, 81, 102, 105, 108, 109

Glass, Carter, 19, 20, 64, 105, 116, 172, 183
Green, William, 133
Grinnell College, 12, 107
Guffey coal bill, 41, 48
Guffey, Joseph, 17, 38, 63, 88, 101, 177

Hague, Frank, 5, 61, 115, 132, 159, 195
Hanes, John, 180
Harper, Fowler, 138
Harrison, Pat, 22, 33, 39, 43, 66, 95, 152, 178, 179
Harvard Law School, 10, 52
Hatch Act, 93, 96, 102, 118
Hatch, Carl, 38, 96
Hearst, William Randolph, 46, 139, 140
Heflin, Thomas, 67
Heil, Julius, 75
Helvering, Guy, 137
Henderson, Leon, 10, 106
Henry, Robert, 75
Herring, Clyde, 70, 109, 174, 179
Hess, Henry, 69, 71
High, Stanley, 11, 16, 32
Hill, Lister, 32, 67, 172
Hillman, Sidney, 129, 133, 159, 180
Hitler, Adolph, 14, 136
Hodges, George, 97
Hoey, Clyde, 151
Holt, Hamilton, 181
Holt, Rush, 105
Hoover, Herbert, 4, 158
Hoover, J. Edgar, 101
Hopkins, Ernest, 181
Hopkins, Harry, 8, 10, 11, 33, 51, 53, 58, 59, 62, 65, 67, 69, 71, 75, 76, 79, 81, 86, 87, 92, 95, 98, 101, 103, 104-107, 108, 110, 112, 117, 118, 132, 148, 159, 160, 162, 166, 167, 168, 169, 170-171, 174, 175, 177, 179, 181, 186, 187, 192
Horner, Henry, 131, 146
Hughes, James, 101
Hull, Cordell, 23, 25, 26, 33, 54, 69, 73, 83, 85, 87, 96, 101, 103, 104, 112, 121, 129-131, 139, 140, 141, 142, 151, 152, 160, 161, 165, 171, 172, 173, 194
Hurja, Emil, 97, 184
Hutchins, Robert, 175, 193
House Labor Committee, 99

House Rules Committee, 21, 45, 68
House Subcommittee on Deficiencies, 43

Ikes, Harold, 8, 33, 44, 65, 67, 69, 71, 81, 87, 88, 98, 101, 109, 119-120, 126, 130-131, 132, 134, 146, 147-148, 149, 155, 159, 161, 166, 167, 168, 169, 175, 178, 179, 184, 185, 186, 187, 193, 195
Illinois primary campaign of 1940, 146
Indiana Democratic Editorial Association, 60
Indiana University football banquet, 120
Indiana University Law School, 27
Insurance Advertising Convention, 89
International Labor Organization, 89, 90
International Ladies Garment Workers' Union, 133
Interior, Department of, 120, 169
Inter-Parliamentary Congress, 82
Interstate Commerce Commission, 93
Iowa primary campaign of 1938, 69, 70, 71, 72, 81, 109

Jackson, Andrew, 124
Jackson, Robert, 10, 57-58, 65, 86, 98, 101, 103, 106, 130, 132, 159, 162, 168, 173, 179
James, Marquis, 125
Jefferson, Thomas, 172, 179
Johnson, Edwin, 120, 135, 171
Johnson, Hiram, 36, 40, 70
Johnson, Hugh, 3, 9, 33
Johnson, Jed, 11
Johnson, Louis, 174
Johnson, Lyndon, 149
Johnson, Paul Burney, 152
Johnston, Alva, 136
Jones, Charles, 62, 63
Jones, Jesse, 23, 26, 32, 33, 54, 84-85, 109-110, 122, 139-140, 148, 174, 176, 186, 193
Jones, Sam, 177
Justice, Department of, 10, 57

Keenan, Joseph, 65
Keller, Gustave, 144, 145

Kelly, Edward, 5, 39, 61, 115, 131, 132, 159, 162, 166, 167, 170, 172, 187, 195
Kennedy, Joseph, 125, 171
Kennedy, Thomas, 62, 63
Kent, Frank, 95
Ketcham, Mrs. Carl, 182
Keynes, John Maynard, 10, 106
King, William, 15, 40, 45, 77, 100, 189
Kintner, Robert, 82, 87, 119, 134
Knox, Frank, 158
Kornbein, Philip, 176
Kraschel, Nelson, 70, 75
Kremer, J. Bruce, 51
Krock, Arthur, 32, 37, 59, 77, 139

Labor, Department of, 10, 118
Labor's Nonpartisan League, 5, 118, 147
La Follette, Philip, 61, 62, 75, 78, 134
La Follette, Robert, Jr., 16, 62, 115, 134, 144, 149
La Follette, Robert, Sr., 36
La Guardia, Fiorello, 25, 87, 159
Lamey, Arthur, 157
Lamneck, Arthur, 59
LaMotte, Leo, 181
Landon, Alfred, 1, 5, 97
Laski, Harold, 129
Lawrence, David, 62, 63
Lawson, Roberta Campbell, 180
Lee, Josh, 114, 153
Lehman, Herbert, 53, 56, 142, 159, 177, 182
Lerner, Max, 187
Lewis, John L., 5, 17, 40, 41, 42, 47, 48, 62, 63, 86, 99, 100, 117, 118, 121, 123, 124, 128, 132, 133, 134, 136, 140, 155, 158, 159, 180, 181, 187, 188, 189, 190
Liberal Democratic Party of Wisconsin, 144
Liberty magazine, 15
Lilienthal, David, 187
Lincoln, G. Gould, 89
Lindley, Ernest, 128, 141
Littel, Norman, 117, 118
Logan, Marvel, 38, 52
Longworth, Alice Roosevelt, 13
Look magazine, 98, 101
Lubell, Samuel, 188, 189
Lubin, Isador, 10

Lucas, Scott, 174, 176, 187
Lundeen, Ernest, 115

MacArthur, Douglas, 112
McAdoo, William Gibbs, 146, 147
McCarran, Pat, 37, 70, 101, 115, 135
McCloskey, Matthew, 63
McClugage, David, 89
McCormack, John, 141, 160
McGarry, Thomas, 220
McHale, Frank, 53, 73, 77, 111, 179
McIntyre, Marvin, 49
McNaboe, John, 145
McNutt, Paul, 27, 28, 37, 53, 60, 61, 62, 73, 77, 78, 111, 112, 119, 120, 129, 135, 136-138, 141, 144, 146, 153, 156, 159, 174, 176, 179, 194, 195
McReynolds, Sam, 11, 43
Maginot Line, 154
Mahoney, Jeremiah, 25
Mahoney, Willis, 149, 185
Margiotti, Charles, 63, 64
Martin, Charles, 69, 71, 81, 149
Massachusetts primary campaign of 1940, 141
Maverick, Maury, 43, 90, 159, 169
Mayflower Hotel, 132
Mayo Clinic, 12, 58, 107
Mellon, Andrew, 46
Michelson, Charles, 142, 185
Miller, Leslie, 187
Miller, Roy, 83, 97, 98, 124, 139, 146
Miller, Tom, 50, 148
Minton, Sherman, 13, 54, 60, 79, 111, 178, 189
Moley, Raymond, 6, 25, 32, 47, 58, 111, 147
Morgenthau, Henry, 31, 44, 105, 106
Morning News, Dallas, 148
Morrow, Wright, 173
Mullen, Arthur, 20
Mundelein, William Cardinal, 101, 103
Murphy, Frank, 24, 41, 74, 79, 87, 92, 95, 98, 101, 102, 103, 159
Murray, James, 52, 89, 135, 157
Mussolini, Benito, 14, 136, 154, 156

N.A.A.C.P., 134, 158
Nation, 14, 92, 101, 136

National Association of Manufacturers, 94, 121
National Industrial Recovery Act, 6, 20
National Labor Relations Board, 69
National Maritime Union, 181
National Progressive Party, 61, 62, 75
National Youth Administration, 111, 128
Nebraska primary campaign of 1940, 146, 189
New Hampshire primary campaign of 1940, 141, 143
New Republic, 35, 101, 112, 136, 137, 146, 181
Newsweek, 108
New York City primary campaign of 1940, 145
New York World's Fair, 104, 127
Niebuhr, Reinhold, 129
Niles, David, 10, 11, 65, 133
Norris, George, 3, 57, 69, 113, 134, 149, 161
North Dakota primary campaign of 1940, 103
Nye, Gerald, 36

Observer, Boston, 110
O'Connell, Jerry, 52, 78
O'Connor, James, 52
O'Connor, John, 21, 68, 72, 100, 179
Ohio primary campaign of 1940, 150
Oklahoma primary campaign of 1940, 153
Oliphant, Herman, 10
Olson, Culbert, 74, 146, 174
O'Mahoney, Joseph, 36, 37, 38
Oregon primary campaign of 1938, 69, 71, 81
Oregon primary campaign of 1940, 149, 150
Ousler, Charles, 15

Parker, Alton, 72
Patman, Wright, 88
Patterson, Ellis, 147, 148
Pearson, Drew, 32, 98, 135, 136
Pendergast, Thomas, 5, 39, 50, 61, 151
Pennsylvania primary campaign of 1938, 62, 63, 88

Pepper, Claude, 67, 68, 93, 132, 153, 156, 159, 175, 178
Perkins, Frances, 8, 41, 67, 69, 160, 169, 170, 178, 187
Perkins, Fred, 14
Phillips, Leon, 166, 177
Phillips, William, 62
Pinchot, Amos, 36
Pittman, Key, 43
Political Science, Academy of, 45
Post Office, Department of, 25, 120
Post, Robert, 14
Post, Washington, 142
Press, Pittsburgh, 14
Price, James, 92, 151
Progressives for Roosevelt, 11
Progressive Party (1924), 36
Progressives, Wisconsin, 16, 134, 144, 146
Public Welfare, Department of, 59
Public Works Administration, National Power Policy Committee of, 10

Quezon, Manuel, 78
Quigley, Jim, 182
Quill, Mike, 181

Rainey, Henry, 4
Rankin, William H., Co., 140
Raskob, John, 178
Rauch, Basil, 66
Rayburn, Sam, 32, 42, 45, 100, 110, 146, 148-149, 173, 174, 187
Reconstruction Finance Corporation, 9, 10, 23
Reed, James, 178, 179
Reed, Stanley, 57
Reorganization Act, 111
Revenue Act of 1938, 66
Rivers, E. E., 152, 154
Roberts, Floyd, 92
Robinson, Edgar, 178, 192
Robinson, Joseph, 22, 33, 39, 41, 42, 43, 48, 49
Rochester, University of, 180
Rollins College, 180
Roosevelt, Eleanor, 117, 170, 176
Roosevelt, Elliott, 95, 176
Roosevelt, James, 65, 68, 70
Roosevelt, Hotel, 7

Roper, Dan, 23, 58, 77, 83, 84, 105
Rosenman, Samuel, 10, 36, 160, 162
Rowe, James, 160
Rural Electrification Administration, 108
Russell, Richard, 152
Russo-Finnish War, 127

Saturday Evening Post, 32, 60, 136
Sawyer, Charles, 150
Schricker, Henry, 73
Schwellenbach, Lewis, 33, 80, 82
Securities and Exchange Commission, 10, 109, 121
Senate Judiciary Committee, 37
Seymour, Charles, 180
Shelley, Carl, 64
Sheppard, Morris, 139
Sherwood, Robert, 12, 58, 87, 107
Shipstead, Henrik, 36, 115
"sitzkrieg," 127
Sloan, Alfred, Jr., 17
Slocum, John, 144
Smathers, William, 33, 80, 96, 101
Smietanka, Julius, 146
Smith, Al, 18, 116, 144, 178, 179
Smith, Al, Jr., 145
Smith, "Cotton Ed," 20, 72, 80, 116, 153, 183
Smith, Young B., 180
Snell, Bertrand, 45
Social Security Commission, 111
Stark, Lloyd, 101, 116, 151, 174, 175
State of the Union Address, 1937, 34
Stevens Hotel, 168, 172
Stimson, Henry L., 158
Stokes, Thomas, 49, 76
Sullivan, John L., 141, 143
Supreme Court, 8, 10, 13, 14, 34-39, 40, 121, 135, 183
Surplus Commodities Corporation, 108

Taft, Robert, 186
Tammany Hall, 61, 145, 184
Tarver, Malcolm, 59
Teamsters' Union, 160
Temporary National Economic Committee, 66, 98
Texas Gulf Sulphur Company, 83, 97

Texas primary campaign of 1940, 148, 149
Texas State Democratic Executive Committee, 82, 97
Thomas, Elbert, 72
Thomas, Norman, 129
Thompson, Dorothy, 155
Thorkelson, Jackob, 78
Time, 102, 106, 109, 137
Times, New York, 14, 24, 37, 77
Timmons, Bascom, 85, 176
Tobin, Dan, 160, 184
Townsend, Clifford, 53, 73
Transport Workers, 181
Treasury, Department of, 10, 136, 137, 141
Tribune, Minneapolis, 110
Truman, Harry, 39, 41
Tugwell, Rex, 3, 32, 131, 193
Tully, Grace, 15, 25
Two Percent Club, 27, 61, 138
Tydings, Millard, 20, 35, 36, 72, 105, 110, 115, 151, 172, 173, 178, 183, 184
Tennessee Valley Authority (T. V. A.), 44, 65, 66

Unemployed Citizens' League, 4
United Auto Workers, 40, 181
United Mine Workers, 86, 133, 134, 136, 181
United Mine Workers' Convention, 86, 133
United Press, 15
United States Employment Service, 111
Utilities Holding Company Bill, 20

Valentine, Alan, 180, 184
Vandenburg, Arthur, 37, 48, 105, 161
Van Devanter, Willis, 40
Van Nuys, Frederick, 36, 40, 53, 60, 61, 73, 77, 102, 116, 178, 183
Villard, Oswald Garrison, 36, 92, 101, 121
Voorhis, Jerry, 43, 147

Wages and Hours Act, 66, 67, 69
Wagner Act, 93
Wagner, Robert, 20, 58, 159, 187
Walker, Frank, 7, 25, 26, 31, 47, 161

Wallace, Henry, 8, 11, 12, 16, 33, 53, 69, 71, 75, 77, 79, 86, 87, 95, 107, 108, 109, 116, 150, 173, 174-179, 187
Walsh, David, 20, 31, 36, 115, 141, 171
Walsh, Thomas, 51
Warren, Lindsey, 96
Washington Commonwealth Federation, 4, 117
Wearin, Otha, 69, 70, 108, 109
Wehle, Louis, 160
Welles, Sumner, 193
Wells, John, 176
West Coast Longshoremen and Warehousemen, 181
Wheeler, Burton, 14, 15, 35, 36, 50, 51, 52, 53, 70, 78, 79, 89, 116, 117, 118, 120, 121, 132, 133, 134, 135, 136, 141, 147, 156, 157, 158, 171, 172, 174, 183, 189, 194
White, William Allen, 3, 36, 136, 194
Whose Constitution? 53
Wickard, Claude, 138
Wilcox, J. Mark, 68
Wilkinson, Ignatius, 180
Willis, Raymond, 77

Willkie, Wendell, 170, 180, 181, 185, 188, 189, 195
Wilson, Richard, 69
Wilson, Samuel, 63
Wilson, Woodrow, 4, 146, 180
Winant, John, 89, 90
Wirtz, Alvin, 148, 169
Wisconsin primary campaign of 1938, 75
Wisconsin primary campaign of 1940, 144, 145
Wisconsin, University of, 61
Women's Democratic Club, 52
Woodring, Harry, 23, 85, 86, 171
Woodrum, Clifton, 43
Workers' Alliance, 43
Workers' Defense League, 137
Works Projects Administration, 11, 43, 76, 95, 98

Yale University, 180
Yarnell, H. E., 60
Young Democratic Clubs of America, 169
Young Democratic Convention, 114